PREVENTION'S Healthy

One-Dish
Meals in Minutes

200 No-Fuss, Low-Fat
Recipes for Busy People

From the Food Editors of

PREVENTION Magazine Health Books

Edited by Jean Rogers

Rodale Press, Inc.
Emmaus, Pennsylvania

Front cover recipe: Shrimp and Feta Skillet Dinner (page 76)

Library of Congress Cataloging-in-Publication Data

Prevention's healthy one-dish meals in minutes: 200 no-fuss, low-fat
    recipes for busy people / from the food editors of Prevention
    Magazine Health Books; edited by Jean Rogers.
       p.   cm.
    Includes index.
    ISBN 0–87596–269–6 hardcover
    1. Low-fat diet—Recipes. 2. Salt-free diet—Recipes. 3. Quick
and easy cookery. I. Rogers, Jean, date. II. Prevention
Magazine Health Books.
RM237.7.P734 1996
641.5'638—dc20   95–36867

Distributed in the book trade by St. Martin's Press

2 4 6 8 10 9 7 5 3 1 hardcover

—————— OUR MISSION ——————

We publish books that empower people's lives.

—— RODALE  BOOKS ——

Prevention's Healthy One-Dish Meals in Minutes Editorial Staff

Managing Food Editor: Jean Rogers
Contributing Writers: Jenna Holst, Mary Carroll, Susan Weaver
Contributing Editors: Mary Goodbody, Leslie Cohen
Recipe Development: Mary Carroll, Nancy Baggett, Ruth Glick, Anita Hirsch, JoAnn Brader, Nancy Zelko, Tom Ney
Nutrition Consultant: Linda Yoakam, M.S., R.D.
Copy Editor: Kathy Diehl
Book and Cover Designer: Elizabeth Youngblood
Associate Art Director: Faith Hague
Studio Manager: Joe Golden
Photo Editor: Susan Pollack
Photographer: Alison Miksch
Food Stylist: William Smith
Prop Stylist: Lora P. Zarubin
Production Manager: Helen Clogston
Manufacturing Coordinator: Melinda B. Rizzo

Rodale Health and Fitness Books

Vice-President and Editorial Director: Debora T. Yost
Art Director: Jane Colby Knutila
Research Manager: Ann Gossy Yermish
Copy Manager: Lisa D. Andruscavage

Contents

Comforting Soups 87

The Salad Bowl 119

Planning for the Rush

What's for dinner? Is that question all too familiar? Every day, week-in and week-out, today's busy cook has to bring the answer straight from the kitchen to the table. Few of you have unlimited time to spend in the kitchen, even on weekends.

The time you used to have for cooking is now devoted to other things: juggling work, children, car pools, after-school activities, exercise classes, shopping, evening meetings and more. Throw in the occasional evening of entertaining friends, and you see how overscheduled you really are. You need a new strategy to help you get dinner on the table.

How can you make healthy dinners that take little time and effort to prepare? In this book you can rediscover the ease and joys of the one-dish meal—delicious homestyle food that is always a hit.

One-dish meals are quick and easy to make. Whether you're talking traditional family casseroles, myriad types of stir-fries, skillet suppers, pasta dishes, main-dish salads or hearty soups, these foods will delight both your family and your friends. This back-to-basics approach to menu planning is a great way to cook and is your solution to quick but satisfying and nutritionally balanced meals.

One-dish meals are time-savers. It's a snap to combine fresh ingredients—vegetables, poultry, fish, meats and grains—with frozen, canned or dried staples to create tasty, healthy entrées. With usually only one or two pots on the stove or in the oven, cleanup is easier and quicker, too. The preparation and cooking time for many of the one-dish meals in this book is only 20 to 30 minutes. What we call Express Meals (starting on page 41) can be ready in record time, generally 15 minutes or less from start to finish. Casseroles generally need 20 to 30 minutes to assemble before you pop them into the oven—leaving you time to do other chores, relax or entertain friends until dinnertime.

Stocking Your Kitchen

In order to keep last-minute shopping time to a minimum, it's helpful to have certain staples on hand at all times. These items can be in your pantry, your refrigerator or your freezer. You don't need a large quantity of each item, just a good variety to give you maximum flexibility when you cook.

Some refrigerated items, such as parsley and lemons, may not have a long shelf life, but they have so many uses that it's wise to consider them staples, too. Along with the basics, keep on hand those items you know your family really likes. And stock a few optional items for unusual dishes, such as sesame oil or hoisin sauce for Chinese meals.

If you have a good-size freezer, you will have a virtual grocery store at your fingertips. Here are some rules for best preserving meat, poultry and fish. Double-wrap them in plastic, then wrap again in foil, freezer paper or special freezer bags. Label everything well and date the packages. Once meat, poultry or fish has completely or partially thawed, for saftey reasons never refreeze it. If, by chance, any items have gotten freezer burn, discard them.

Post a list in your kitchen and note when you run out of staples so you remember to pick them up on your next supermarket trip.

The following lists highlight ingredients used often in recipes throughout this book. They're divided first by storage area then further broken into "basics" and "optional" items. With a well-stocked kitchen at your fingertips, you can literally throw together a meal in a flash, even for company.

Cool, Dry Place
Basics
- Garlic
- Onions
- Potatoes *(baking and new or red)*
- Sweet potatoes or yams
- Winter squash *(such as acorn or butternut)*

Refrigerator
Basics
- Butter or margarine
- Eggs or egg substitute
- Milk *(skim or 1% low-fat)*
- Orange juice
- Parmesan cheese
- Sour cream *(nonfat or low-fat)*
- Yogurt *(plain nonfat or low-fat)*
  •
- Apples *(such as Granny Smith, Rome, McIntosh)*
- Carrots *(regular or baby)*
- Celery
- Cucumbers
- Fresh ginger
- Lemons
- Mushrooms
- Parsley
- Scallions

Freezer
Basics
- Egg substitute
- Lemon juice
  •
- Bread
- Bread dough
- English muffins
- Pita bread
- Pizza dough
- Rolls
- Tortillas *(corn and flour)*
  •
- Artichoke hearts
- Corn
- Green beans *(cut)*
- Peas
- Pearl onions
- Pepper strips *(mixed)*
- Spinach
- Stir-fry vegetable combinations
- Succotash
- Vegetable combinations *(such as peas and carrots)*
  •
- Salmon or other fish *(individually packed)*
- Shrimp *(peeled)*

Pantry Shelves

Basics
- Apple juice
- Beans (assorted canned varieties)
- Beef broth (preferably reduced-sodium)
- Bread crumbs
- Brown sugar
- Canola oil
- Chicken broth (preferably reduced-sodium)
- Clams, chopped
- Cornmeal
- Cornstarch
- Couscous
- Flour (unbleached all-purpose)
- Green chili peppers (chopped)
- Honey
- Hot-pepper sauce
- Ketchup
- Lentils (red and brown)
- Mayonnaise (preferably nonfat)
- Molasses
- Mushrooms (dried shiitake, porcini or other varieties)
- Mustard (Dijon and honey-mustard blend)
- Noodles (broad and fine, preferably yolk-free)
- No-stick spray
- Olive oil
- Pasta (assorted varieties)
- Peanut oil
- Raisins
- Rice (regular or quick-cooking white and brown, basmati)
- Salsa or picante sauce
- Spaghetti sauce
- Sugar
- Tomato juice or spicy vegetable juice
- Tomato paste
- Tomato sauce (preferably reduced-sodium)
- Tomatoes (whole, chopped and stewed, preferably reduced-sodium)
- Tuna (preferably water-packed)
- Vinegar (such as cider, white-wine or red-wine)
- Worcestershire sauce

Optional
- Apricot preserves
- Balsamic vinegar
- Barbecue sauce
- Clam juice
- Hoisin sauce
- Hot-chili oil
- Mango chutney
- Maple syrup
- Peanuts (preferably dry-roasted and un-salted)
- Pimentos
- Rice vinegar
- Roasted red peppers
- Sesame oil
- Soy sauce (preferably reduced-sodium)
- Sun-dried tomatoes (dry or packed in oil)
- Tahini
- Teriyaki sauce (preferably reduced-sodium)

Spice Rack

Basics
- Basil
- Bay leaf
- Black pepper
- Chili powder
- Chives
- Cinnamon
- Cumin
- Curry powder
- Garlic powder
- Ginger
- Marjoram
- Mustard (dry)
- Oregano
- Paprika
- Red pepper (ground)
- Red-pepper flakes
- Rosemary
- Sage
- Salt or herbal salt
- Thyme

Optional
- Allspice
- Caraway seeds
- Cardamom
- Celery seeds
- Cloves
- Coriander
- Fennel seeds
- Hungarian sweet paprika
- Italian herb seasoning
- Lemon-pepper seasoning
- Nutmeg
- Savory
- Tarragon

Perfect for Today's Lifestyle

In short, one-dish meals are perfect for today's hectic lifestyle. They're great for busy weeknights and make entertaining a few friends, or even a crowd, a breeze. Everyone can relax and enjoy, including the cook.

The recipes in this book update a classic way to cook and address our modern health and dietary concerns. This is the way families used to cook, but now it's faster, easier and healthier. Taste is enhanced, never sacrificed. Dishes are lower in cholesterol, fat and sodium but still deliver full flavor and satisfaction.

Our new American cooking preserves our taste for regional and traditional American fare. Recipes also reflect our desire to experience different ethnic cuisines. So today's cook literally uses ingredients from all over the globe. Fortunately, these ingredients are readily available in most major supermarkets. And that's the terrific thing about these recipes—no special shopping is needed to make any dish. Who has time to run around to find the right gourmet or specialty shop?

Using this book, you can feast on old favorites and discover new or exotic ones. Whether you hanker for Smothered Chicken and Sweet Potatoes, Kansas Oven-Fried Chicken and Vegetables, Indonesian Rice with Chicken, Vegetable Quesadillas, Spaghetti Carbonara, Cold Sesame Noodle Salad, Creole Fish Chowder, Italian Vegetable-Bean Soup, Greek Lemon-Rice Salad, Irish Stew, Szechuan Shrimp or Chicken Potpie with Thyme Biscuits, there is something here to satisfy both your soul and your taste buds. This is food you can be proud to serve to anyone who shares your table.

How Fast Can You Make Dinner?

That depends on two things—your culinary skills and your penchant for planning. Skill takes time to develop, but proper planning lets anyone cook like a pro. Even new cooks needn't fret—with very little experience, they too will be able to cook quickly and well.

Whether you are making your first dinner or your millionth, you can make a fabulous meal if you choose your recipe and begin to plan. The rest will fall into place.

Planning involves setting up your kitchen correctly. And that means having the right ingredients in your pantry, refrigerator and freezer as well as having the right equipment for the job. You also need to know how to plan your food week—from selecting menus to organizing your shopping list so you don't waste valuable time in the store.

Plan Your Food Week

Where do you begin? When planning your menus for the week, following a few guidelines can ensure that you and your family have healthy and delicious meals. Start by choosing a few traditional or favorite dishes to take care of several nights' meals. Then round them out with at least one new recipe each week that has characteristics you like, such as flavors from a favorite ethnic cuisine.

On weekends, you may want to stretch your taste buds a little and try a dish that is more exotic. Ask your family for suggestions. You might even want to get the entire family to help make a new recipe. Participation in meal preparation almost guarantees success.

The Right Tools for the Job

To be an efficient home chef, you should outfit your kitchen with certain equipment. Although there is an abundance of cookware on the market to choose from, you don't need everything. Choose what you really need from this list. If you can purchase a food processor or blender, you'll save yourself considerable preparation time.

When choosing utensils, keep in mind that plastic or wooden utensils are best for no-stick cookware. For kitchen efficiency and safety, keep your knives sharp (more accidents happen with dull knives than with sharp ones).

If you don't have a casserole or baking dish that is exactly the same size as the one called for in a recipe, use a dish that has the same surface area measurement or the same volume. If you have a microwave, it's a good idea to purchase casseroles that are usable in both the oven and the microwave.

Disposable Items
- Aluminum foil
- Freezer paper
- Paper towels
- Parchment paper
- Plastic wrap
- Self-sealing plastic bags *(regular and freezer)*
- Wax paper

Cookware
- 6-quart Dutch oven or soup pot with lid *(preferably with ovenproof handles)*
- 1½-quart saucepan with lid
- 2½- or 3-quart saucepan with lid
- 10″ or 12″ no-stick frying pan

Bakeware and Casseroles
- Baking sheet
- Broiler pan
- Jelly-roll pan
- 7″ × 11″ or 8″ × 12″ baking dish
- 8″ × 8″ baking dish
- 9″ × 13″ baking dish
- 9″ deep-dish pie plate
- 2- or 3-quart casserole

Equipment and Utensils
- Colander
- Cutting board
- Food processor or blender
- Grater *(preferably four-sided)*
- Measuring cups for dry ingredients
- Measuring cups for liquid ingredients *(preferably glass)*
- Measuring spoons
- Mixing bowls *(graduated set of stainless steel, glass or ceramic)*
- Salad bowl
- Serving platters
- Storage containers for leftovers *(preferably microwave-safe)*
- Wire rack

- Chef's knife *(preferably 8″)*
- Knife sharpener
- Paring knife
- Serrated slicing knife
- Slicing knife *(at least 8″)*

- Kitchen fork
- Ladle
- Meat mallet
- Melon baller
- Slotted spoon
- Solid spoon
- Spatula *(rubber and metal)*
- Tongs
- Toothpicks *(preferably wooden)*
- Vegetable peeler

Variety in your diet is also important. Few people want to eat chicken or pasta every night. And no matter how much they like Mexican or Chinese food, for instance, a steady diet of the cuisine wears thin quickly. Try to balance the week by selecting recipes that use a wide range of ingredients. You can use the different chapters of this book for easy ideas. Have a favorite chicken dish one night, a creamy pasta dish a second night and a hearty salad on a third night.

The great thing about meal planning is that there are infinite combinations. You literally never have to repeat a week's menu unless you want to or you get a special request. Here are some suggestions, using recipes in this book, for two weeks' worth of dinners.

Week One
Monday: Szechuan Shrimp
Tuesday: Polenta with Ratatouille
Wednesday: Enchilada Casserole (freeze leftovers in single servings for future lunches)
Thursday: Chicken Mallorca
Friday: Italian Sausage Sandwiches
Saturday: Singapore Noodles
Sunday: Hungarian Goulash (serve leftovers with noodles for lunch tomorrow)

Week Two
Monday: Mexican Red Rice and Beans
Tuesday: Curried Chicken Salad with Chutney (use leftovers in a pita for lunch)
Wednesday: Pesto Focaccia
Thursday: Turkey Tenderloin with Orange Marmalade Glaze
Friday: Lean Sloppy Joes (kids can have leftovers for lunch on Saturday)
Saturday: Spaghetti Carbonara
Sunday: Herbed Fish and Vegetables

The versatility of one-dish meals will also make your life easier. Many of the recipes in this book can be made ahead and frozen for times when you're just too tired or busy to cook. By the same token, leftovers make quick future lunches—especially brown-bag fare. See the tips scattered throughout the recipe section for details.

Leftovers can also make an appearance at a second dinner in a new guise. All it takes is a little improvisation. You might, for instance, use some leftover seafood, chicken or meat stir-fry as a filling for sandwiches or burritos. Or you could turn the leftovers into a main-dish salad or soup. You could even sprinkle them over pizza or focaccia for a novel topping. With a little imagination, anything goes! Again, look for the "Encore!" tips that accompany many of the recipes in this book.

Company's Coming

Planning a meal for guests is really no different than planning for your family. Today's entertaining is relaxed, and people expect good home cooking, not fancy restaurant-style food that takes hours to prepare. Cook for others just as you would when making a special meal for your family. Select a recipe that *you* will enjoy making and eating.

Make It Pretty!

Garnishes add color and a finishing touch or complementary taste to a dish. Since they're not the focus of the dish, a little bit is all that's needed. And they can be quite simple, so you don't have to spend more time perfecting the garnish than making the dish in the first place.

Fresh herbs are the easiest and most appropriate garnish. Unless you use a general garnish such as chopped fresh parsley or snipped chives, make sure the garnish reflects the flavors or ingredients that are used in the recipe. For example, use rosemary as a garnish only if the dish contains rosemary.

You need to keep in mind the ethnic origin of a dish when choosing a garnish. Parmesan cheese, for instance, would not be appropriate for a Chinese stir-fry. You can, however, use ingredients that traditionally accompany or complement a dish. Nonfat sour cream and chopped cilantro, for example, are always appropriate for a Mexican entrée. And you can't go wrong by putting a few chopped tomatoes or slices of red peppers on fish.

Think of garnishes, too, when serving dessert. The hearty one-dish meals in this book go very well with simple fruit desserts or light cakes such as angel food. A quickly fashioned garnish dresses up these foods immeasurably.

Garnishes for Entrées
- Black olives, finely chopped
- Cheese *(such as grated Parmesan or Romano cheese or crumbled feta or goat cheese)*
- Citrus wedges or curled strips of rind *(such as lemon, lime or orange)*
- Fresh herbs, finely chopped or in small sprigs *(such as basil, chervil, chives, cilantro, lemon balm, marjoram, mint, oregano, rosemary, sage and thyme)*
- Nonfat sour cream or yogurt
- Peanuts or other nuts, finely chopped or slivered
- Vegetables, finely chopped *(such as peppers, carrots, scallions and seeded tomatoes)*

Garnishes for Desserts
- Cocoa powder
- Confectioner's sugar
- Curled strips of citrus rind
- Fresh berries
- Fruit puree
- Mint sprigs

The first rule of entertaining is never to serve a dish that you haven't made before. If you come across a new recipe that sounds perfect for company, try it out on your family first to make sure everything will go smoothly. That's doubly important if you are new at entertaining.

It's so easy to turn an easy one-dish entrée into a meal special enough for guests. Start the meal with a modestly dressed-up garden salad as an appetizer, accompany the main course with warm rolls or crusty bread from a good bakery and finish the dinner with fresh fruit or a make-ahead baked or frozen dessert.

One aspect of entertaining that is sometimes overlooked is presentation. A beautifully set table with candles and fresh flowers gives the evening a festive flair and enhances any meal. Another important aspect of presentation is garnishing. Garnishes don't need to be elaborate. In fact, the simpler your garnishes are, the better. Often, a sprinkle of chopped parsley or snipped chives is all it takes to add just a modicum of panache.

Super Market Strategies

Shopping is always easier when you know precisely what you're in the store for. You also don't end up wasting money on impulse items that you may or may not use. So the first order of business, obviously, is a good shopping list. And one thing that makes it "good" is organizing it so you don't have to backtrack in the store.

If you know how your store is laid out, shopping will be easier. Are the Mexican items across from the canned tomatoes or are they next to the baked goods? Every store has its own unique design, and it's a good idea to try to shop in one you are familiar with when you are in a hurry.

Divide your shopping list into categories that make sense for the way your favorite market is laid out. Some suggestions include produce, meat, fish, dairy, frozen food, bakery, deli, staples, canned goods and household nonfood merchandise. Remember to take a pencil or pen along so you can cross out items as you put them into your shopping cart.

You might want to take advantage of the salad bar to purchase precut vegetables and other convenience items. Many produce departments also stock ready-to-cook bagged vegetables, singly or in interesting combinations. Many meat counters cut meat and poultry into slices or cubes that are perfect for stir-fries and stews. These items generally cost more per pound, but you may find that the trade-off in time saved later is well worth the additional expense.

One problem frequently encountered by shoppers is that what they need for a particular recipe is not available or is too costly. A willingness to be flexible and experiment a little can keep your meal plans on track. You can generally make simple ingredient substitutions without jeopardizing the recipe. If the snow peas in the store look limp and lifeless, use sugar snap peas or string beans instead. If there are no scallops available, try shrimp. You can almost always replace one fresh herb with another. The same goes for canned beans. Many types of pasta are interchangeable, and so are the various colors of peppers. You get the idea.

Try Something Else

Cooking should be fun and should allow you the culinary equivalent of poetic license. If you don't have the exact ingredients that a recipe calls for, you can often make simple substitutions that will give you slightly different, but equally delicious, results. Below are some ideas for easy ingredient switches.

Ingredient	Substitution
Boneless, skinless chicken breasts =	Turkey cutlets
Bottom round of beef =	Beef chuck steak
Round or top round steak =	Sirloin steak
Flounder =	Sea bass or sole
Monkfish =	Halibut
Red snapper =	Any firm white fish
Swordfish =	Mako shark
Baby carrots =	Carrots, cut into small pieces
Bok choy or Chinese cabbage =	Napa cabbage
Boston lettuce =	Leaf lettuce or other soft lettuce
Butternut squash =	Acorn or other winter squash
Cauliflower =	Broccoflower or broccoli
Fennel bulb =	Celery or celery root
New or red potatoes =	Baking potatoes, cut small
Peppers of a certain color =	Substitute another color
Savoy cabbage =	Napa cabbage
Snow peas =	Sugar snap peas or string beans
Spinach =	Swiss chard
Sweet potatoes =	Yams
Zucchini =	Yellow squash
Arborio rice =	Converted rice
Basmati or jasmine rice =	White rice
Bow-tie pasta =	Fusilli or small shells
Orzo =	Pastina
Penne =	Rigatoni or macaroni
Spaghetti =	Linguine or angel hair
Apple juice =	White grape or pear juice
Balsamic vinegar =	Raspberry or fruit vinegar
Chicken or beef broth =	Vegetable broth or low-salt bouillon
Honey mustard =	Dijon mustard mixed with honey
Rice vinegar =	White-wine vinegar
Tomato sauce =	Chopped or pureed tomatoes

Organization Is Key

Preparing a meal requires some organization. There are three basic rules that will make your cooking easier.

Rule one: Read the recipe through before you start cooking. Get as familiar with it as you can. Get it straight in your mind what you are going to do and in what order. Keep the recipe handy as a guide so you can refer to it when you need to.

Rule two: Be prepared to cook. Set out all the ingredients you will need and prepare those things that you can. For instance, do all the chopping at once and put the ingredients in separate small bowls, in piles on a baking sheet or on the cutting board in the area of the kitchen where you will be using them, such as on the counter near the stove.

Next, get out all the equipment you will need—pots, lids, spoons, tongs and such. One thing that makes cooking difficult is not being ready to cook. It's counter-productive to have to search for ingredients or utensils in the middle of a recipe. You have enough on your mind without making things harder on yourself.

Rule three: Be ready to serve. If you're preparing a quick dinner, have your table set before you start cooking. Make sure that serving platters and bowls or dinner plates are right where you'll need them. When the food is cooked, you'll be in a position to serve it immediately. If you are making a casserole or another longer-cooking dish, you can wait for a lull in the action to take care of setting the table and assembling serving dishes. Just be sure to attend to these chores before the food is scheduled to be done.

This method of cooking may take a little getting used to at first, but the results are well worth it. With time and with practice, it will become second nature and you will be able to get dinner ready effortlessly.

Making Healthy Meals

The last few years have seen important changes in the way we eat. We tend to consume less meat and more grains and vegetables. In some dishes, meat has become more of an accent rather than the centerpiece it once was. If we eat steak, it is rarely the eight-ounce serving we used to consider standard. Instead, we keep the portion down to four to six ounces.

We also cook with less fat and use vegetable oils in place of more saturated fats. We use no-stick pans and no-stick sprays. We use nonfat or reduced-fat dairy products. When we do splurge by using butter, we use less than before. We've lowered our cholesterol consumption. And we try to keep our fat intake to 30 percent or less of our total calories for the day.

Have we lost anything? Not really. We are eating better, more nutritious and tastier food. We have replaced salt with flavorful herbs and spices. We have added texture to food by using more grains and crunchier vegetables that are not overcooked. We are also incorporating more ethnic and regional dishes, such as Mediterranean foods, into our diets and enjoy the health benefits inherent in those cuisines.

Our markets now offer a greater variety of fresh foods. Once-rare fresh produce and herbs are commonplace. Organic and hormone-free items are also widely available. Many cuts of meat are leaner, with excess fat removed from around the edges and less fat marbled throughout the meat. Food companies have responded to our desire to eat healthier foods by marketing reduced-fat and lower-salt products.

With so many choices, sometimes it's hard to know just what to buy. One good way to start is by checking the labels on prepackaged items for fat and sodium contents. Know how much of both you're getting per serving and make sure that the serving size is realistic—one that you would eat. You might also want to check that the amount of sugar (which can come in the form of corn syrup, sucrose, fructose and glucose) has not been boosted to compensate for less fat.

Make a habit of using skim or 1% low-fat milk. Take advantage of nonfat sour cream and low-fat or nonfat yogurt and cheese. Recognize that sometimes it is advisable to use a part-skim cheese rather than a nonfat one because it will melt more evenly. You may have to do some experimenting to find which products work best in which situations, but you should be willing to be adventuresome.

The recipes in this book are designed for people who want to eat nutritious, delicious and satisfying food. They present a wide range of culinary styles. In the pages that follow, you can rediscover traditional favorites, uncover appetizing new combinations and learn to make exciting ethnic dishes. We hope you'll discover that one-dish meals are not only an adventure in good eating but also a winning combination: easy for the cook and a delight for the lucky diners who get to enjoy them.

Baked Chicken Cutlets and Potato Wedges with Pesto
(page 14) ⟶

Starting with Poultry

Baked Chicken Cutlets and Potato Wedges with Pesto

Herbed chicken cutlets and potatoes—moist inside, golden brown outside—get a zesty pesto garnish that uses bread crumbs in place of the usual fatty nuts and oil.

Makes 4 servings

Chicken and Potatoes

1 cup	**dry bread crumbs**
2 teaspoons	**paprika**
1 teaspoon	**dried thyme leaves**
1 teaspoon	**garlic powder**
½ teaspoon	**salt**
½ teaspoon	**freshly ground black pepper**
¼ teaspoon	**ground allspice**
4	**boneless, skinless chicken breast halves (4 ounces each)**
2	**large all-purpose potatoes, cut into eighths**

Pesto

½ cup	**packed fresh basil**
½ cup	**packed spinach**
3	**large cloves garlic, minced**
⅓ cup	**dry bread crumbs**
2 tablespoons	**grated Parmesan cheese (optional)**

●

To make the chicken and potatoes

Preheat the oven to 400°. Cover a baking sheet with aluminum foil.

●

In a heavy-duty self-sealing plastic bag, combine the bread crumbs, paprika, thyme, garlic powder, salt, pepper and allspice. Shake to combine. Add the chicken and potatoes; shake the bag to coat.

●

Transfer the chicken and potatoes to the baking sheet; lightly coat them with no-stick spray.

●

Bake for 15 to 20 minutes, or until the chicken is cooked through and the potatoes are tender.

●

To make the pesto

Place the basil, spinach and garlic in a food processor; process until smooth. Add the bread crumbs and Parmesan (if using); process just until combined.

●

Serve the pesto with the chicken and potatoes.

Hands-on time: 15 minutes
Total time: 35 minutes

Per serving: 306 calories
3.9 g. total fat (11% of calories)
0.9 g. saturated fat
46 mg. cholesterol
562 mg. sodium

Take It Along

Easy Chicken Lunch
For a working lunch, pack a chicken cutlet and 4 potato wedges in a microwave-safe container; scoop a few spoonfuls of pesto into a separate lidded jar. Wrap up some slices of crusty rye bread and some carrot sticks or broccoli florets. At work, reheat the chicken and potatoes in the microwave on high power for 3 minutes (or crisp them in a 400° oven for 15 minutes). Spread the pesto on the bread or use it as a dipping sauce for the vegetables.

Middle Eastern Chicken with Peppers

This dish is wonderfully spicy and pleasing to the eye—with or without its traditional Middle Eastern garnish of fresh cilantro.

Makes 4 servings

1 pound	**cubed boneless, skinless chicken breasts**
1	**large onion, chopped**
2	**cloves garlic, minced**
2½ teaspoons	**olive oil**
3 cups	**frozen mixed pepper strips, rinsed with hot water, drained and coarsely chopped**
⅔ cup	**defatted reduced-sodium chicken broth**
⅓ cup	**raisins**
1	**large tomato, peeled and cubed**
1 tablespoon	**chopped fresh ginger**
2 teaspoons	**ground coriander**
1½ teaspoons	**chili powder**
½ teaspoon	**ground allspice**
3 cups	**hot cooked orzo or rice**
¼ cup	**chopped fresh cilantro (optional)**

●

In a large no-stick frying pan, combine the chicken, onions, garlic and oil. Cook over medium-high heat, stirring, for 5 minutes, or until the chicken and onions begin to brown.

●

Add the peppers and cook, stirring, for 5 minutes, or until most of the liquid evaporates from the pan.

●

Stir in the broth, raisins, tomatoes, ginger, coriander, chili powder and allspice. Bring to a boil. Adjust the heat so that the mixture simmers gently and cook for 15 minutes, or until it cooks down slightly.

●

Serve over the orzo or rice. Sprinkle with the cilantro (if using).

Hands-on time: 15 minutes
Total time: 30 minutes

Per serving: 403 calories
5.8 g. total fat (13% of calories)
1.1 g. saturated fat
46 mg. cholesterol
139 mg. sodium

Encore!

Middle Eastern Chicken Wraps

For Sunday supper, wrap 4 large flour tortillas in a damp paper towel and microwave on high power for 1 minute. Spread each tortilla with 1 teaspoon prepared mango chutney, then top with ½ cup leftover Middle Eastern Chicken with Peppers. Roll tightly and put on a microwave-safe tray. Cover with plastic wrap and micro-wave on high power for 3 to 5 minutes. Top each roll with a dollop of plain nonfat yogurt and chopped fresh cilantro.

Chicken Mallorca

A colorful mélange of vegetables and a hint of the Mediterranean distinguish this dish. If you'd rather not use sherry, substitute apple juice.

Makes 4 servings

1½ cups **sliced mushrooms**
2 teaspoons **olive oil**
1¼ cups **mixed green and sweet red pepper cubes**
1 **large onion, cut into eighths**
1 **large clove garlic, minced**
4 **boneless, skinless chicken breast halves (4 ounces each)**
1 can (14½ ounces) **Italian-style stewed tomatoes**
2 **large carrots, thinly sliced**
3 tablespoons **sherry or apple juice**
1½ tablespoons **chopped oil-cured black olives**
1 teaspoon **dried thyme leaves**
¾ teaspoon **paprika**
½ teaspoon **dried marjoram leaves**
Salt (optional)
3 cups **hot cooked rice**

•

In a large no-stick frying pan, combine the mushrooms and 1 teaspoon of the oil. Cook over high heat, stirring, for 5 minutes, or until the mushrooms are lightly browned. Remove the mushrooms from the pan and set aside.

•

Add the peppers, onions, garlic and the remaining 1 teaspoon oil to the pan. Cook for 5 minutes, or until the onions are limp.

•

Add the chicken to the pan and cook, turning the pieces occasionally, for 3 minutes.

•

Stir in the tomatoes, carrots, sherry or apple juice, olives, thyme, paprika and marjoram. Adjust the heat so the mixture simmers. Cook, stirring occasionally, for 25 minutes, or until the chicken is very tender.

•

Add the reserved mushrooms and cook for 5 minutes. Season with the salt (if using). Serve over the rice.

Hands-on time: 20 minutes
Total time: 55 minutes

Per serving: 399 calories
5.6 g. total fat (13% of calories)
1.1 g. saturated fat
46 mg. cholesterol
334 mg. sodium

Chicken stuffed with mushrooms and Monterey Jack nests on a bed of colorful sautéed spinach (which gives the dish its Florentine name). Elegant but easy!

Makes 4 servings

½ cup + 2 tablespoons	**defatted reduced-sodium chicken broth**
2 cups	**minced mushrooms**
2 teaspoons	**minced garlic**
2 ounces	**reduced-fat Monterey Jack cheese, shredded**
½ cup	**crushed corn flakes**
½ teaspoon	**lemon-pepper seasoning**
	Pinch of dried thyme leaves
4	**boneless, skinless chicken breast halves (4 ounces each)**
1 pound	**fresh spinach**
2 tablespoons	**lemon juice**
1 tablespoon	**cornstarch**
4 cups	**hot cooked rice**

Preheat the oven to 425°. Lightly coat a 9″ × 13″ baking dish with no-stick spray.

Bring ¼ cup of the broth to a boil in a large no-stick frying pan over medium heat. Add the mushrooms and garlic. Cook, stirring frequently, for 7 minutes, or until the liquid evaporates.

Remove the pan from the heat and stir in the Monterey Jack.

In a small bowl, combine the corn flakes, lemon-pepper seasoning and thyme.

Place the chicken pieces between 2 sheets of plastic wrap or parchment paper. Using a meat mallet, pound each piece to ¼″ thickness.

Divide the mushroom mixture among the breasts, placing it in the center of each piece. Roll up the pieces to enclose the filling; secure the rolls with wooden toothpicks.

Dredge the rolls in the corn flake mixture to coat them evenly. Place the rolls, seam side down, in the prepared baking dish. Add ¼ cup of the remaining broth to the dish and cover with foil.

Bake for 25 to 30 minutes, or until the chicken is cooked through.

Wash the spinach in cold water; do not dry. Remove and discard any tough stems. Place the spinach in a large pot. Cover and cook over medium heat for 2 to 3 minutes, or until the spinach begins to wilt. Stir in the lemon juice.

In a small saucepan, mix the cornstarch with the remaining 2 table-spoons broth until smooth. Carefully drain the liquid from the spinach into the pan. Cook over medium heat, whisking, for 3 minutes, or until the liquid begins to thicken.

Serve the chicken on a bed of rice and spinach. Top with the sauce.

Hands-on time: 20 minutes
Total time: 50 minutes

Per serving: 506 calories
6.4 g. total fat (11% of calories)
2.4 g. saturated fat
67 mg. cholesterol
365 mg. sodium

Italian TV Dinner
Assemble your own ready-to-heat TV dinners with leftover Chicken Florentine, then freeze them for easy weeknight suppers. Place portions of the cooked greens, rice and stuffed chicken on individual microwave-safe trays and cover tightly with plastic wrap, pressing the plastic around the food. Seal tightly with the tray lids and freeze for up to 6 weeks. To reheat, thaw overnight in the refrigerator or remove the lid and thaw in the microwave at 50% power for 3 to 5 minutes. Then microwave on high power for 3 to 4 minutes, or until the chicken is heated through.

Chicken and Chilies

Chopped green chili peppers and black beans turn this chicken skillet dinner into a south-of-the-border fiesta! A tossed salad is a perfect accompaniment.

Makes 4 servings

12 ounces	**cubed boneless, skinless chicken breasts**
¼ teaspoon	**ground black pepper**
¼ teaspoon	**salt** (optional)
2 teaspoons	**olive oil**
1	**medium onion, chopped**
2	**cloves garlic, minced**
1 cup	**defatted reduced-sodium chicken broth**
1 can (8 ounces)	**reduced-sodium tomato sauce**
1 can (15 ounces)	**black beans, rinsed and drained**
1 can (4½ ounces)	**chopped mild green chili peppers**
1 teaspoon	**chili powder**
½ teaspoon	**ground cumin**
1–2 teaspoons	**sugar** (optional)
3 cups	**hot cooked rice**

Sprinkle the chicken with the black pepper and salt (if using).

Coat a large no-stick frying pan with no-stick spray. Add the chicken and cook over medium-high heat for 5 minutes, or until the pieces begin to brown. Transfer to a bowl and set aside until the chicken is cool enough to handle. Cut into small strips.

In the same pan, combine the oil, onions, garlic and 2 tablespoons of the broth. Cook, stirring frequently, for 5 to 6 minutes, or until the onions are soft.

Add the tomato sauce, beans and remaining broth to the pan. Stir to mix well. Add the chili peppers, chili powder, cumin and reserved chicken. Bring to a boil.

Reduce the heat and simmer for 15 minutes, or until the chicken is tender and the liquid has thickened.

Taste the sauce. If it's acidic, add the sugar. Serve with the rice.

Hands-on time: 20 minutes
Total time: 35 minutes

Per serving: 288 calories
5 g. total fat (14% of calories)
0.8 g. saturated fat
34 mg. cholesterol
776 mg. sodium

To Your Health

Chili Peppers

Chili peppers contain vitamin C and beta-carotene. The peppers are said to help increase metabolism, burn calories and speed weight loss. They may also block the formation of cancer-causing compounds that are found in cured meats. The super healing powers of chili peppers are attributed to capsaicin, the substance that makes them hot.

Cajun Chicken

Black-eyed peas (or cowpeas, as they're sometimes called) help give this stick-to-your-ribs chicken dish real down-home flavor.

Makes 4 servings

12 ounces	**cubed boneless, skinless chicken breasts**
2 teaspoons	**olive oil**
1 cup	**chopped onions**
2	**cloves garlic, minced**
½ cup	**defatted reduced-sodium chicken broth**
1 can (15 ounces)	**reduced-sodium tomato sauce**
1 can (15 ounces)	**black-eyed peas, rinsed and drained**
1	**bay leaf**
¾ teaspoon	**dried thyme leaves**
¼ teaspoon	**dried sage leaves**
¼ teaspoon	**dry mustard**
2–3 drops	**hot-pepper sauce**
⅛ teaspoon	**freshly ground black pepper**
1 teaspoon	**sugar (optional)**
¼ teaspoon	**salt (optional)**
3 cups	**hot cooked rice**
2 tablespoons	**chopped fresh parsley**

Encore!

Cajun Chicken Soup

For a quick soup, bring 2 cups chicken broth to a simmer over medium-high heat. Add 1 cup chopped frozen spinach and 2 cups leftover Cajun Chicken. Season with hot-pepper sauce. Stir in ¼ cup low-fat sour cream before serving. For a thicker soup, puree 1 cup of the soup in a blender, then return it to the pan.

Coat a large no-stick frying pan with no-stick spray. Add the chicken and cook, stirring frequently, over medium-high heat for 5 minutes, or until the pieces begin to brown. Transfer to a bowl and set aside.

In the same pan, combine the oil, onions, garlic and 3 tablespoons of the broth. Cook, stirring frequently, for 5 minutes, or until the onions are soft. If the liquid begins to evaporate, add more broth.

Add the tomato sauce, peas, bay leaf, thyme, sage, mustard, hot-pepper sauce, black pepper and the remaining broth. Mix well. Stir in the reserved chicken. Bring to a boil.

Cover, reduce the heat and simmer for 10 minutes, or until the chicken is cooked through.

Taste the sauce. If it's acidic, add the sugar. Then add the salt (if using). Remove and discard the bay leaf.

Serve over the rice. Sprinkle with the parsley.

Hands-on time: 20 minutes
Total time: 30 minutes

Per serving: 297 calories
4.5 g. total fat (14% of calories)
0.9 g. saturated fat
34 mg. cholesterol
345 mg. sodium

Moroccan Chicken

Raisins and onions add a bit of sweetness to this mix of flavors and textures that brings the cuisine of North Africa to your table.

Makes 4 servings

12 ounces	**cubed boneless, skinless chicken breasts**
1	**large onion, chopped**
1	**clove garlic, minced**
1 cup	**defatted reduced-sodium chicken broth**
1 can (16 ounces)	**reduced-sodium tomatoes (with juice)**
1 can (15 ounces)	**chick-peas, rinsed and drained**
½ cup	**raisins**
3 tablespoons	**chopped fresh parsley**
1 teaspoon	**dried thyme leaves**
1 teaspoon	**ground cumin**
¼ teaspoon	**ground cinnamon**
	Freshly ground black pepper
	Salt (optional)
3 cups	**hot cooked rice**

Coat a large no-stick frying pan with no-stick spray. Add the chicken and cook over medium heat, turning frequently, for about 5 minutes, or until the pieces begin to brown.

Combine the onions, garlic and 3 tablespoons of the broth in a 2-cup glass measuring cup. Cover with wax paper and microwave on high power for a total of 3 minutes; stop and stir after 1½ minutes.

Transfer the onion mixture and the remaining broth to a large saucepan. Add the tomatoes (with juice) and break them up with a large spoon. Stir in the chick-peas, raisins, parsley, thyme, cumin and cinnamon.

Bring to a boil, reduce the heat and simmer, stirring occasionally, for 20 minutes, or until the chicken is tender and the sauce has cooked down slightly. Season with the pepper and salt (if using). Serve over the rice.

Hands-on time: 15 minutes
Total time: 45 minutes

Per serving: 338 calories
4.1 g. total fat (11% of calories)
0.8 g. saturated fat
34 mg. cholesterol
464 mg. sodium

Indonesian Rice with Chicken

Indonesian Rice with Chicken

This is a lower-fat version of a typical Indonesian dish. Tender-crisp vegetables add crunch and fiber. Serve garnished with chopped peppers, tomatoes and scallions.

Makes 4 servings

1½ tablespoons	**reduced-sodium soy sauce**
1 tablespoon	**molasses**
1 teaspoon	**mild curry powder**
½ teaspoon	**ground ginger**
	Pinch of red-pepper flakes
2 cups + 3 tablespoons	**defatted reduced-sodium chicken broth**
1 cup	**uncooked white rice**
2 teaspoons	**peanut oil**
4 cups	**thinly sliced bok choy**
1	**sweet red pepper, diced**
¼ cup	**thinly sliced scallions**
1 cup	**cubed cooked chicken breast**
¼ cup	**chopped roasted peanuts**
1 teaspoon	**rice vinegar**

In a medium saucepan, stir together the soy sauce, molasses, curry powder, ginger, pepper flakes and 2 cups of the broth. Add the rice.

Cover and bring to a boil. Reduce the heat and simmer for 20 minutes, or until the liquid is absorbed and the rice is tender.

Place the oil and the remaining 3 tablespoons broth in a large no-stick frying pan. Add the bok choy, peppers and scallions. Cook over medium-high heat, stirring, for 3 to 4 minutes, or until the vegetables soften slightly.

Add the rice, chicken, peanuts and vinegar. Cook for 3 to 4 minutes, or until the chicken is heated through.

Hands-on time: 10 minutes
Total time: 35 minutes

Per serving: 387 calories
9.4 g. total fat (22% of calories)
1.8 g. saturated fat
48 mg. cholesterol
525 mg. sodium

Fried Rice Dinner
Cooked rice dishes, such as this one, freeze beautifully. Spoon portions of Indonesian Rice with Chicken into 1-cup self-sealing plastic freezer bags. Flatten the bags to remove excess air, then seal and label. Freeze for up to 6 weeks. Thaw overnight in the refrigerator, then cook, stirring frequently, in a covered no-stick frying pan with ¼ cup chicken broth for 5 minutes.

Chicken Cacciatore

Cacciatore means "hunter style" in Italian. This version of the classic dish is perfect over polenta or pasta. To vary it, add a cup of sliced mushrooms in the last 5 minutes of cooking.

Makes 4 servings

Chicken

2 teaspoons	**olive oil**
1 pound	**cubed boneless, skinless chicken breasts**
¼ cup	**dry white wine or chicken broth**
1	**medium red onion, thinly sliced**
1	**yellow or orange pepper, cut into ¾" cubes**
1	**clove garlic, minced**
1 can (14½ ounces)	**sodium-free diced tomatoes (with juice)**
2	**bay leaves**
½ teaspoon	**dried rosemary**
2 tablespoons	**chopped fresh parsley**
¼ teaspoon	**freshly ground black pepper**

Polenta

3 cups	**defatted reduced-sodium chicken broth or water**
1 cup	**yellow cornmeal**
2 tablespoons	**sliced fresh basil**

•

To make the chicken

Coat a large no-stick frying pan with no-stick spray. Add the oil and place over medium-high heat. Add the chicken and cook, stirring, for 5 minutes, or until lightly browned. Remove with a slotted spoon and set aside.

•

Pour the wine or broth into the pan. Add the onions, yellow or orange peppers and garlic and cook for 2 minutes, or until slightly softened.

•

Add the tomatoes (with juice), bay leaves, rosemary, parsley and black pepper. Bring to a boil.

•

Return the chicken to the pan. Reduce the heat to low; cover and simmer for 15 minutes, or until the chicken and vegetables are tender. Remove and discard the bay leaves.

To make the polenta

While the chicken is cooking, bring the broth or water to a full boil in another large frying pan. Slowly whisk in the cornmeal. Smooth the top of the mixture with a spatula. Reduce the heat to very low. Cook without stirring for 10 to 12 minutes, or until the mixture is firm. Invert the polenta onto a serving platter and cover loosely with foil to keep warm.

Spoon the chicken over the polenta and sprinkle with the basil.

Hands-on time: 10 minutes
Total time: 35 minutes

Per serving: 400 calories
9.6 g. total fat (22% of calories)
2 g. saturated fat
103 mg. cholesterol
134 mg. sodium

Chicken Fricassee

The aroma of this rich-tasting chicken stew—in French, *fricassee*—will call your family to the table for you. Here, it's served over toasted baguette slices, but you could use rice or noodles instead.

Makes 4 servings

1 teaspoon **olive oil**
1 **frying chicken (3–3½ pounds),
cut into serving pieces and skinned**
3 cups **defatted reduced-sodium chicken broth**
1 **large onion, chopped**
1 **carrot, diced**
2 cups **sliced mushrooms**
2 cups **frozen cut green beans**
1 **large tomato, diced**
2 tablespoons **chopped fresh parsley**
1 tablespoon **chopped fresh chives**
1 **bay leaf**
½ teaspoon **dried marjoram leaves**
½ teaspoon **dried rosemary**
¼ teaspoon **freshly ground black pepper**
Pinch of saffron
2 tablespoons **cornstarch**
3 tablespoons **cold water**
8 slices **French bread, toasted**

Preheat the oven to 400°.

Lightly coat a Dutch oven with no-stick spray. Add the oil and set the pot over medium-high heat until the oil is hot but not smoking. Add the chicken pieces and brown them on both sides. Transfer the chicken to a plate.

Pour ½ cup of the broth into the pot and scrape the bottom of the pot with a wooden spoon to loosen any browned bits.

Bring to a simmer, add the onions, reduce the heat to low and cover the pot. Cook the onions for 10 minutes, or until softened.

Add the carrots, mushrooms, beans, tomatoes, parsley, chives, bay leaf, marjoram, rosemary, pepper and saffron. Cover the pot and cook for 5 minutes, or until the vegetables soften.

Add the chicken and the remaining 2½ cups broth. Cover and bake for 25 minutes, or until the chicken is cooked through. Remove the chicken to a serving platter and cover loosely with foil to keep warm.

In a cup, mix the cornstarch and water. Stir into the broth and cook over medium heat until the broth thickens. Remove and discard the bay leaf. Serve the chicken and sauce over the bread.

Hands-on time: 20 minutes
Total time: 1 hour

Per serving: 671 calories
11.5 g. total fat (15% of calories)
2.4 g. saturated fat
86 mg. cholesterol
845 mg. sodium

Kansas Oven-Fried Chicken and Vegetables

Mmm! Crisp and crunchy outside, moist and mellow inside! The secret of this no-fry chicken-and-vegetable recipe is corn flakes and oven-roasting.

Makes 4 servings

4	**skinless, bone-in chicken breast halves**
⅓ cup	**buttermilk**
¾ cup	**corn flakes**
½ cup	**unbleached flour**
¾ teaspoon	**salt**
¾ teaspoon	**freshly ground black pepper**
½ teaspoon	**paprika**
2	**large baking potatoes**
2	**large carrots**
2	**medium zucchini or yellow squash**

Preheat the oven to 400°. Cover a baking sheet with aluminum foil and coat lightly with no-stick spray.

Place the chicken and buttermilk in a large self-sealing plastic bag. Close the bag and shake well. Refrigerate for 5 minutes.

In a blender or food processor, combine the corn flakes, flour, salt, pepper and paprika. Process until finely ground. Transfer the mixture to another large self-sealing plastic bag.

Cut the potatoes, carrots and zucchini or squash into long wedges. Add them to the corn flake mixture. Close the bag and shake well to coat. Transfer the vegetables to the baking sheet.

Using tongs, remove the chicken from the buttermilk, one piece at a time, and place in the bag with the corn flake mixture. Close the bag and shake well to coat. Transfer to the baking sheet with the vegetables. Lightly mist the chicken and vegetables with no-stick spray.

Bake for 45 minutes, or until the vegetables are tender. Remove the vegetables to a plate.

Carefully turn the chicken over, mist the top with no-stick spray and bake for 10 minutes, or until the chicken is browned and cooked through.

Return the vegetables to the baking sheet; bake for 5 minutes to reheat.

Hands-on time: 15 minutes
Total time: 1¼ hours

Per serving: 269 calories
2.5 g. total fat (9% of calories)
0.7 g. saturated fat
46 mg. cholesterol
523 mg. sodium

Encore!

Mandarin Chicken Salad
Thinly slice 2 cups leftover Kansas Oven-Fried Chicken and Vegetables. Toss in a large salad bowl with 4 cups mixed greens, 1 drained 8-ounce can mandarin oranges, ½ cup bean sprouts or diced cucumbers and ½ cup diced red peppers. In a small jar, combine ¼ cup orange juice, 2 to 3 tablespoons rice vinegar, 1 tablespoon honey, 1 teaspoon dark sesame oil, salt and pepper. Shake well and toss with the salad.

Smothered Chicken and Sweet Potatoes

This is real comfort food from the Deep South—tender chicken and sweet potatoes in rich-tasting, low-fat gravy. And we aren't just whistling Dixie.

Makes 4 servings

⅔ cup **unbleached flour**
1 **frying chicken (3–3½ pounds), cut into serving pieces and skinned**
3 cups **defatted reduced-sodium chicken broth**
½ **large onion, sliced**
2 cups **halved mushrooms**
2 **large sweet potatoes, cut into eighths**
2 tablespoons **cornstarch**
2 tablespoons **cold water**
3 cups **hot cooked rice or noodles**

•

Preheat the oven to 350°.

•

Place ⅓ cup of the flour in a self-sealing plastic bag. Add the chicken, close the bag and shake to coat the pieces with the flour.

•

Coat a Dutch oven with no-stick spray. Set the pot over medium-high heat until hot. Add the chicken. Brown the pieces on both sides. Remove from the pot and set aside.

•

Pour ½ cup of the broth into the pot and scrape the bottom with a wooden spoon to loosen any browned bits. Bring to a simmer. Add the onions, reduce the heat to low and cook for 5 minutes. Add the mushrooms and cook for 5 minutes, or until softened.

•

Add the remaining ⅓ cup flour and cook, stirring, for 2 minutes (the mixture will be dry). Add 1 cup of the remaining broth and stir to break up any lumps of flour.

•

Add the sweet potatoes, chicken and the remaining 1½ cups broth. Bring to a boil, cover and transfer the pot to the oven.

•

Bake for 1 hour, or until the chicken is cooked through and the sweet potatoes are tender. Remove the chicken and sweet potatoes from the pot to a serving platter.

•

In a cup, mix the cornstarch and water. Pour into the pot. Cook, stirring, over medium heat until the broth is thickened. Serve over the chicken, sweet potatoes and rice or noodles.

Encore!

**Creamy
Sweet Potato Soup**
Puree 2 cups leftover broth and vegetables from Smothered Chicken and Sweet Potatoes in a blender or food processor. Add cubed cooked chicken, diced parsley and pepper. Warm through. If desired, thin the soup with additional broth or thicken it with cooked orzo or other small pasta.

Hands-on time: 15 minutes
Total time: 1½ hours

Per serving: 558 calories
7.5 g. total fat (12% of calories)
2 g. saturated fat
86 mg. cholesterol
446 mg. sodium

Chicken Thighs and Sweet Onions with Fruit Sauce

This is a "berry good" barbecue recipe for grilling or broiling all year long. Frozen berries let you capture summer's flavor any time with this tangy sauce.

Makes 4 servings

¼ cup **reduced-sodium soy sauce**
¼ cup **honey mustard**
¼ teaspoon **freshly ground black pepper**
4 **large skinless, bone-in chicken thighs**
1 cup **fresh or frozen blackberries or boysenberries**
½ cup **honey**
1 tablespoon **balsamic vinegar**
2 teaspoons **cornstarch**
¼ cup **orange juice**
2 **large Vidalia or other sweet onions, quartered**
3 cups **hot cooked rice**

Preheat the grill or the broiler.

In a cup, mix the soy sauce, mustard and pepper. Pour into a large self-sealing plastic bag. Add the chicken, close the bag and shake well to coat the chicken.

In a small saucepan, mix the berries, honey and vinegar. Bring to a boil over medium-high heat. Reduce the heat and simmer, stirring occasionally, for 5 minutes, or until the berries have softened.

In a cup, mix the cornstarch and orange juice. Add to the berries and cook, stirring constantly, for 30 seconds, or until the sauce thickens slightly. Remove from the stove, cover and keep warm.

Grill the chicken over medium-hot coals or under a broiler 5″ from the heat for 15 minutes, turning the pieces every 5 minutes, or until nicely browned. Add the onions to the grill or broiler pan and lightly mist with no-stick spray. Cook for 10 minutes, turning both the onions and chicken once.

Lightly brush the chicken and onions with about 1 tablespoon of the berry sauce. Cook for 5 minutes. Turn the pieces and brush with another tablespoon of sauce. Cook for 5 minutes more, or until the chicken is cooked through. Serve over the rice with the remaining berry sauce.

Hands-on time: 15 minutes
Total time: 50 minutes

Per serving: 556 calories
6.5 g. total fat (11% of calories)
1.6 g. saturated fat
49 mg. cholesterol
681 mg. sodium

Chicken Pilaf

Simply delicious! This pilaf with chicken, mushrooms and herbs wins the low-fat contest over any packaged alternative—and it's a meal in itself.

Makes 4 servings

¾ cup **chopped onions**
½ cup **chopped celery**
2 cups **chopped cooked chicken breast**
1 cup **sliced mushrooms**
Pinch of dried thyme leaves
1 can (16 ounces) **reduced-sodium chicken broth, defatted**
½ cup **dry white wine or apple juice**
½ cup **water**
¼ cup **minced fresh parsley**
1 tablespoon **minced garlic**
1 teaspoon **curry powder**
1½ cups **uncooked white rice**

•

Lightly coat a Dutch oven with no-stick spray and set it over medium-high heat. When the pot is hot, add the onions, celery, chicken, mushrooms and thyme. Sauté, stirring frequently, for 5 minutes, or until the onions are soft but not browned.

•

Add the broth, wine or apple juice, water, parsley, garlic and curry powder. Bring to a boil, then stir in the rice.

•

Reduce the heat to medium-low, cover and cook for 20 minutes, or until the liquid is absorbed and the rice is tender.

Hands-on time: 15 minutes
Total time: 35 minutes

Per serving: 390 calories
2.6 g. total fat (6% of calories)
0.6 g. saturated fat
43 mg. cholesterol
292 mg. sodium

Spicy Turkey Pot Roast Dinner

Here's a new take on pot roast using the fresh turkey breast halves sold in many supermarkets. If yours doesn't carry them, ask the butcher to halve and debone a small whole breast for you.

Makes 4 servings

¾ cup **defatted reduced-sodium chicken broth**
1 **onion, chopped**
3 tablespoons **packed brown sugar**
1½ tablespoons **lemon juice**
2½ teaspoons **chili powder**
¾ teaspoon **dried thyme leaves**
¾ teaspoon **dry mustard**
¼ teaspoon **ground allspice**
1 **boneless, skinless turkey breast half**
3 **large red potatoes, cut into eighths**
1 pound **baby carrots**
1 bag (10 ounces) **frozen pearl onions**
⅓ cup **ketchup**
¼ teaspoon **salt** (**optional**)
⅛ teaspoon **freshly ground black pepper**

•

In a Dutch oven, mix together the broth, chopped onions, brown sugar, lemon juice, chili powder, thyme, mustard and allspice. Add the turkey.

•

Bring to a boil over medium-high heat. Reduce the heat to a simmer and cook for 15 minutes, turning the turkey occasionally to prevent sticking.

•

Add the potatoes and carrots. Cover and simmer, stirring occasionally to prevent sticking, for 20 minutes. Stir in the pearl onions. Cover and simmer for 10 to 15 minutes, or until the vegetables and turkey are tender. Stir in the ketchup, salt (if using) and pepper.

•

Transfer the turkey to a cutting board and cut crosswise into slices. Serve surrounded by the vegetables, with the sauce spooned over the top.

Hands-on time: 15 minutes
Total time: 1 hour

Per serving: 475 calories
3.7 g. total fat (7% of calories)
1 g. saturated fat
62 mg. cholesterol
435 mg. sodium

Pot Roast
Pot roast of any sort—even turkey—freezes well for impromptu suppers later in the month. Submerge the hot cooking pot in a sinkful of ice water to cool, then strain out the potatoes (which become mealy when frozen). Package the cooled pot roast in 4-cup plastic freezer containers and seal. Freeze for up to 4 weeks. To serve, thaw overnight in the refrigerator, then heat in a covered saucepan for 15 minutes.

Asian-Spiced Turkey Cutlets

In this feast from the East, a paste of fragrant spices adds a hint of the exotic to turkey and vegetables—and plays up the flavor of both.

Makes 4 servings

¼ cup	**defatted reduced-sodium chicken broth**
1½ tablespoons	**lemon juice**
1½ tablespoons	**canola oil**
2½ teaspoons	**chili powder**
2¼ teaspoons	**ground coriander**
1½ teaspoons	**paprika**
1 teaspoon	**ground ginger**
¼ teaspoon	**ground cloves**
3	**large onions, quartered**
3	**large boiling potatoes, peeled and cut into 1″ chunks**
4	**large carrots, cut into ½″ lengths**
1 pound	**turkey breast cutlets**
¼ teaspoon	**salt (optional)**

Preheat the oven to 400°. Coat a jelly-roll pan with no-stick spray.

In a large glass or ceramic bowl, stir together the broth, lemon juice, oil, chili powder, coriander, paprika, ginger and cloves to make a paste. Remove half of the paste and set aside for seasoning the turkey.

Add the onions, potatoes and carrots to the bowl, tossing them with the remaining paste until evenly coated. Spread the vegetables in the prepared pan. Bake, stirring once or twice, for 20 minutes.

Meanwhile, lay the cutlets between 2 pieces of plastic wrap. Using a meat mallet, pound to ⅛″ thickness. Transfer to the bowl that held the vegetables.

Add the reserved seasoning paste. Toss the turkey with the paste until coated.

Add the turkey to the baking pan. Continue baking, stirring occasionally, for 12 to 18 minutes longer, or until the turkey and vegetables are just tender. Sprinkle with the salt (if using).

Hands-on time: 15 minutes
Total time: 50 minutes

Per serving: 333 calories
8.3 g. total fat (22% of calories)
1.2 g. saturated fat
49 mg. cholesterol
126 mg. sodium

Turkey Étouffée

Étouffée means "smothered." In this Creole-style dish, turkey is smothered in a festive confetti of celery, onions, sweet peppers and ham.

3 tablespoons **unbleached flour**
1½ tablespoons **canola oil**
1¾ cups **defatted reduced-sodium chicken broth**
1 **pound boneless, skinless turkey breast, cut into 4 large pieces**
1 **large onion, coarsely chopped**
¾ cup **coarsely chopped celery**
1 teaspoon **dried thyme leaves**
½ teaspoon **dried oregano leaves**
¼ teaspoon **freshly ground black pepper**
2 **bay leaves**
¼ cup **diced lean trimmed ham**
1 cup **coarsely chopped mixed green and sweet red peppers**
¼ cup **finely chopped fresh parsley**
3 cups **hot cooked rice**

•

In a Dutch oven, stir together the flour and oil. Place over medium-high heat and cook, stirring, for 6 minutes, or until the flour turns a rich brown color.

•

Using a wire whisk and a brisk whisking motion, slowly add the broth to the pot and whisk until completely smooth.

•

Add the turkey, onions, celery, thyme, oregano, black pepper and bay leaves.

•

Bring the mixture to a boil over high heat. Reduce the heat and simmer for 30 minutes, or until the turkey is cooked through.

•

Transfer the turkey to a cutting board and cut into bite-size pieces. Return to the pot.

•

Add the ham, green and red peppers and parsley. Simmer for 10 minutes, or until the peppers are just cooked. Remove and discard the bay leaves.

•

Serve over the rice in shallow soup bowls.

Hands-on time: 15 minutes
Total time: 55 minutes

Per serving: 423 calories
8.5 g. total fat (19% of calories)
1.4 g. saturated fat
52 mg. cholesterol
376 mg. sodium

Turkey Cutlets with Cranberry Stuffing

You needn't roast a whole bird to enjoy turkey with stuffing—not when you can make this speedy skillet version that's studded with fruit and nuts.

Makes 4 servings

Stuffing

2 teaspoons	**butter or margarine**
1	**onion, chopped**
1	**large stalk celery, diced**
½ teaspoon	**dried thyme leaves**
1 cup	**defatted reduced-sodium chicken broth**
½ cup	**dried cranberries**
¼ cup	**diced dried pineapple**
2 cups	**seasoned reduced-sodium crumb-style stuffing mix**
2 tablespoons	**chopped pecans**

Turkey

1 teaspoon	**butter or margarine**
½ teaspoon	**dried thyme leaves**
⅛ teaspoon	**freshly ground black pepper**
12–16 ounces	**turkey breast cutlets**

●

To make the stuffing

In a large no-stick frying pan, combine the butter or margarine, onions, celery, thyme and 3 tablespoons of the broth. Cook over medium heat, stirring frequently, for 6 to 7 minutes, or until the onions are softened. If the liquid begins to evaporate, add more broth.

●

Stir in the cranberries, pineapple and the remaining broth. Bring to a boil, reduce the heat and simmer for 2 to 3 minutes, or until the liquid has thickened slightly.

●

Stir in the stuffing mix and pecans. If the stuffing seems too dry, add water or more broth. Reduce the heat and cook for 2 minutes, stirring frequently. Arrange the stuffing on a heat-proof platter and keep warm while the turkey cooks.

●

To make the turkey

Wash and dry the frying pan. Add the butter or margarine and melt over medium heat. Sprinkle the thyme and pepper evenly over the turkey. Working in batches if needed, sauté the turkey in the pan for 2 minutes per side, or until cooked through. Serve with the stuffing.

Hands-on time: 15 minutes
Total time: 30 minutes

Per serving: 211 calories
5.7 g. total fat (24% of calories)
1.3 g. saturated fat
40 mg. cholesterol
371 mg. sodium

Turkey Curry

A quickly prepared curry dish makes a marvelous change of pace. Adjust the "heat" to suit your own taste buds by varying the amount of curry powder and choosing either a mild or spicy blend.

Makes 4 servings

1	**large onion, coarsely chopped**
1 cup	**coarsely chopped celery**
¾ cup	**chopped Golden Delicious apples**
½ cup	**chopped mushrooms**
2 teaspoons	**canola oil**
1 pound	**cubed boneless, skinless turkey breasts**
1 tablespoon	**unbleached flour**
1⅓ cups	**defatted reduced-sodium chicken broth**
1½ teaspoons	**curry powder**
2–4 tablespoons	**canned chopped mild green chili peppers**
1½ tablespoons	**tomato paste**
3 cups	**hot cooked rice**
3 tablespoons	**chopped fresh cilantro (optional)**

In a Dutch oven, combine the onions, celery, apples, mushrooms and oil. Cook over medium-high heat, stirring occasionally, for 8 to 10 minutes, or until the vegetables are lightly browned.

Stir in the turkey and cook, stirring, for 5 minutes, or until the meat begins to brown.

Stir in the flour. Cook, stirring, for 1 minute. Vigorously stir the broth into the flour until completely smooth. Add the curry powder, peppers and tomato paste. Reduce the heat and simmer, stirring occasionally, for 10 to 12 minutes, or until the turkey is tender.

Serve over the rice. Sprinkle with the cilantro (if using).

Hands-on time: 15 minutes
Total time: 35 minutes

Per serving: 387 calories
5.5 g. total fat (13% of calories)
1.1 g. saturated fat
49 mg. cholesterol
296 mg. sodium

Encore!

Turkey Burritos

Create spicy turkey burritos with leftover Turkey Curry. Wrap 4 large flour tortillas in a damp paper towel and microwave on high power for 1 minute. Warm 2 cups of leftover curry (without the rice) in a covered saucepan over low heat, then divide it among the tortillas. Top with chopped scallions and red peppers. Roll tightly and serve with plain nonfat yogurt on the side.

Easy Chicken-and-Black-Bean Skillet
(page 54) ➤

Express
Meals

Ginger Chicken

No chopping and dicing for this stir-fry, thanks to frozen mixed vegetables. In this colorful combo, water chestnuts provide authentic crunch.

Makes 4 servings

1 package (16 ounces) **frozen mixed broccoli, carrots and water chestnuts or a similar combination**
12 ounces **cubed boneless, skinless chicken breasts**
1 teaspoon **ground ginger**
2 cups **water**
2 cups **uncooked instant rice**
¼ cup **reduced-sodium teriyaki sauce**

•

Cook the vegetables according to the package directions. Do not drain.

•

Sprinkle the chicken with the ginger.

•

Coat a large no-stick frying pan with no-stick spray. Add the chicken and cook over medium heat, turning frequently, for 5 minutes, or until the cubes begin to brown.

•

Meanwhile, bring the water to a boil in a medium saucepan. Stir in the rice. Remove from the heat, cover and allow to stand for 5 minutes to absorb the water.

•

Stir the teriyaki sauce into the cooked vegetables. Add the vegetable mixture to the pan with the chicken and stir to mix well. Cook for 2 or 3 minutes longer, or until heated through.

•

Fluff the rice with a fork. Serve the chicken and vegetable mixture over the rice.

Hands-on time: 5 minutes
Total time: 15 minutes

Per serving: 516 calories
2.6 g. total fat (5% of calories)
0.7 g. saturated fat
34 mg. cholesterol
364 mg. sodium

Chinese Chicken Roll-Ups with Hoisin Sauce

These quick and easy roll-ups make a hit at parties and picnics and in lunch boxes. Look for hoisin sauce in the Asian food section of your supermarket.

Makes 4 servings

2 cups **shredded cooked chicken breast**
¼ cup **orange juice**
⅓ cup **hoisin sauce**
4 **flour tortillas (8″ diameter)**
2 cups **shredded green cabbage**

•

Place the chicken, orange juice and hoisin sauce in a medium saucepan. Cook over medium heat for 5 to 6 minutes, or until the chicken absorbs most of the sauce.

•

Stack the tortillas, wrap them loosely in plastic wrap and microwave on high power for 1 minute.

•

Divide the chicken mixture among the tortillas. Top with the cabbage. Roll to enclose the filling.

Hands-on time: 5 minutes
Total time: 10 minutes

Per serving: 219 calories
3.6 g. total fat (15% of calories)
0.5 g. saturated fat
43 mg. cholesterol
251 mg. sodium

Chicken Chutney Sandwiches

The flavor secret of these broiled chicken sandwiches? Store-bought chutney. For extra eye appeal, garnish the sandwiches with pineapple rings and slices of red onion on the side.

Makes 4 servings

4 **boneless, skinless chicken breast halves**
¼ cup **mango chutney**
¼ cup **nonfat mayonnaise**
4 **whole-wheat sandwich rolls, split and toasted**
1 cup **shredded romaine lettuce**

●

Preheat the broiler. Line a small broiler pan with aluminum foil.

●

Place the chicken on the foil and broil about 5″ from the heat for 5 minutes. Turn the pieces.

●

Take 1 tablespoon of the chutney and divide it among the chicken breasts, spreading it with a spatula. Broil about 5″ from the heat for 2 minutes, or until the chicken is cooked through and the chutney glaze is lightly browned.

●

In a small bowl, mix the mayonnaise and the remaining 3 tablespoons chutney. Spread on the rolls.

●

Slice each piece of chicken across the grain on the diagonal and arrange in the rolls. Top with the lettuce.

Hands-on time: 10 minutes
Total time: 15 minutes

Per serving: 233 calories
2.9 g. total fat (11% of calories)
0.5 g. saturated fat
46 mg. cholesterol
431 mg. sodium

Chicken Dinner with Mustard Sauce

Dash by your grocery's salad bar or produce section for a suitable assortment of precut fresh vegetables and this recipe is half-made. In a pinch, you could even use mixed frozen vegetables.

Makes 4 servings

Encore!

Chicken and Orzo with Mustard Sauce

Chop leftover chicken and vegetables into bite-size pieces, then heat in a covered no-stick frying pan with 1 cup chicken broth, 1 tablespoon brown sugar and chopped fresh thyme, basil or tarragon to taste. Mix 1 tablespoon cornstarch and 2 tablespoons apple cider; add to the pan. Heat, stirring, until the sauce thickens. Add 2 cups cooked orzo and ½ cup low-fat sour cream.

5 tablespoons **Dijon mustard**
1½ tablespoons **sugar**
1 tablespoon **lemon juice**
1¾ cups **water**
4 **boneless, skinless chicken breast halves (4 ounces each)**
4 cups **mixed chopped vegetables**
Salt (optional)
Freshly ground black pepper
¾ cup **uncooked couscous**

●

In a large no-stick frying pan, stir together the mustard, sugar, lemon juice and ¼ cup of the water. Bring to a boil over high heat.

●

Add the chicken and reduce the heat slightly. Cover and simmer, turning the pieces occasionally, for 5 minutes, or until the chicken turns opaque.

●

Add the vegetables and cook, uncovered, for 5 to 6 minutes, or until the vegetables and chicken are just cooked through. Season with the salt (if using) and pepper.

●

While the chicken is cooking, bring the remaining 1½ cups water to a boil in a medium saucepan. Stir in the couscous. Remove the pan from the heat and allow to stand for 5 minutes. Fluff with a fork. Serve the chicken and vegetables over the couscous.

Hands-on time: 5 minutes
Total time: 15 minutes

Per serving: 279 calories
3.6 g. total fat (12% of calories)
0.6 g. saturated fat
46 mg. cholesterol
317 mg. sodium

Turkey Tenderloin with Orange Marmalade Glaze

Lovely and luscious, this hot glazed turkey breast with vegetable wedges beats the clock for a fast way to put dinner on the table. Serve with rice or couscous.

Makes 4 servings

2 **medium zucchini or yellow squash**
2 **large carrots**
1 pound **turkey tenderloin, cut into pieces about ½″ thick**
1 tablespoon **orange marmalade**
1 tablespoon **honey mustard**

●

Preheat the broiler. Line a broiler pan with aluminum foil.

●

Cut the zucchini or squash and carrots lengthwise into long wedges. Place them on the pan. Add the turkey. Broil about 5″ from the heat for 5 to 8 minutes, watching carefully to prevent scorching.

●

In a small saucepan, mix the marmalade and mustard. Cook over medium-low heat, stirring, for 2 to 3 minutes, or until warm.

●

Turn the turkey pieces and brush lightly with the marmalade mixture. Broil for 2 minutes, or until the turkey is cooked through. Serve with additional glaze.

Hands-on time: 10 minutes
Total time: 15 minutes

Per serving: 272 calories
4.8 g. total fat (16% of calories)
1.5 g. saturated fat
99 mg. cholesterol
130 mg. sodium

Minted Lamb Kabobs with Pita

As in the Middle East, these kabobs are cooked without vegetables. For variety, add chopped cucumbers, peppers and other fresh vegetables to the sandwiches before serving.

Makes 4 servings

1½ pounds **trimmed boneless leg of lamb, cut into ¾″ cubes**
Salt (optional)
Freshly ground black pepper
1½ cups **plain low-fat yogurt**
½ cup **chopped fresh mint**
¼ cup **finely minced red onions**
4 **large pita breads**
1 cup **diced tomatoes**

•

Preheat the grill or the broiler.

•

Sprinkle the lamb with the salt (if using) and pepper. Thread onto metal skewers, leaving space between the cubes. Grill or broil about 5″ from the heat, turning once, for 10 minutes, or until cooked through. Remove the lamb from the skewers.

•

In a small bowl, mix the yogurt, mint and onions.

•

Stack the pitas, wrap them loosely in plastic wrap and microwave on high power for 1 minute. Serve topped with the lamb and tomatoes. Drizzle with the yogurt sauce.

Hands-on time: 5 minutes
Total time: 15 minutes

Per serving: 351 calories
9.4 g. total fat (25% of calories)
3.5 g. saturated fat
91 mg. cholesterol
342 mg. sodium

Lean Sloppy Joes

In no time, you can whip up these messy, delicious sandwiches that everybody loves. Leftover sloppy joe filling tastes even better the next day. Use the leanest ground beef you can find and be sure to drain as much excess fat as possible.

Makes 4 servings

1 pound **extra-lean ground beef**
¾ cup **finely chopped onions**
½ cup **chopped green peppers**
¾ cup **reduced-calorie mild barbecue sauce**
4 **whole-wheat sandwich rolls, split and toasted**

●

Crumble the beef into a large no-stick frying pan. Cook over medium-high heat, breaking up the meat with a wooden spoon, for 5 minutes, or until lightly browned. Remove from the heat and pour off any excess fat.

●

Return the pan to the stove and add the onions and peppers. Cook for 5 minutes, or until the beef is cooked through and the vegetables are softened.

●

Add the barbecue sauce and cook for 3 minutes, or until heated through. Serve on the rolls.

Hands-on time: 5 minutes
Total time: 15 minutes

Per serving: 354 calories
15.6 g. total fat (40% of calories)
5.5 g. saturated fat
70 mg. cholesterol
638 mg. sodium

Sausage-Potato Supper

Reduced-fat sausage forms the base of this homestyle skillet. Be sure to read labels in the store to choose sausage that's significantly lower in fat than regular sausage.

8 ounces **reduced-fat pork and turkey bulk sausage**
2 **scallions, chopped**
2 **medium red potatoes, cubed**
1 package (10 ounces) **frozen succotash, rinsed with hot water and drained**
1¼ cups **defatted reduced-sodium chicken broth**
Salt (optional)
Freshly ground black pepper

Makes 4 servings

Crumble the sausage into a large no-stick frying pan. Sprinkle with the scallions. Place over high heat and cook, breaking up the meat with a wooden spoon, for 5 minutes, or until the meat is lightly browned.

Transfer to a platter lined with several layers of paper towels and drain well.

Using a paper towel, wipe any fat from the pan. Add the potatoes, succotash and broth to the pan. Stir in the sausage and scallions.

Bring to a boil, cover and simmer for 7 to 9 minutes, or until the potatoes are just tender. If necessary, add a little water to the pan to prevent sticking. Season with the salt (if using) and pepper.

Hands-on time: 5 minutes
Total time: 15 minutes

Per serving: 232 calories
6.8 g. total fat (25% of calories)
0.1 g. saturated fat
0 mg. cholesterol
841 mg. sodium

Encore!

Spicy Sausage Stew
Chop 2 cups of leftover sausage and vegetables. Place in a medium saucepan with 10 ounces canned stewed tomatoes, ½ cup chopped kale, ¼ cup salsa, 2 table-spoons chopped fresh cilantro and 2 teaspoons minced garlic. Bring to a boil and simmer for 5 minutes, or until thick. Add ½ teaspoon crushed fennel seeds. Serve with toasted French bread croutons.

Gazpacho with Shrimp

Adding shrimp to gazpacho, that great Spanish soup, makes this classic even better! A food processor makes speedy work of this refreshing, chilled soup. To reduce the sodium content, choose a reduced-sodium juice.

Makes 4 servings

1 **cucumber, peeled, halved lengthwise and seeded**
1 **small red onion, coarsely chopped**
4 cups **chilled spicy tomato-vegetable juice**
12 ounces **cooked, deveined and peeled shrimp, coarsely chopped**
Freshly ground black pepper
Chopped fresh cilantro

In a food processor fitted with a metal blade, chop the cucumber. Transfer to a large bowl.

Add the onion to the food processor and finely chop. Transfer to the bowl with the cucumbers. Stir in the tomato-vegetable juice and shrimp.

Season with the pepper. Serve sprinkled with the cilantro.

Hands-on time: 10 minutes
Total time: 10 minutes

Per serving: 144 calories
1.2 g. total fat (8% of calories)
0.3 g. saturated fat
166 mg. cholesterol
1,075 mg. sodium

To Your Health

Tomatoes
Tomatoes are one of the richest sources of lycopene. A close relative of beta-carotene, the substance is the plant pigment that makes tomatoes red. Just like beta-carotene, lycopene may help prevent cancer. The difference between low and high intakes? One tomato a day. Fortunately, even tomato sauce and tomato paste contain high amounts of lycopene.

Substantial and spicy, this Mexican rice, beans and chicken recipe takes almost no prep time if you use a time-saver package of precut chicken breast cubes.

Makes 4 servings

1 pound **cubed boneless, skinless chicken breasts**
2 teaspoons **olive oil**
⅔ cup **salsa or picante sauce**
¾ cup **uncooked instant rice**
⅓ cup **water**
1 can (15 ounces) **black beans, rinsed and drained**
Salt (optional)
Freshly ground black pepper

In a large no-stick frying pan, combine the chicken and oil. Cook over high heat, stirring, for 4 minutes, or until the chicken begins to brown.

Stir in the salsa or picante sauce. Cook for 3 minutes. Add the rice, water and beans. Bring to a simmer.

Cover and simmer for 8 to 10 minutes, or until the chicken and rice are cooked through. Fluff with a fork before serving. Season with the salt (if using) and pepper.

Hands-on time: 5 minutes
Total time: 15 minutes

Per serving: 333 calories
6.3 g. total fat (16% of calories)
0.9 g. saturated fat
46 mg. cholesterol
419 mg. sodium

Easy Freeze

Next Week's Dinner
Make enough of this recipe to use next week as a filling for burritos or as a topping for salad or baked potatoes. Spoon leftovers into 1-cup plastic microwave-safe containers and freeze for up to 6 weeks. Defrost in the microwave on 50% power for 5 minutes, then heat in a no-stick frying pan with a few tablespoons water for 5 minutes, stirring frequently.

Speedy Ham, Vegetable and Rice Skillet

A few flavor-packed ingredients make mealtime magic in this colorful, quick-as-a-wink entrée. Cleanup is just as easy.

Makes 4 servings

1 bag (16 ounces) **mixed frozen corn, sweet red peppers and broccoli**
1 cup **coarsely diced lean smoked ham**
1½ teaspoons **olive oil**
1 can (14½ ounces) **Italian-style stewed tomatoes**
⅔ cup **uncooked instant rice**
Salt (optional)
Freshly ground black pepper

•

In a large no-stick frying pan, combine the corn, red peppers and broccoli, ham and oil. Cook over high heat, stirring frequently, for 3 minutes, or until the vegetables are heated.

•

Stir in the tomatoes and rice; break up the tomatoes with a spoon. Bring to a boil, reduce the heat, cover and simmer for 5 minutes.

•

Remove from the heat and let stand for 3 minutes, or until all the liquid is absorbed.

•

Season with the salt (if using) and pepper. Fluff with a fork before serving.

Hands-on time: 5 minutes
Total time: 15 minutes

Per serving: 224 calories
4 g. total fat (16% of calories)
0.9 g. saturated fat
18 mg. cholesterol
697 mg. sodium

German Green Bean, Potato and Ham Dinner

German Green Bean, Potato and Ham Dinner

The herb savory, often paired with green beans in German cookery, gives a flavor boost to this hearty one-pot dinner. If you don't have savory, you can use a bay leaf.

Makes 4 servings

6 **medium red potatoes, cut into ½″ cubes**
1⅓ cups **defatted reduced-sodium chicken broth**
½ teaspoon **dried savory leaves**
3 cups **frozen cut green beans,
   rinsed with hot water and drained**
1¼ cups **coarsely chopped lean smoked ham
   Freshly ground black pepper**

●

In a large saucepan, combine the potatoes, broth and savory. Cover and bring to a boil over high heat. Reduce the heat and gently boil for 5 minutes.

●

Add the beans and ham. Cover and cook, stirring occasionally, for 10 minutes, or until the potatoes and beans are tender. Season with the pepper.

Hands-on time: 5 minutes
Total time: 20 minutes

Per serving: 185 calories
2.4 g. total fat (12% of calories)
0.8 g. saturated fat
13 mg. cholesterol
660 mg. sodium

Pork Skillet Pronto

Always in season, frozen mixed sweet pepper strips put dinner on the fast track and contribute to a beautiful, fresh-tasting sauce.

Makes 4 servings

12 ounces	**lean boneless, center-cut loin pork chops, trimmed and cut into ¼″ × 2″ strips**
2½ cups	**frozen mixed pepper strips, rinsed with hot water and drained**
1 can (14½ ounces)	**stewed tomatoes, drained**
2¼ teaspoons	**dried Italian seasoning**
	Salt (optional)
	Freshly ground black pepper
2 cups	**hot cooked orzo or rice**

Coat a large no-stick frying pan with no-stick spray. Add the pork and cook over medium-high heat, stirring occasionally, for 3 minutes, or until the pork is lightly browned. Transfer to a bowl.

Add the pepper strips, tomatoes and Italian seasoning to the pan. Bring to a boil and cook, stirring, for 4 to 5 minutes, or until the liquid has reduced by about half.

Return the pork to the pan, reduce the heat slightly and simmer, stirring frequently, for 3 minutes, or until the pork is just cooked through. Season with the salt (if using) and black pepper. Serve with the orzo or rice.

Hands-on time: 5 minutes
Total time: 15 minutes

Per serving: 235 calories
6.3 g. total fat (24% of calories)
2 g. saturated fat
38 mg. cholesterol
292 mg. sodium

Hurry-Up Shrimp Curry

Simply outstanding and outstandingly simple, this shrimp curry is a good way to utilize cooked rice you may have on hand—and serve up the romance of the tropics.

Makes 4 servings

1 can (14½ ounces) **stewed tomatoes**
2 teaspoons **curry powder**
2 tablespoons **canned chopped mild green chili peppers**
12 ounces **peeled and deveined shrimp**
Salt (optional)
Freshly ground black pepper
3 cups **hot cooked rice**

•

In a large no-stick frying pan, combine the tomatoes, curry powder and chili peppers. Bring to a simmer over high heat and cook, stirring to break up the tomatoes, for 5 minutes.

•

Stir in the shrimp and simmer for 3 minutes, or until the shrimp are pink. Season with the salt (if using) and black pepper. Serve over the rice.

Hands-on time: 5 minutes
Total time: 15 minutes

Per serving: 295 calories
1.4 g. total fat (4% of calories)
0.3 g. saturated fat
131 mg. cholesterol
464 mg. sodium

To Your Health

Rice

Rice is a carbohydrate—the kind of starchy food that the American Heart Association says should make up 55 percent of our calories. It's also extremely low in fat, contains no cholesterol and has only about 90 calories in a half-cup serving. Although white rice is a perfectly respectable food, brown rice has more fiber. A one-cup serving of cooked brown rice has about 3.5 grams of fiber, compared with less than 0.5 gram for white rice. Fiber may help prevent colon cancer and seems to play a role in reducing blood cholesterol levels.

Classic Omelet with Scallions and Potatoes

Here's a classic omelet minus the cholesterol, courtesy of fat-free egg substitute. This entrée makes a satisfying supper or brunch.

Makes 4 servings

1½ tablespoons **olive oil**
1 **medium potato, very thinly sliced**
4 **scallions, sliced**
2 cups **fat-free egg substitute**
¼ cup **water**
¼ cup **canned roasted red peppers, sliced**

●

Coat a large no-stick frying pan with no-stick spray. Add ½ tablespoon of the oil and warm over medium heat. Add the potatoes and scallions and cook for 5 minutes, or until the potatoes are golden and fork-tender.

●

In a medium bowl, beat together the egg substitute, water and peppers.

●

Add the remaining 1 tablespoon oil to the pan and warm over low heat. Add the egg mixture and cook for 1 minute, or until the edges begin to set. Lift the edges with a pancake turner and tilt the pan slightly to allow any uncooked mixture to run underneath.

●

Cook for 1 to 2 minutes, or until the eggs are just cooked through. Fold the omelet in half and cook for 30 seconds. Slide from the pan onto a serving platter and cut into 4 wedges.

Hands-on time: 5 minutes
Total time: 15 minutes

Per serving: 129 calories
5.1 g. total fat (29% of calories)
0.7 g. saturated fat
0 mg. cholesterol
165 mg. sodium

Vegetable Quesadillas

A Mexican treat in minutes! You may find these quesadillas so popular at your house that you'll decide to keep the makings on hand all the time.

Makes 4 servings

¼ cup **thinly sliced scallions**
2 cups **frozen corn kernels**
1 cup **mild salsa**
4 **flour tortillas** (**8″ diameter**)
1¼ cups **shredded reduced-fat sharp Cheddar cheese**

•

Preheat the oven to 375°.

•

In a medium saucepan, combine the scallions and corn. Cook according to the corn package directions. Drain well and return the vegetables to the pan.

•

Stir in the salsa and cook over low heat for 1 to 2 minutes, or until the salsa is heated through.

•

Arrange the tortillas in a single layer on 1 or 2 baking sheets. Sprinkle evenly with the Cheddar. Bake for 2 or 3 minutes, or until the cheese begins to melt.

•

Remove the tortillas from the oven. Divide the vegetable-salsa mixture evenly among the tortillas and spread it over them. Roll the tortillas into loose cylinders.

Hands-on time: 5 minutes
Total time: 15 minutes

Per serving: 268 calories
7.1 g. total fat (23% of calories)
3 g. saturated fat
15 mg. cholesterol
612 mg. sodium

Linguine with Savory Mushroom Sauce
(page 80)

Pasta Presto

Pepper Chicken with Tomato Sauce and Pasta

Sun-dried tomatoes, sliced peppers and a few oil-cured black olives help create a dish alive with taste and color.

Makes 4 servings

2 teaspoons **olive oil**

1 **clove garlic, minced**

1 bag (16 ounces) **frozen pepper stir-fry combo (mixed peppers and onions), rinsed with hot water and drained**

12 ounces **boneless, skinless chicken breasts, cut into 2″ × ⅛″ strips**

1 can (8 ounces) **tomato sauce**

½ cup **water**

¼ cup **tomato paste**

3 tablespoons **diced oil-packed sun-dried tomatoes**

1 tablespoon **finely chopped oil-cured black olives**

2 teaspoons **dried marjoram leaves**

1 teaspoon **dried basil leaves**

Pinch of red-pepper flakes

¼ teaspoon **salt (optional)**

8 ounces **uncooked vermicelli**

•

In a large no-stick frying pan, combine the oil and garlic and cook over medium heat for 3 minutes, or until fragrant. Raise the heat to high and add the pepper-and-onion combo. Cook, stirring, for 5 minutes, or until most of the liquid has evaporated.

•

Add the chicken and cook for 3 minutes, or until the meat is opaque.

•

Reduce the heat to medium. Stir in the tomato sauce, water, tomato paste, tomatoes, olives, marjoram, basil and pepper flakes.

•

Cover and simmer, stirring occasionally, for 20 minutes. Stir in the salt (if using).

•

While the sauce is cooking, cook the vermicelli in a large pot of boiling water until just tender. Drain. Serve topped with the sauce.

Hands-on time: 10 minutes
Total time: 35 minutes

Per serving: 365 calories
6.5 g. total fat (16% of calories)
1.1 g. saturated fat
35 mg. cholesterol
530 mg. sodium

Penne with Roasted Pepper Sauce

Roasted red peppers add a delectable depth to this pasta sauce, which puts leftover cooked chicken to good use. It's an interesting change from tomato sauce.

Makes 4 servings

¼ cup **defatted reduced-sodium chicken broth**
1 teaspoon **olive oil**
1 cup **chopped onions**
1 cup **diced cooked chicken breast**
1 cup **minced green peppers**
1 jar (7 ounces) **roasted red peppers, drained and finely chopped**
¼ cup **chopped fresh parsley**
8 ounces **uncooked penne**
¼ cup **grated Parmesan cheese**

Bring the broth and oil to a simmer in a large no-stick frying pan over medium-high heat. Add the onions and cook, stirring frequently, for 3 minutes, or until the onions soften slightly.

Add the chicken, green peppers and red peppers. Cook, stirring occasionally, for 5 minutes, or until the peppers soften. Remove from the heat and add the parsley.

While the sauce is cooking, cook the penne in a large pot of boiling water until just tender. Drain. Serve topped with the sauce. Sprinkle with the Parmesan.

Hands-on time: 5 minutes
Total time: 15 minutes

Per serving: 409 calories
6.4 g. total fat (14% of calories)
1.9 g. saturated fat
100 mg. cholesterol
181 mg. sodium

To Your Health

Red Peppers

Scientists tell us that most peppers are bursting with cancer-fighting vitamin C and heart-healthy beta-carotene. A half-cup of sweet red peppers provides 150 percent of your daily need for vitamin C and one-fifth of your daily supply of beta-carotene. Beta-carotene, which is found in both hot and sweet peppers, has also been found to help protect a diseased heart from further damage.

Skillet Noodles with Turkey Ham and Artichoke Hearts

Skillet Noodles with Turkey Ham and Artichoke Hearts

The nip of cilantro and mild green chilies combine with artichoke hearts to add a classy touch to a down-home, quick-fix skillet meal.

Makes 4 servings

1 tablespoon **olive oil**
1 cup **sliced mushrooms**
3 tablespoons **chopped canned mild green chili peppers**
1 package (10 ounces) **frozen artichoke hearts, thawed and chopped**
4 ounces **lean turkey ham, diced**
⅔ cup **frozen corn kernels**
3 tablespoons **chopped fresh cilantro**
⅓ cup **nonfat sour cream (optional)**
Salt (optional)
Freshly ground black pepper
8 ounces **uncooked egg noodles**

•

Warm the oil in a large no-stick frying pan over medium-high heat. Add the mushrooms, chili peppers and artichokes. Cook, stirring frequently, for 5 minutes, or until the vegetables begin to soften.

•

Add the ham, corn and cilantro and cook for 1 to 2 minutes, or until heated through. Remove from the heat and stir in the sour cream (if using). Season with the salt (if using) and black pepper.

•

While the sauce is cooking, cook the noodles in a large pot of boiling water until just tender. Drain. Return the noodles to the pot and toss with the sauce.

Hands-on time: 10 minutes
Total time: 15 minutes

Per serving: 332 calories
7.2 g. total fat (19% of calories)
1 g. saturated fat
66 mg. cholesterol
357 mg. sodium

Spaghetti with Italian Turkey Sausage

This is a festive Italian dish with the best flavors of pizza—only it's served over pasta for a change of pace. This is a sauce you'll be asked to make again and again.

Makes 4 servings

5 ounces **Italian bulk turkey sausage**
2 teaspoons **olive oil**
1 **small onion, finely chopped**
1 cup **sliced mushrooms**
3 **cloves garlic, minced**
2 **large sweet red or yellow peppers, diced**
¼ cup **minced fresh basil**
2 teaspoons **minced fresh oregano**
¼ cup **tomato paste**
8 ounces **uncooked spaghetti**

Coat a large no-stick frying pan with no-stick spray. Crumble the sausage into the pan. Cook over medium-high heat, breaking up the meat with a wooden spoon, for 4 to 5 minutes, or until lightly browned.

Line a platter with several thicknesses of paper towels. Transfer the sausage to the plate and drain well.

Wipe out the pan with a paper towel. Add the oil and onions. Cook, stirring, for 5 minutes, or until the onions are softened but not browned.

Add the mushrooms, garlic, peppers, basil and oregano. Cook, stirring occasionally, for 5 minutes, or until the mushrooms begin to soften.

Add the tomato paste and sausage. Cook, stirring occasionally, for 10 minutes, or until the vegetables are tender.

While the sauce is cooking, cook the spaghetti in a large pot of boiling water until just tender. Drain. Serve topped with the sauce.

Hands-on time: 15 minutes
Total time: 30 minutes

Per serving: 312 calories
8.3 g. total fat (23% of calories)
0.3 g. saturated fat
0 mg. cholesterol
133 mg. sodium

Pasta with Meat Sauce

Whole tomatoes give pleasing texture to this delicious but uncomplicated meat sauce. To remove even more fat from the cooked beef, place it in a colander and rinse it with hot water. Pat it dry with paper towels.

Makes 4 servings

8 ounces **extra-lean ground beef**
¼ cup **defatted reduced-sodium chicken broth**
1 cup **chopped onions**
2 **cloves garlic, minced**
4 cups **drained canned tomatoes, chopped**
1 teaspoon **dried basil leaves**
¼ teaspoon **dried oregano leaves**
2 tablespoons **tomato paste**
Salt (optional)
Freshly ground black pepper
8 ounces **uncooked spaghetti**
2 tablespoons **grated Parmesan cheese** (**optional**)

●

Coat a large no-stick frying pan with no-stick spray. Crumble the beef into the pan. Cook over medium-high heat, breaking up the meat with a wooden spoon, for 4 to 5 minutes, or until lightly browned.

●

Line a platter with several thicknesses of paper towels. Transfer the beef to the plate and drain well.

●

Wipe out the pan with a paper towel. Add the broth and onions. Cook over medium-high heat, stirring frequently, for 10 minutes, or until softened. Add the garlic, tomatoes, basil, oregano, tomato paste and beef.

●

Bring the sauce to a boil and simmer, stirring occasionally, for 15 minutes. Season with the salt (if using) and pepper.

●

While the sauce is cooking, cook the spaghetti in a large pot of boiling water until just tender. Drain. Serve topped with the sauce. Sprinkle with the Parmesan (if using).

Hands-on time: 15 minutes
Total time: 35 minutes

Per serving: 369 calories
9.1 g. total fat (22% of calories)
3 g. saturated fat
84 mg. cholesterol
150 mg. sodium

Spaghetti Carbonara

Carbonara sauce goes light! This version owes its creaminess to nonfat sour cream and its delicious flavor to lean Canadian bacon, peas and mushrooms.

Makes 4 servings

⅔ cup **defatted reduced-sodium chicken broth**

1 **medium onion, diced**

3 ounces **lean Canadian bacon, thinly sliced into strips**

3 cups **sliced mushrooms**

1 cup **frozen peas**

1 ounce **Parmesan cheese, grated**

2 tablespoons **nonfat sour cream**

8 ounces **uncooked spaghetti**

●

Bring the broth to a boil over medium-high heat in a large no-stick frying pan. Add the onions and cook, stirring frequently, for 3 minutes. Add the bacon and mushrooms and continue to cook, stirring frequently, for 5 to 8 minutes, or until the mushrooms are very soft.

●

Add the peas and heat through. Remove from the heat and stir in the Parmesan and sour cream.

●

While the sauce is cooking, cook the spaghetti in a large pot of boiling water until just tender. Drain. Return to the pot. Add the sauce and toss well.

Hands-on time: 5 minutes
Total time: 20 minutes

Per serving: 342 calories
5 g. total fat (13% of calories)
1.9 g. saturated fat
16 mg. cholesterol
497 mg. sodium

Herbed Pasta with Ham and Red Peppers

Who says you need tomatoes in pasta sauce? Delightfully different but still Italian, this one features ham, zucchini and herbs.

Makes 4 servings

1¼ **cups uncooked ziti**
1 **large onion, chopped**
½ cup **coarsely chopped green peppers**
2 teaspoons **olive oil**
1¼ cups **defatted reduced-sodium chicken broth**
⅓ cup **water**
8 ounces **cubed lean smoked ham**
1 jar (4 ounces) **chopped red peppers, drained**
1 tablespoon **dried basil leaves**
½ teaspoon **dried thyme leaves**
½ teaspoon **dried oregano leaves**
⅛ teaspoon **freshly ground black pepper**
1 **large zucchini, cut into ¾″ cubes**

•

Cook the pasta in a large pot of boiling water for 7 minutes, or until it begins to soften but is only partially cooked. Drain in a colander, rinse under cold water, drain and set aside.

•

Set the pot over medium-high heat and add the onions, green peppers and oil. Cook, stirring, for 5 minutes, or until the onions are soft and beginning to brown. Add the broth, water, ham, red peppers, basil, thyme, oregano and black pepper.

•

Stir in the pasta. Bring to a boil and cook for 5 minutes, or until the pasta is al dente. Stir in the zucchini and simmer for 4 minutes, or until the zucchini is cooked through.

Hands-on time: 5 minutes
Total time: 25 minutes

Per serving: 262 calories
6.2 g. total fat (16% of calories)
1.4 g. saturated fat
30 mg. cholesterol
839 mg. sodium

Creamy Pasta with Vegetables and Ham

Cauliflower and Cheddar are a great combo, especially when paired with green peas and ham in a creamy-tasting, super-quick sauce.

Makes 4 servings

2 cups **chopped cauliflower florets**

1 cup **chopped onions**

1 **clove garlic, minced**

2 tablespoons **cornstarch**

2 cups **1% low-fat milk**

½ teaspoon **dried thyme leaves**

½ teaspoon **dried basil leaves**

¼ teaspoon **dry mustard**

⅛ teaspoon **freshly ground black pepper**

⅛ teaspoon **salt** (**optional**)

¾ cup **shredded reduced-fat sharp Cheddar cheese**

6 ounces **cubed lean ham steak**

1 cup **frozen peas**

8 ounces **uncooked linguine**

Combine the cauliflower, onions and garlic in a 4-cup glass measuring cup. Cover with wax paper and microwave on high power for a total of 6 to 7 minutes, or until the onions are tender; stop and stir the mixture halfway through the cooking period. Set aside.

In a large saucepan, mix the cornstarch and ¼ cup of the milk until smooth. Stir in the thyme, basil, mustard, pepper, salt (if using) and the remaining 1¾ cups milk.

Bring to a simmer over medium heat, stirring frequently. Reduce the heat to medium-low and cook, stirring, for 2 to 3 minutes, or until the sauce thickens. Add the Cheddar and stir until the cheese melts.

Add the ham, peas and cauliflower mixture. Heat through.

While the sauce is cooking, cook the linguine in a large pot of boiling water until just tender. Drain. Serve topped with the sauce.

Hands-on time: 15 minutes
Total time: 30 minutes

Per serving: 464 calories
7.8 g. total fat (15% of calories)
3.4 g. saturated fat
27 mg. cholesterol
731 mg. sodium

Encore!

Baked Creamy Pasta Casserole

In a bowl, mix 2 cups leftover Creamy Pasta with Vegetables and Ham, 2 eggs (or ½ cup egg substitute) and 2 cups additional cooked linguine. Coat a 9″ × 13″ baking dish with no-stick spray and add the mixture, smoothing the top. Sprinkle generously with toasted bread crumbs. Bake at 350° for 25 minutes. Cut into squares as you would lasagna.

Spicy Noodle-and-Pork Stir-Fry

The Malaysian dish that inspired this is usually served with very fine rice vermicelli or Chinese wheat noodles. But regular vermicelli does nicely.

Makes 4 servings

8 ounces **uncooked vermicelli, broken into 3″ lengths**
3½ tablespoons **reduced-sodium soy sauce**
1½ teaspoons **minced fresh ginger**
1¼ teaspoons **curry powder**
8 ounces **trimmed boneless pork loin,**
  cut into thin 2″ strips
1 teaspoon **canola oil**
1 **small onion, coarsely chopped**
2 **large stalks celery, thinly sliced**
½ **medium red or green pepper,**
  cut into 1¼″ strips
½ cup **defatted reduced-sodium chicken broth**
1½ teaspoons **sesame oil**

•

Cook the vermicelli in a large pot of boiling water until just tender. Drain, rinse with cold water and set aside.

•

Meanwhile, in a medium bowl, stir together the soy sauce, ginger, curry powder and pork. Set aside to marinate for 10 minutes.

•

In a large no-stick frying pan, warm the canola oil over medium-high heat until hot but not smoking. Add the onions, celery and peppers and cook, stirring, for about 4 minutes, or until the onions soften slightly.

•

Stir in the pork and marinade. Cook, stirring, for about 3 minutes, or until the pork strips are almost cooked through.

•

Stir in the broth, sesame oil and vermicelli. Bring to a boil. Cook, stirring, for 1 to 2 minutes, or until most of the liquid is absorbed.

Hands-on time: 12 minutes
Total time: 20 minutes

Per serving: 238 calories
7.3 g. total fat (27% of calories)
1.6 g. saturated fat
25 mg. cholesterol
560 mg. sodium

**Savory
Leftover Stir-Fry**
If you make extra, this stir-fry freezes well. Transfer cooled leftovers to 1-cup self-sealing plastic freezer bags, flattening each bag to remove excess air. Freeze flat. To use, thaw overnight in the refrigerator, then transfer to a no-stick wok or frying pan. Add ¼ cup chicken broth. Cover and heat through, stirring occasionally. Adjust seasonings, adding more curry powder if desired.

Shrimp and Feta Skillet Dinner

Feta cheese is just assertive enough to make a fine foil for succulent shrimp and ripe tomatoes. Use canned whole tomatoes if ripe ones are out of season.

Makes 4 servings

3 tablespoons **defatted reduced-sodium chicken broth**
2 teaspoons **olive oil**
¼ cup **thinly sliced scallions**
1 **clove garlic, minced**
1 teaspoon **dried oregano leaves**
2 teaspoons **lemon juice**
¼ cup **chopped fresh parsley**
12 ounces **peeled and deveined shrimp**
4 **plum tomatoes, chopped**
½ cup **cubed feta cheese**
8 ounces **uncooked f**

•

In a large no-stick frying pan, co.... .e broth, oil, scallions and garlic. Cook over medium heat, stir frequently, for 2 to 3 minutes, or until the scallions soften. Stir in the oregano, lemon juice and parsley and mix well.

•

Stir in the shrimp, cover and cook for 3 to 4 minutes, or until the shrimp turn pink.

•

Stir in the tomatoes and feta. Cook for 2 minutes, or until the tomatoes are hot.

•

While the sauce is cooking, cook the fusilli in a large pot of boiling water until just tender. Drain. Serve topped with the sauce.

Hands-on time: 10 minutes
Total time: 30 minutes

Per serving: 350 calories
8 g. total fat (21% of calories)
2.9 g. saturated fat
192 mg. cholesterol
351 mg. sodium

Linguine with Fresh Salmon and Tomato Sauce

In this easy, economical salmon dinner, fresh tomatoes and herbs complement the fresh fish. The delectable sauce is enriched with nonfat sour cream.

Makes 4 servings

8 ounces **skinless salmon fillet, cut crosswise into 2″ pieces**
1 teaspoon **dried dill**
¼ teaspoon **salt** (**optional**)
¼ teaspoon **freshly ground black pepper**
2 cups **cubed tomatoes**
½ cup **thinly sliced scallions**
2 tablespoons **chopped fresh parsley**
1 **clove garlic, minced**
2 teaspoons **olive oil**
⅓ cup **nonfat sour cream**
8 ounces u**** **ked linguine**

Sprinkle the salmon with th**** ll, salt (if using) and pepper.

Coat a large no-stick frying pan with no-stick spray. Add the salmon and cook over medium heat for 11 to 12 minutes, or until the pieces are cooked through. Remove from the pan and break into bite-size pieces.

In the same pan, combine the tomatoes, scallions, parsley, garlic and oil. Cook over medium heat, stirring frequently, for 4 to 5 minutes, or until the tomatoes are soft. Stir in the sour cream and salmon. Cook for 1 to 2 minutes, or until heated through.

While the sauce is cooking, cook the linguine in a large pot of boiling water until just tender. Drain. Serve topped with the sauce.

Hands-on time: 10 minutes
Total time: 30 minutes

Per serving: 338 calories
7.7 g. total fat (21% of calories)
1.1 g. saturated fat
80 mg. cholesterol
70 mg. sodium

To Your Health

Salmon

Salmon is a super source of heart-healthy omega-3 fatty acids. All told, scientists have discovered that the omega-3's reduce or inhibit at least 17 different factors suspected of putting you at risk for heart disease and increase at least 7 different factors that may protect you.

Fish and Pasta Stew

In this mouthwatering stew, delicate-flavored haddock marries well with tomatoes, peppers, sherry and the piquancy of a little fresh lime juice.

Makes 4 servings

2 cups **uncooked medium pasta shells**

1 tablespoon **olive oil**

1 **large onion, chopped**

⅔ cup **coarsely chopped mixed sweet red and green peppers**

2 **large cloves garlic, minced**

2 cups **defatted reduced-sodium chicken broth**

½ cup **dry sherry or apple juice**

½ teaspoon **dried thyme leaves**

⅛ teaspoon **ground red pepper**

1 can (14½ ounces) **tomatoes (with juice), chopped**

2 tablespoons **lime juice**

Salt (optional)

Freshly ground black pepper

1 pound **haddock or other mild white fish fillets, cubed**

Cook the shells in a large pot of boiling water for 6 minutes, or until softened but only partially cooked. Drain in a colander, rinse under cold water and set aside.

Add the oil, onions, chopped peppers and garlic to the pot. Cook over high heat, stirring, for about 5 minutes, or until the onions are browned. Add the broth, sherry or apple juice, thyme and red pepper. Bring to a boil and cook for 5 minutes.

Add the shells to the pot and boil for 5 minutes.

Stir in the tomatoes (with juice), lime juice, salt (if using) and black pepper.

Add the fish and simmer for 3 to 4 minutes, or until the fish flakes when tested with a fork and the pasta is al dente.

Hands-on time: 10 minutes
Total time: 30 minutes

Per serving: 395 calories
5.4 g. total fat (12% of calories)
0.8 g. saturated fat
65 mg. cholesterol
486 mg. sodium

Take It Along

Stew for Lunch
This stew tastes even better the next day, when flavors have a chance to meld. Package the stew in 1-cup microwave-safe containers. Reheat on high power for 3 to 5 minutes. Toast a few thick slices of French bread. Serve your lunchtime stew French-style by placing the toast at the bottom of a bowl and ladling fish and pasta over it.

Linguine with Savory Mushroom Sauce

This meatless sauce has an intriguing earthy taste and meaty texture, thanks to sun-dried tomatoes and dried shiitake mushrooms, available in most produce sections.

Makes 4 servings

1 ounce **dried shiitake mushrooms**

3 ounces **sun-dried tomatoes** (**not oil-packed**)

1 cup **boiling water**

1 cup **defatted reduced-sodium chicken broth**

2 **cloves garlic, minced**

3 cups **sliced fresh mushrooms**

1 can (14½ ounces) **Italian-style stewed tomatoes**

12 ounces **uncooked linguine**

Place the shiitake mushrooms, sun-dried tomatoes and water in a small bowl. Let soak for 10 minutes.

In a large no-stick frying pan, bring the broth to a boil over medium-high heat. Add the garlic and fresh mushrooms. Simmer for 5 minutes, or until the mushrooms soften.

Add the soaked mushrooms and sun-dried tomatoes with the soaking liquid. Cook for 5 minutes, or until slightly thickened.

Remove the pan from the heat and let the vegetables cool slightly. Transfer them to a food processor and chop to a coarse puree. Return the puree to the pan. Add the stewed tomatoes and heat through.

While the sauce is cooking, cook the linguine in a large pot of boiling water until just tender. Drain. Return to the pot, add the sauce and toss well to combine.

Hands-on time: 10 minutes
Total time: 25 minutes

Per serving: 417 calories
2.9 g. total fat (6% of calories)
0.4 g. saturated fat
73 mg. cholesterol
420 mg. sodium

Rotini with Eggplant-Pepper Sauce

Rotini, or spiral pasta, grab this satisfying sauce perfectly. The technique of salting the eggplant draws out its bitter juices. Just remember to rinse the eggplant well to remove the salt.

Makes 4 servings

1	**small eggplant, peeled and diced**
1 teaspoon	**salt**
½ cup	**white wine or apple juice**
1	**small onion, chopped**
2 cups	**chopped sweet red peppers**
2 cups	**chopped green peppers**
2 cups	**chopped yellow peppers**
1 can (16 ounces)	**plum tomatoes (with juice)**
2	**large cloves garlic, minced**
1 teaspoon	**honey**
2 tablespoons	**chopped fresh basil**
12 ounces	**uncooked rotini**

•

Place the eggplant in a medium bowl; sprinkle lightly with the salt and let stand for 15 minutes to absorb the salt and release excess moisture. Rinse well to remove the salt; pat dry with paper towels. Spread the eggplant in a single layer on paper towels.

•

Bring the wine or apple juice to a boil in a large no-stick frying pan. Add the onions and simmer, stirring frequently, for 3 minutes, or until softened. Add the red, green and yellow peppers, tomatoes (with juice), garlic, honey and basil. Reduce the heat to medium and simmer, stirring occasionally, for 10 minutes, or until the peppers are very soft.

•

Add the eggplant and simmer for 10 minutes, or until the sauce is thick.

•

While the sauce is cooking, cook the rotini in a large pot of boiling water until just tender. Drain. Return to the pot. Add the sauce and toss well to combine.

Hands-on time: 15 minutes
Total time: 40 minutes

Per serving: 393 calories
3 g. total fat (7% of calories)
0.4 g. saturated fat
73 mg. cholesterol
204 mg. sodium

Make-Ahead Weeknight Supper
Eggplant-Pepper Sauce tastes even richer after it's been frozen, so make extra for busy weeknight suppers. Separately freeze the cooked pasta in self-sealing plastic freezer bags and the sauce in tightly lidded containers. Reheat the sauce in a covered saucepan over low heat for 15 minutes, stirring frequently, or microwave on high power for 3 minutes. Immerse frozen cooked pasta in boiling water for 2 to 3 minutes, or until hot.

———

Tortelloni and Vegetables

Here's a different and delicious twist on an impromptu pasta dinner. Tortelloni are the large form of tortellini, which you may also use if the bigger pasta is not available.

1 **large onion, chopped**
1 cup **sliced mushrooms**
2 teaspoons **olive oil**
2 **cloves garlic, minced**
½ cup **defatted reduced-sodium chicken broth**
1 can (15 ounces) **reduced-sodium tomato sauce**
1 **large green pepper, chopped**
1 cup **diced zucchini**
2 tablespoons **dry sherry or apple juice**
1½ teaspoons **dried Italian seasoning**
9 ounces **uncooked reduced-fat cheese-filled tortelloni**
Salt (optional)
Freshly ground black pepper
●

Coat a large saucepan with no-stick spray. Add the onions, mushrooms, oil, garlic and 3 tablespoons of the broth. Cook over medium heat, stirring frequently, for 5 to 6 minutes, or until the onions soften. If the liquid evaporates, add more broth.
●

Stir in the tomato sauce, green peppers, zucchini, sherry or apple juice, Italian seasoning and the remaining broth. Add the tortelloni.
●

Cover and simmer for 15 minutes. Season with the salt (if using) and black pepper.

Hands-on time: 10 minutes
Total time: 30 minutes

Per serving: 284 calories
4 g. total fat (13% of calories)
1.1 g. saturated fat
4 mg. cholesterol
371 mg. sodium

Makes 4 servings

Encore!

Tortelloni and Vegetable Soup
For a speedy, rich soup, mix 2 cups leftover Tortelloni and Vegetables, 2 cups chicken broth, 1 cup chopped mixed fresh or frozen vegetables and 2 tablespoons chopped fresh basil in a saucepan. Bring to a boil, then simmer for 15 minutes, or until the vegetables are crisp-tender. Season with salt, pepper and Parmesan cheese.

Vegetables in Creamy Tomato Sauce over Pasta

To add variety to your pasta repertoire, try this vegetable medley in creamy tomato sauce. The secret of its wonderfully rich taste: nonfat sour cream.

Makes 4 servings

2 tablespoons **sherry or apple juice**
2 teaspoons **olive oil**
1 cup **chopped onions**
1 **large clove garlic, minced**
1 can (15 ounces) **reduced-sodium tomato sauce**
2 cups **coarsely chopped cauliflower florets**
1 **large carrot, thinly sliced**
1½ cups **diced zucchini**
2 teaspoons **dried Italian seasoning**
¼ teaspoon **dry mustard**
⅛ teaspoon **freshly ground black pepper**
½ cup **nonfat sour cream**
¼ teaspoon **salt** (**optional**)
8 ounces **uncooked linguine**

In a large no-stick frying pan, combine the sherry or apple juice, oil, onions and garlic. Cook over medium-high heat, stirring frequently, for 5 to 7 minutes, or until the onions soften.

Stir in the tomato sauce, cauliflower, carrots, zucchini, Italian seasoning, mustard and pepper. Bring to a boil over high heat, cover, reduce the heat and simmer for 15 to 20 minutes, or until the vegetables are tender.

Remove the pan from the heat and stir in the sour cream until well-combined. Add the salt (if using).

While the sauce is cooking, cook the linguine in a large pot of boiling water until just tender. Drain. Serve topped with the sauce.

Hands-on time: 10 minutes
Total time: 30 minutes

Per serving: 373 calories
3.6 g. total fat (9% of calories)
0.5 g. saturated fat
0 mg. cholesterol
89 mg. sodium

Zesty Ziti

An unusual, time-saving feature of this recipe is that you don't cook the ziti before assembling the casserole. Leftovers reheat well in a 250° oven for 15 minutes (or microwave them on high power for about 2 minutes per serving).

Makes 4 servings

1 tablespoon **olive oil**
1 **clove garlic, minced**
2 cups **baby carrots**
8 **stalks fresh asparagus, cut into 2″ lengths**
4 **scallions, cut into 2″ lengths**
2 cups **frozen wax beans or Italian green beans**
1 can (16 ounces) **reduced-sodium chicken broth, defatted**
1 can (14½ ounces) **Italian-style stewed tomatoes**
1 can (16 ounces) **vegetarian beans in tomato sauce**
1 cup **water**
3 cups **uncooked ziti**
1 cup **shredded part-skim mozzarella cheese**
1 tablespoon **grated Romano cheese**
¼ cup **seasoned dry bread crumbs**

Preheat the oven to 400°. Lightly coat a 9″ × 13″ baking dish with no-stick spray.

In a large pot, warm the oil over medium-high heat. Add the garlic and cook for 1 minute, or until softened but not browned. Add the carrots, asparagus, scallions and wax or green beans; mix well.

Add the broth, tomatoes, vegetarian beans and water. Bring to a boil.

Spread the ziti evenly over the bottom of the baking dish.

When the vegetables come to a boil, carefully pour or spoon the mixture over the ziti. Make sure the ziti is covered completely.

Bake for 20 minutes, or until hot and bubbling.

Sprinkle with the mozzarella and Romano. Top with the bread crumbs and bake for 10 minutes, or until the crumbs brown. Let stand for 10 minutes before serving.

Hands-on time: 5 minutes
Total time: 45 minutes

Per serving: 628 calories
10.6 g. total fat (15% of calories)
3.9 g. saturated fat
17 mg. cholesterol
962 mg. sodium

Cold Sesame Noodle Salad

Tahini dressing and cilantro—a pungent green herb also known as fresh coriander or Chinese parsley—give this salad its distinctive flavor.

Makes 4 servings

1 tablespoon **tahini**
¼ cup **plain nonfat yogurt**
1 tablespoon **reduced-sodium soy sauce**
1 tablespoon **honey**
2 **scallions, chopped**
⅓ cup **diced peeled cucumbers**
1 tablespoon **minced fresh cilantro**
3 cups **chilled cooked spaghetti, udon noodles or other strand pasta**
2 cups **finely shredded romaine lettuce or green cabbage**

•

In a large bowl, stir together the tahini, yogurt, soy sauce and honey until smooth. Add the scallions, cucumbers, cilantro and pasta. Mix well.

•

Serve on a bed of lettuce or cabbage.

Hands-on time: 10 minutes
Total time: 10 minutes

Per serving: 199 calories
2.8 g. total fat (12% of calories)
0 g. saturated fat
2 mg. cholesterol
147 mg. sodium

Take It Along

Asian Feast at the Office
For a workday lunch treat, take leftover Cold Sesame Noodle Salad in a two-cup Thermos, with the shredded lettuce or cabbage wrapped separately to stay crisp. Add a small bag of carrot sticks, sliced daikon radishes or sliced peppers. If desired, top the salad with slivers of cold grilled chicken breast.

Spicy Minestrone
(page 110) ➙

Comforting
Soups

Caribbean Chicken-Vegetable Soup

Zesty and aromatic! Turn up or tone down this soup's tropic heat by your choice of curry and chili powders. For example, curry labeled "madras" is hot.

Makes 4 servings

2½ teaspoons **canola oil**
1 cup **chopped onions**
½ cup **chopped celery**
½ cup **diced sweet red or green peppers**
4½ cups **defatted reduced-sodium chicken broth**
1 cup **water**
2 **large bay leaves**
1 teaspoon **chili powder**
½ teaspoon **curry powder**
½ teaspoon **dried thyme leaves**
¼ teaspoon **ground allspice**
⅛ teaspoon **freshly ground black pepper**
1¼ pounds **skinless, bone-in chicken breast halves**
¼ cup **uncooked white rice**
1 can (14½ ounces) **black beans, rinsed and drained**

•

In a large pot, combine the oil, onions, celery and red or green peppers. Cook over high heat, stirring, for 5 minutes, or until the vegetables soften. If needed, add a little water to prevent burning.

•

Stir in the broth, water, bay leaves, chili powder, curry powder, thyme, allspice and black pepper. Add the chicken and bring to a boil.

•

Reduce the heat and simmer, stirring occasionally, for 25 minutes, or until the chicken is cooked through. Transfer the chicken to a plate and set aside until cool enough to handle.

•

Stir the rice and beans into the pot. Cover and simmer for 15 minutes, or until the rice is just tender.

•

Remove the chicken from the bone and cut into bite-size pieces. Add to the pot and cook for 5 minutes. Remove and discard the bay leaves.

Hands-on time: 15 minutes
Total time: 1 hour

Per serving: 299 calories
6.5 g. total fat (18% of calories)
0.9 g. saturated fat
57 mg. cholesterol
704 mg. sodium

Easy Freeze

Better Beans

Some people say that freezing cooked beans makes them easier to digest. Whether or not that's true, Caribbean Chicken-Vegetable Soup freezes very well for future meals. Thaw the soup in the microwave on 50% power, then heat through on high power. Before serving, adjust the spiciness and garnish each bowl with chopped red peppers and nonfat yogurt.

Curried Chicken-and-Lentil Soup

This hearty soup calls for red lentils (found at most health food stores). The red lentils cook especially fast; allow extra time if using other lentils.

Makes 4 servings

2 cups **chopped onions**
2 **large cloves garlic, minced**
5 cups **defatted reduced-sodium chicken broth**
6–8 ounces **boneless, skinless chicken breasts, cubed**
¾ cup **red lentils, rinsed and drained**
2 cups **frozen carrots and peas**
2 teaspoons **curry powder**
¼ teaspoon **ground ginger**
¼ teaspoon **freshly ground black pepper**
½ cup **2% low-fat milk**
½ teaspoon **salt (optional)**

●

In a large pot, combine the onions, garlic and 3 tablespoons of the broth. Cook over medium heat, stirring frequently, for 5 minutes, or until the onions are softened. Add the chicken, lentils, carrots and peas, curry powder, ginger, pepper and the remaining broth.

●

Bring to a boil. Reduce the heat, cover and simmer for 25 to 30 minutes, or until the lentils are cooked but not soft.

●

Add the milk and salt (if using). Heat through.

Hands-on time: 10 minutes
Total time: 40 minutes

Per serving: 240 calories
4 g. total fat (15% of calories)
0.6 g. saturated fat
19 mg. cholesterol
90 mg. sodium

Take It Along

Picnic in the Park

Heat some leftover Curried Chicken and Lentil Soup and pack it in a Thermos for lunch in the park. Take along a small bag of minced scallions and parsley to garnish each bowl, plus some low-salt bread-sticks as an accompaniment. If you really want to get fancy, add some chopped dried apricots, raisins or other dried fruit for extra sweetness.

Charlie

Chicken Soup with Dumplings

This mild-flavored, ultra-easy soup begins with canned chicken broth and boneless, skinless chicken breasts. Even the homemade dumplings are a snap.

Makes 4 servings

2 **eggs**
½ cup **matzo meal**
2 cups **defatted reduced-sodium chicken broth**
1 **carrot, chopped**
½ **stalk celery, chopped**
½ cup **chopped onions**
2 **boneless, skinless chicken breast halves**
   (**4 ounces each**)
3 tablespoons **chopped fresh parsley**

•

In a small bowl, beat the eggs with a fork until frothy. Slowly beat in the matzo meal. Cover and refrigerate for at least 10 minutes.

•

In a large pot, bring the broth to a boil over high heat. Add the carrots, celery, onions and chicken. Reduce the heat to medium, cover and cook for 10 minutes, or until the chicken is cooked through.

•

Remove the chicken with a slotted spoon and set aside until cool enough to handle.

•

Form the matzo mixture into 8 balls. (For each ball, use about 1 tablespoon of the mixture. Dampen your hands with cold water and roll the mixture between your palms into a ball.)

•

Bring the broth back to a gentle boil. Drop the dumplings into the pot. Cover and cook for 10 minutes, or until the dumplings are cooked through.

•

Cut the chicken into bite-size pieces and add to the pot. Stir in the parsley. Cook for 3 minutes, or until the chicken is hot.

Hands-on time: 15 minutes
Total time: 35 minutes

Per serving: 254 calories
7.5 g. total fat (28% of calories)
2 g. saturated fat
165 mg. cholesterol
734 mg. sodium

Big Bowls of Comfort

Chicken soup has always been good for what ails you. And if nothing ails you, no matter—chicken soup is just downright delicious. Here are 20 quick variations on the theme, giving you something to fit your every mood.

The following recipes serve 4. Most use 12 ounces of boneless, skinless chicken breast. If you want to cut back on meat, you could easily reduce it to 6 ounces and still get delicious results.

Greek Soup with Broccoli and Dill

In a 3-quart saucepan, **sauté** 12 ounces cubed chicken breast, 1 tablespoon minced garlic and a pinch of black or red pepper in 2 tablespoons olive oil. **Add** 32 ounces chicken broth; bring just to the boiling point. **Add** 1 to 2 cups frozen broccoli florets and 1 cup cooked rice. Bring back to the boiling point and **remove** from the heat. **Whisk** together 1 egg and 2 teaspoons lemon juice; quickly **stir** into the soup. **Add** 1 tablespoon chopped fresh dill.

Egg Drop and Snow Pea Soup

In a 3-quart saucepan, **mix** 12 ounces cubed chicken breast, 1 tablespoon chopped garlic, 1 tablespoon cornstarch, 2 teaspoons sesame oil, 2 teaspoons soy sauce, 1 teaspoon chopped ginger, 1 teaspoon honey and a pinch of black pepper. **Cook**, stirring, until the chicken is opaque. **Add** 32 ounces chicken broth and bring to a boil. **Add** 1 to 2 cups snow peas and 1 cup cooked rice. Reduce the heat. Lightly **whisk** an egg and **pour** in a thin stream into the pan, stirring gently to form ribbons.

Mexican Meatball Soup

Soak 3 slices white bread in water, then squeeze dry. **Place** in a food processor with 6 ounces cubed chicken breast, 1 egg, chopped scallions, ½ teaspoon minced garlic and a pinch of cumin. **Process** until just blended; **form** into small meatballs. In a 3-quart saucepan, **sauté** 1 teaspoon minced garlic, 1 bay leaf and a pinch of black pepper in 1 teaspoon olive oil. **Add** 16 ounces chopped tomatoes and 16 ounces chicken broth. Bring to a boil. Carefully **add** the meatballs, a few at a time. **Simmer** gently for 10 minutes. **Remove** and discard the bay leaf. Serve garnished with avocado slices and chopped cilantro.

Hungarian Chicken Soup

In a 3-quart saucepan, **sauté** 2 cups chopped onions and 1 cup sliced red peppers in 2 teaspoons butter until the vegetables are soft. **Add** 12 ounces cubed chicken breast and **sauté** until opaque. Stir in ¼ cup raisins, 1 tablespoon flour, 1 tablespoon paprika and 2 teaspoons salt. **Sauté** for 1 minute. Gradually **add** 2 cups chicken broth, stirring constantly. Bring to a boil. **Add** 1 teaspoon honey. **Simmer** for 5 minutes. **Stir** in 1 tablespoon low-fat sour cream just before serving.

Chicken Florentine Soup

In a 3-quart saucepan, **sauté** 12 ounces cubed chicken breast, 1 tablespoon minced garlic, a pinch of black pepper and a pinch of nutmeg in 2 teaspoons olive oil or butter. **Add** 32 ounces chicken broth, 4 cups chopped fresh spinach and 1 cup cooked rice. Bring to a boil, then **simmer** for 5 minutes; **remove** from the heat. **Whisk** 1 egg with 2 teaspoons lemon juice; quickly **stir** into the soup. Serve sprinkled with Parmesan.

Tortilla Soup

Cut 5 corn tortillas into wedges; **toss** with 1 teaspoon olive oil and **crisp** on a baking sheet in a 375° oven until deep golden brown. In a 3-quart saucepan, **sauté** 1 cup chopped celery, 1 cup chopped onions, 1 tablespoon minced garlic, ½ teaspoon minced orange rind (optional) and ¼ teaspoon cumin in 1 teaspoon olive oil. **Add** 12 ounces cubed chicken breast; **cook** until opaque. **Add** 16 ounces black beans, 16 ounces chicken broth, 1 cup chopped carrots, 4½ ounces canned chopped green chili peppers and ¼ cup orange juice. Bring to a boil, then **simmer** for 5 to 10 minutes. **Add** the tortillas and **simmer** until softened. Serve garnished with chopped cilantro and low-fat sour cream.

Chicken Soup with Crispy Wontons

Cut 20 wonton wrappers into strips; **toss** with 1 teaspoon sesame oil and crisp on a baking sheet in a 375° oven until golden brown. In a 3-quart saucepan, **mix** 12 ounces diced chicken breast, 1 teaspoon minced ginger, 1 teaspoon minced garlic, chopped scallions, 2 teaspoons cornstarch, 1 teaspoon soy sauce, 1 teaspoon brown sugar, 1 teaspoon sesame oil and a pinch of white pepper. **Cook**, stirring, until the chicken is opaque. **Add** 32 ounces chicken broth and 4 cups frozen oriental vegetables. Bring to a boil. Serve topped with the crisped wontons.

Italian Greens Soup

In a 3-quart saucepan, **mix** 12 ounces cubed chicken breast, 2 teaspoons minced garlic, 2 teaspoons cornstarch, 1 teaspoon olive oil and a pinch of black pepper. **Cook**, stirring, until the chicken is opaque. **Add** 32 ounces chicken broth, 2 cups diced carrots and 1 cup cooked rice. Bring to a boil, then **simmer** for 5 to 10 minutes. **Add** 3 cups shredded escarole and **simmer** for 5 minutes. Serve sprinkled with Parmesan.

Hearty Chicken and Egg Noodle Soup

In a 3-quart saucepan, bring 32 ounces chicken broth to a boil. **Add** 12 ounces cubed chicken breast, 1 cup cooked egg noodles and 1 cup mixed frozen vegetables. **Simmer** until the vegetables are hot and the chicken is cooked through (about 5 minutes). Stir in chopped parsley.

(continued)

Chick-Pea and Tomato Soup

In a 3-quart saucepan, **sauté** 12 ounces cubed chicken breast, 2 teaspoons garlic and a pinch of black pepper in 2 teaspoons olive oil until the chicken is opaque. **Add** 16 ounces chicken broth, 16 ounces crushed tomatoes and 1 cup canned chick-peas. Bring to a boil, then **simmer** for 10 minutes. Serve sprinkled with Parmesan and chopped basil.

Alphabet Soup

In a 3-quart saucepan, **sauté** 12 ounces cubed chicken breast, 1 table-spoon chopped onions and 1 tablespoon chopped celery in 2 teaspoons olive oil until the chicken is opaque. **Add** 16 ounces chicken broth and 16 ounces crushed tomatoes. Bring to a boil and **add** 2 cups frozen diced vegetables and 1 cup cooked alphabet noodles. **Simmer** until vegetables are heated through.

Spanish Sweet Potato Soup

In a 3-quart saucepan, **sauté** 12 ounces cubed chicken breast, ¼ cup chopped scallions, 2 teaspoons minced garlic, 2 teaspoons chopped green olives and a pinch of saffron in 2 teaspoons olive oil until the chicken is opaque. **Add** 16 ounces chicken broth, 16 ounces crushed tomatoes and 12 ounces frozen sweet potatoes. Bring to a boil, then **simmer** for 15 minutes, or until the sweet potatoes are cooked through. Break up the sweet potatoes with a wooden spoon. **Add** 1 cup cooked rice.

Chili Chicken Soup

In a 3-quart saucepan, **sauté** 12 ounces cubed chicken breast, 1 cup chopped onions, 2 teaspoons minced garlic and ¼ teaspoon cumin in 2 teaspoons oil until the chicken is opaque. **Add** 16 ounces pinto beans, 2 cups chopped tomatoes, 1 cup chicken broth and 1 cup cooked rice. Bring to a boil, then **remove** from the heat. **Stir** in 2 tablespoons shredded Cheddar cheese and 2 tablespoons chopped mild green chili peppers.

Hot-and-Sour Soup

Rehydrate 1 ounce sliced dried shiitake mushrooms in 2 cups boiling water; set aside. In a 3-quart saucepan, **sauté** 12 ounces cubed chicken breast, ¼ cup chopped scallions, 2 teaspoons minced garlic and 2 teaspoons chopped ginger in 2 teaspoons olive oil until the chicken is opaque. **Add** 16 ounces chicken broth and bring to a boil. **Mix** 1 table-spoon cornstarch, 2 teaspoons vinegar, 2 teaspoons sesame oil, 1 teaspoon brown sugar and 1 teaspoon soy sauce. **Stir** into the soup. **Add** the mushrooms and their liquid and 2 cups frozen peas. **Cook**, stirring, until slightly thickened.

Potpie Soup

In a 3-quart saucepan, **sauté** 12 ounces cubed chicken breast in 2 teaspoons butter or olive oil until the chicken is opaque. **Stir** in 2 tablespoons flour, a pinch of dried thyme and a pinch of black pepper; stir for 2 minutes. **Add** 2 cups 2% low-fat milk, 16 ounces chicken broth and 2 cups frozen mixed vegetables. Bring to a boil, then **simmer** for 10 minutes.

Mediterranean Soup with Peppers

In a 3-quart saucepan, **sauté** 12 ounces cubed chicken breast, 2 cups sliced red peppers, 1 cup sliced onions and 2 teaspoons minced garlic in 2 teaspoons olive oil until the chicken is opaque. **Stir** in 32 ounces chicken broth and 2 cups cooked rice. Bring to a boil, then **stir** in 2 teaspoons chopped basil and 2 teaspoons fresh chopped mint.

Italian Bean Soup

In a 3-quart saucepan, **sauté** 12 ounces cubed chicken breast and 2 teaspoons minced garlic in 2 teaspoons olive oil until the chicken is opaque. **Add** 16 ounces Great Northern beans, 16 ounces chopped tomatoes and 1 cup water. Bring to a boil, then **stir** in 1 tablespoon minced basil, 2 teaspoons chopped parsley and 1 tablespoon Parmesan.

Japanese Chicken and Noodles

In a 3-quart saucepan, **sauté** 12 ounces cubed chicken breast, ¼ cup sliced scallions, 2 teaspoons minced garlic, 2 teaspoons chopped ginger and 1 teaspoon brown sugar in 2 teaspoons sesame oil until the chicken is opaque. **Add** 32 ounces chicken broth, 2 cups cooked linguine, 1 cup sliced mushrooms and 2 teaspoons soy sauce. Bring to a boil.

Chicken Stew with Winter Vegetables

In a 3-quart saucepan, **brown** 2 tablespoons flour in 2 teaspoons butter and 2 teaspoons olive oil, stirring constantly. **Add** 12 ounces cubed chicken breast, 1 cup sliced mushrooms and 1 cup chopped onions; **sauté** until the chicken is opaque. **Add** 32 ounces chicken broth and 2 cups frozen mixed vegetables. Bring to a boil, then **simmer** for 5 minutes. **Stir** in 1 tablespoon chopped parsley.

Primavera Soup

In a 3-quart saucepan, **sauté** 12 ounces cubed chicken breast, 1 cup chopped zucchini, 1 cup sliced red peppers, 1 cup sliced mushrooms, ¼ cup sliced scallions and 2 teaspoons minced garlic in 1 tablespoon olive oil until the chicken is opaque. **Add** 16 ounces chopped tomatoes and 16 ounces chicken broth. Bring to a boil. **Add** 2 cups cooked rotini, 1 tablespoon shredded basil and 1 tablespoon Parmesan.

German Beef, Barley and Cabbage Soup

This robust soup could easily become your family's favorite. The combination of beef or pork, cabbage, caraway and paprika is popular in German cookery.

Makes 4 servings

8 ounces **extra-lean ground beef**
1 **large onion, chopped**
1 **large carrot, chopped**
3½ cups **defatted reduced-sodium beef broth**
1½ cups **water**
1 **medium pork hock**
¼ cup **uncooked quick-cooking barley**
1 **large tart apple, chopped**
1½ tablespoons **paprika**
2 **large bay leaves**
½ teaspoon **dried thyme leaves**
½ teaspoon **caraway seeds**
¼ teaspoon **freshly ground black pepper**
2½ cups **coarsely shredded green cabbage**
¼ cup **tomato paste**

Coat a large pot with no-stick spray. Crumble the beef into the pot. Cook over medium-high heat, breaking up the meat with a wooden spoon, for 4 to 5 minutes, or until lightly browned.

Line a platter with several thicknesses of paper towels. Transfer the beef to the plate and drain well.

Wipe out the pot with a paper towel. Add the beef, onions, carrots, broth, water, pork hock, barley, apples, paprika, bay leaves, thyme, caraway seeds and pepper. Bring to a boil over high heat.

Reduce the heat to a simmer, cover and cook, stirring occasionally, for 20 minutes. Add the cabbage.

Remove ¼ cup of the broth and mix it with the tomato paste until well-blended. Stir the mixture into the pot. Simmer for 10 minutes, or until the cabbage is crisp-tender and the barley is tender.

Remove and discard the pork hock and bay leaves.

Hands-on time: 10 minutes
Total time: 45 minutes

Per serving: 257 calories
8.9 g. total fat (30% of calories)
3.2 g. saturated fat
39 mg. cholesterol
653 mg. sodium

Encore!

Hearty German-Style Potatoes

Scrub and bake or microwave 2 large russet potatoes, then split them in half and lightly fluff the flesh with a fork. Place them, cut side up, on a baking sheet covered with aluminum foil. Top each with ½ cup strained left-over German Beef, Barley and Cabbage Soup and 1 tablespoon shredded low-fat Cheddar cheese. Bake at 400° for 15 to 20 minutes, or until heated through.

Beef, Cabbage and Beet Borscht

A slimmed-down version of a traditional Russian vegetable soup, this borscht needs to simmer vigorously to cook the cabbage as quickly as possible.

Makes 4 servings

6 ounces **extra-lean ground beef**
1 **clove garlic, minced**
1 cup **chopped onions**
4 cups **chopped cabbage**
2 cans (14½ ounces each) **reduced-sodium stewed tomatoes**
1¾ cups **water**
3 cups **shredded raw beets**
1 tablespoon **lemon juice**
2 tablespoons **packed brown sugar**

•

Coat a large pot with no-stick spray. Crumble the beef into the pot. Cook over medium-high heat, breaking up the meat with a wooden spoon, for 4 to 5 minutes, or until lightly browned.

•

Line a platter with several thicknesses of paper towels. Transfer the beef to the plate and drain well.

•

Wipe out the pot with a paper towel. Add the garlic, onions and cabbage. Sauté over medium heat for 15 minutes, or until the cabbage is softened; if needed, add a few tablespoons water to the pot to prevent sticking.

•

Add the beef, tomatoes, water, beets, lemon juice and brown sugar. Bring to a boil over high heat.

•

Cover, reduce the heat to medium and cook for 10 minutes, or until the beets are tender.

Hands-on time: 10 minutes
Total time: 40 minutes

Per serving: 241 calories
7.5 g. total fat (27% of calories)
2.9 g. saturated fat
28 mg. cholesterol
167 mg. sodium

Take It Along

Russian Carryout

Borscht gets better-tasting as it stands, so pack some in a microwave-safe container and take it to work. Reheat on high power for 3 to 4 minutes. Serve with a dollop of low-fat sour cream, a sprinkle of minced scallions and fingers of toasted dark rye bread for dipping.

———

Italian Vegetable-Bean Soup

Here's a stick-to-the-ribs, peasant-style soup, perfect for a winter dinner. This handsome soup reflects the three colors of the Italian flag.

Makes 4 servings

8 ounces	**extra-lean ground beef**
1	**large onion, chopped**
2	**large stalks celery, finely chopped**
2	**cloves garlic, minced**
3½ cups	**defatted reduced-sodium chicken broth**
1½ cups	**reduced-sodium spaghetti sauce**
1 can (19 ounces)	**cannellini beans, rinsed and drained**
1½ cups	**chopped zucchini**
2 cups	**chopped cauliflower florets**
⅛ teaspoon	**freshly ground black pepper**
⅓ cup	**uncooked orzo**
¼ teaspoon	**salt (optional)**
3 tablespoons	**grated Parmesan cheese (optional)**

●

Coat a large pot with no-stick spray. Crumble the beef into the pot. Cook over medium-high heat, breaking up the meat with a wooden spoon, for 4 to 5 minutes, or until lightly browned.

●

Line a platter with several thicknesses of paper towels. Transfer the beef to the platter and drain well.

●

Wipe out the pot with a paper towel. Add the onions, celery and garlic. Cook, stirring, over medium heat for 5 minutes, or until the onions are softened; if needed, add a few tablespoons water to prevent sticking.

●

Add the beef, broth, spaghetti sauce, beans, zucchini, cauliflower and pepper. Bring to a boil over high heat.

●

Cover, reduce the heat to medium and simmer for 30 minutes.

●

Meanwhile, in a medium saucepan, cook the orzo according to the package directions and drain in a colander.

●

Stir the orzo into the soup and simmer for 5 minutes. Season the soup with the salt (if using). Serve sprinkled with the Parmesan (if using).

Hands-on time: 15 minutes
Total time: 55 minutes

Per serving: 344 calories
6.2 g. total fat (14% of calories)
1.8 g. saturated fat
55 mg. cholesterol
674 mg. sodium

Ham and Vegetable Soup

Here's further proof that you needn't simmer a pot of soup all day to get rich, homemade flavor.

Makes 4 servings

2 teaspoons **olive oil**
1 cup **chopped onions**
1 **clove garlic, minced**
3½ cups **defatted reduced-sodium chicken broth**
1 **large carrot, finely chopped**
1 can (15 ounces) **reduced-sodium tomato sauce**
1 package (10 ounces) **frozen succotash, rinsed with hot water and drained**
6 ounces **lean reduced-sodium ham steak, trimmed and cubed**
¼ cup **uncooked white rice**
1½ teaspoons **dried Italian seasoning**
⅛ teaspoon **freshly ground black pepper**
Salt (**optional**)

●

In a large pot, combine the oil, onions, garlic and 3 tablespoons of the broth. Cook over medium heat for 5 to 6 minutes, or until the onions soften. If the liquid begins to evaporate, add more broth.

●

Add the carrots, tomato sauce, succotash, ham, rice, Italian seasoning, pepper and the remaining broth.

●

Cover and simmer, stirring occasionally, for 25 minutes, or until the vegetables are tender and the rice is cooked. Season with the salt (if using).

Hands-on time: 10 minutes
Total time: 40 minutes

Per serving: 283 calories
5.1 g. total fat (16% of calories)
1.1 g. saturated fat
13 mg. cholesterol
784 mg. sodium

Spanish Fish Soup with Orzo

You'll love this sensational soup that's full of sunny Mediterranean flavors. You'll find orzo, a tiny rice-shaped pasta, in most supermarkets.

Makes 4 servings

1 tablespoon **olive oil**
¼ cup **white wine or water**
1 **large onion, sliced**
2 **cloves garlic, minced**
1 **bay leaf**
½ teaspoon **dried basil leaves**
⅛ teaspoon **fennel seeds, crushed**
1 can (28 ounces) **plum tomatoes**
⅛ teaspoon **red-pepper flakes**
2 cups **bottled clam juice or defatted fish broth**
2 cups **cubed new potatoes**
1 pound **cod fillets, cubed**
½ cup **uncooked orzo**
⅓ cup **chopped fresh parsley**

In a large pot, bring the oil and wine or water to a simmer over medium-high heat. Add the onions and cook, stirring occasionally, for 8 minutes, or until softened.

Add the garlic, bay leaf, basil, fennel seeds, tomatoes, pepper flakes, clam juice or broth and potatoes.

Bring the soup to a boil, reduce the heat to medium and simmer for 15 minutes, or until the potatoes are tender.

Add the cod and orzo. Cook, stirring often, for 10 minutes, or until the pasta is tender. Remove and discard the bay leaf. Stir in the parsley.

Hands-on time: 15 minutes
Total time: 45 minutes

Per serving: 355 calories
5.5 g. total fat (14% of calories)
0.8 g. saturated fat
66 mg. cholesterol
561 mg. sodium

To Your Health

Fish

Cod, haddock and other mild white-fleshed fish are naturally low in fat and cholesterol. They're a good source of protein, and any fat they do contain is largely poly-unsaturated, which does not raise cholesterol. In addition, even the low-fat fish contain some omega-3 fatty acids, which can help buoy up heart health.

Manhattan Clam Chowder

We bet you'll call this chunky soup the best Manhattan clam chowder you ever tasted. If you like, you can replace the broth with clam juice—just be aware that the sodium content will increase.

Makes 4 servings

1 **medium onion, finely chopped**
1 **small clove garlic, minced**
2 teaspoons **olive oil**
1½ cups **defatted reduced-sodium chicken broth**
1 can (6½ ounces) **chopped clams (with juice)**
2 **medium boiling potatoes, diced**
1½ cups **frozen mixed corn, carrots and peas**
2 ounces **Canadian bacon, cut into thin strips**
1 **bay leaf**
1 can (14½ ounces) **reduced-sodium tomatoes (with juice)**
1 teaspoon **dried Italian seasoning**
½ teaspoon **sugar**
¼ teaspoon **salt (optional)**
⅛ teaspoon **freshly ground black pepper**
Dash of hot-pepper sauce

In a large pot, combine the onions, garlic, oil and 2 tablespoons of the broth. Cook over medium-high heat, stirring frequently, for 5 minutes, or until the onions soften. If the liquid evaporates, add a bit more broth.

Drain the juice from the clams into a small bowl and set the clams aside.

Add the clam juice, potatoes, frozen vegetables, bacon and bay leaf to the pot. Bring to a boil. Cover, reduce the heat and simmer, stirring occasionally, for 10 minutes, or until the potatoes are tender.

Add the tomatoes (with juice), breaking them up with a spoon. Stir in the Italian seasoning, sugar, salt (if using), black pepper, hot-pepper sauce and clams.

Cover and simmer for 5 minutes, or until the clams are heated through. Remove and discard the bay leaf.

Hands-on time: 10 minutes
Total time: 30 minutes

Per serving: 217 calories
4.2 g. total fat (17% of calories)
0.8 g. saturated fat
35 mg. cholesterol
423 mg. sodium

Creole Fish Chowder

For authentic Creole flavor, try to use catfish in this colorful chowder. But if it's unavailable, cod, haddock and flounder work fine.

Makes 4 servings

½ tablespoon **canola oil**
1 cup **chopped scallions**
1 cup **chopped celery**
½ cup **chopped mixed sweet red and green peppers**
1 **large clove garlic, minced**
2¼ cups **defatted reduced-sodium chicken broth**
1 can (14½ ounces) **stewed tomatoes**
2¼ cups **frozen corn kernels or succotash**
1 teaspoon **dried thyme leaves**
1 teaspoon **dried marjoram leaves**
½ teaspoon **dried oregano leaves**
¼ teaspoon **freshly ground black pepper**
Pinch of ground red pepper (**optional**)
1 pound **catfish, cod or other mild white fish fillets, cubed**
1½ teaspoons **butter or margarine**

•

In a large pot, combine the oil, scallions, celery, chopped peppers and garlic. Cook over medium-high heat, stirring, for 5 minutes, or until the scallions soften.

•

Add the broth, tomatoes, corn or succotash, thyme, marjoram, oregano, black pepper and red pepper (if using). Bring to a simmer and cook for 12 to 15 minutes, or until the vegetables are tender.

•

Stir in the fish and butter or margarine. Bring to a simmer and cook for 7 to 10 minutes, or until the fish pieces flake easily when tested with a fork.

Hands-on time: 10 minutes
Total time: 40 minutes

Per serving: 287 calories
8.3 g. total fat (25% of calories)
2.2 g. saturated fat
69 mg. cholesterol
644 mg. sodium

Flavorful Freezing

Fish often loses its fresh taste in the freezer, but the spices in this chowder help keep it flavorful. Cool any leftover Creole Fish Chowder, then freeze it in 2-cup containers for up to 4 weeks. The spices will intensify during the freezing process, so the chowder will still taste rich when reheated. Warm in a covered saucepan over low heat and serve with sliced French bread.

Corn and Potato Chowder

Have you let the pantry get low? No problem. With a few soup vegetables and a package of corn in the freezer, you can still turn out this surprisingly filling country chowder. Whole milk gives this soup extra body, but you may substitute low-fat milk.

Makes 4 servings

1 tablespoon **butter or margarine**
2 **onions, chopped**
1 **stalk celery, diced**
1 **small carrot, diced**
1 tablespoon **unbleached flour**
1¼ cups **defatted reduced-sodium chicken broth**
3 cups **diced potatoes**
1 package (10 ounces) **frozen corn kernels**
1 tablespoon **Worcestershire sauce**
1¼ teaspoons **dried basil leaves**
¾ teaspoon **dry mustard**
½ teaspoon **dried marjoram leaves**
¼ teaspoon **celery salt**
¼ teaspoon **freshly ground black pepper**
2½ cups **milk**

In a large pot, melt the butter or margarine over medium heat. Add the onions, celery and carrots. Cook, stirring frequently, for 5 minutes, or until the onions soften.

Stir in the flour and cook for 1 minute. Add the broth and stir until smooth.

Add the potatoes, corn, Worcestershire sauce, basil, mustard, marjoram, celery salt, pepper and 1½ cups of the milk. Bring to a boil.

Cover, reduce the heat and simmer for 12 to 15 minutes, or until the potatoes are tender.

Using a slotted spoon, scoop 2 cups of vegetables from the pot and transfer them to a blender. Add the remaining 1 cup milk. Process until smooth. Return the puree to the pot.

Simmer for 5 minutes, or until heated through.

Hands-on time: 10 minutes
Total time: 35 minutes

Per serving: 313 calories
8.3 g. total fat (23% of calories)
5 g. saturated fat
28 mg. cholesterol
412 mg. sodium

To Your Health

Corn

Corn is mostly a complex carbohydrate, the kind of starchy food that the American Heart Association says should make up at least half our calories each day. And even though it's a popular source of oil, sweet corn itself is low in both fat and calories. Corn also provides about three grams of fiber per ear. It has both soluble fiber to help lower cholesterol and insoluble fiber for good digestive health.

Tomato-Vegetable Soup with Ham

Ham it up! For a milder soup, you may omit the hot-pepper sauce. But this soup is best when it's a bit zippy.

Makes 4 servings

2½ teaspoons **olive oil**

2 **onions, coarsely chopped**

3 cups **defatted reduced-sodium chicken broth**

1 cup **water**

2 **small ham hocks** (about 1 pound)

½ cup **coarsely chopped celery**

½ cup **coarsely diced carrots**

½ cup **chopped sweet red or green peppers**

¼ cup **brown lentils, rinsed and drained**

2 teaspoons **dried basil leaves**

½ teaspoon **dried oregano leaves**

½ teaspoon **dried thyme leaves**

¼ teaspoon **freshly ground black pepper**

1 package (10 ounces) **frozen succotash**

½ cup **diced, trimmed lean smoked ham**

1 can (14½ ounces) **sodium-free stewed tomatoes**

⅛ teaspoon **hot-pepper sauce**

•

In a large pot, combine the oil and onions. Cook over high heat, stirring frequently, for 5 minutes, or until the onions soften and begin to brown.

•

Add the broth, water, ham hocks, celery, carrots, red or green peppers, lentils, basil, oregano, thyme and black pepper. Bring to a boil over medium-high heat.

•

Reduce the heat, cover and simmer for 30 minutes.

•

Add the succotash, ham, tomatoes and hot-pepper sauce. Simmer, breaking up the tomatoes with a spoon, for 15 to 20 minutes, or until the lentils are tender.

•

Remove and discard the ham hocks.

Hands-on time: 15 minutes
Total time: 1 hour

Per serving: 270 calories
6.7 g. total fat (21% of calories)
1.5 g. saturated fat
16 mg. cholesterol
734 mg. sodium

Lentil and Potato Soup

Try this for a warming, full-flavored, hearty soup. For variety, use small, beige Indian lentils. Like red lentils, they cook quickly; look for them in ethnic grocery stores.

Makes 4 servings

2 teaspoons **olive oil**
1 **large onion, chopped**
2 teaspoons **curry powder**
1 teaspoon **dried thyme leaves**
5 cups **water**
2 cups **chopped cabbage**
1 cup **red lentils, rinsed and drained**
3 teaspoons **reduced-sodium vegetable bouillon granules
   or 3 chicken bouillon cubes**
2 drops **hot-pepper sauce (optional)**
2 **boiling potatoes, cubed**
1 can (15 ounces) **reduced-sodium stewed tomatoes**
½ teaspoon **salt (optional)**
Freshly ground black pepper

●

In a large pot, combine the oil, onions, curry powder, thyme and 3 tablespoons of the water. Cook over medium heat, stirring frequently, for 5 to 6 minutes, or until the onions soften.

●

Add the cabbage, lentils, bouillon, hot-pepper sauce (if using) and the remaining water. Bring to a boil.

●

Reduce the heat, cover and simmer for 10 minutes. Add the potatoes, cover and simmer, stirring occasionally, for 15 minutes, or until the lentils and potatoes are tender.

●

Add the tomatoes. Simmer for 5 minutes. Season with the salt (if using) and pepper.

Hands-on time: 15 minutes
Total time: 50 minutes

Per serving: 305 calories
3.9 g. total fat (11% of calories)
0.5 g. saturated fat
0 mg. cholesterol
28 mg. sodium

To Your Health

Lentils

Lentils are biblical beans that are a major protein source in the Middle East. They provide a rich-flavored base for soups and stews. Half a cup provides five grams of fiber, 89 percent of the Recommended Dietary Allowance (RDA) for blood-building folate and 33 percent of the RDA for iron.

Winter Squash and Potato Chowder

This spicy chowder gets its rich texture from pureed potatoes rather than cream or butter. This soup keeps well and is even better the next day.

Makes 4 servings

1 tablespoon **olive oil**
1 cup **sherry or apple juice**
2 cups **chopped onions**
1 tablespoon **curry powder**
½ teaspoon **ground cinnamon**
¼ teaspoon **ground coriander**
¼ teaspoon **ground cumin**
⅛ teaspoon **ground red pepper**
½ teaspoon **salt**
½ teaspoon **freshly ground black pepper**
3½ cups **defatted reduced-sodium chicken broth**
4 **small red potatoes, diced**
1½ cups **peeled, seeded and diced butternut or acorn squash**
½ teaspoon **dried thyme leaves**
½ cup **chopped fresh parsley**

•

In a large pot, combine the oil, sherry or apple juice, onions, curry powder, cinnamon, coriander, cumin, red pepper, salt and black pepper. Cover and cook over medium-high heat for 5 minutes.

•

Add the broth, potatoes, squash and thyme. Reduce the heat to medium, cover and simmer for 25 minutes, or until the potatoes are tender.

•

Let the soup cool slightly and then transfer 2 cups to a blender. Puree the soup and return it to the pot. Add the parsley.

Hands-on time: 10 minutes
Total time: 40 minutes

Per serving: 258 calories
4.2 g. total fat (14% of calories)
0.6 g. saturated fat
0 mg. cholesterol
705 mg. sodium

To Your Health

Winter Squash

The deep-orange varieties of squash — including butternut, acorn, buttercup, hubbard and pumpkin — are full of cancer-fighting beta-carotene, vitamin C, folate and fiber. A half-cup serving of baked butternut squash, for example, serves up nearly 75 percent of the Recommended Dietary Allowance (RDA) of beta-carotene, over 25 percent of the RDA for vitamin C, 10 percent of your daily folate need and nearly three grams of cholesterol-fighting fiber.

Herbed Broccoli-Cauliflower Soup

Yummy is the word to describe this homey herbed soup. It goes especially well with garlic bread or cheese bread and a tossed garden salad.

Makes 4 servings

1½ teaspoons **butter or margarine**
1 **large onion, chopped**
1 **large stalk celery, chopped**
3 cups **defatted reduced-sodium chicken broth**
3¼ cups **diced potatoes**
1 tablespoon **Dijon mustard**
1 teaspoon **dry mustard**
1 teaspoon **dried tarragon leaves**
¾ teaspoon **dried marjoram leaves**
½ teaspoon **curry powder**
3 cups **mixed fresh or frozen broccoli and cauliflower florets**
1 cup **milk**
Salt (optional)
Freshly ground black pepper

•

In a large pot, melt the butter or margarine over medium heat. Add the onions and celery. Cook, stirring, for 5 minutes, or until the onions soften.

•

Add the broth, potatoes, Dijon mustard, dry mustard, tarragon, marjoram and curry powder. Bring to a boil.

•

Reduce the heat and simmer for 12 to 15 minutes, or until the potatoes are tender.

•

Transfer 2 cups of the soup to a blender. Blend until smooth. Return the puree to the pot and add the broccoli and cauliflower and milk.

•

Bring to a boil. Cook, stirring frequently, for 5 to 8 minutes, or until the florets are crisp-tender. Season with the salt (if using) and pepper.

Hands-on time: 10 minutes
Total time: 35 minutes

Per serving: 198 calories
4 g. total fat (18% of calories)
2.2 g. saturated fat
12 mg. cholesterol
482 mg. sodium

Encore!

Creamy Penne with Vegetables

Spoon 2 cups leftover Herbed Broccoli-Cauliflower Soup into a saucepan and heat to simmering. In a small bowl, whisk together 2 tablespoons skim milk, 1½ tablespoons corn-starch and ½ teaspoon salt. Add to the pan and cook, stirring frequently, until the mixture thickens. Add ¼ cup shredded mozzarella and ¼ cup ricotta; stir until the cheese melts. Then toss with 3 cups hot cooked penne or other pasta.

Mushroom-Barley Soup

Mushrooms and barley seem made for each other in this subtle but satisfying soup. A touch of nonfat sour cream gives it a creamy texture.

Makes 4 servings

1 tablespoon **canola oil**
1 cup **chopped onions**
1 **clove garlic, minced**
1 **carrot, chopped**
2 cups **sliced mushrooms**
3 cups **defatted reduced-sodium chicken broth**
½ cup **uncooked quick-cooking barley**
1 teaspoon **Worcestershire sauce**
⅛ teaspoon **freshly ground black pepper**
2 tablespoons **nonfat sour cream**
1 tablespoon **chopped fresh parsley**

●

In a large saucepan, warm the oil over medium heat. Add the onions and garlic. Cook for 2 minutes.

●

Add the carrots and mushrooms. Cook for 10 minutes.

●

Add the broth and bring to a boil. Add the barley. Cover and cook for 10 minutes, or until the barley is tender.

●

Add the Worcestershire sauce and pepper. Remove from the heat and gently stir in the sour cream. Serve sprinkled with the parsley.

Hands-on time: 10 minutes
Total time: 30 minutes

Per serving: 154 calories
4.6 g. total fat (28% of calories)
1.3 g. saturated fat
0 mg. cholesterol
49 mg. sodium

Take It Along

Midday Winter Warm-Up

Leftover Mushroom-Barley Soup makes a great low-fat lunch that warms body and soul on winter days. To prevent the sour cream from separating, heat the soup very gently, then pack each serving into a one-cup Thermos and cover tightly. Separately carry along some chopped parsley for a garnish and low-fat croutons or breadsticks.

Spinach and Tortelloni Soup

Spinach, tortelloni and just a touch of sherry turn a simple tomato base into an extraordinary soup.

Makes 4 servings

1 **large onion, chopped**
1 **clove garlic, minced**
3 tablespoons **dry sherry or apple juice**
4 cups **defatted reduced-sodium chicken broth**
2 teaspoons **dried Italian seasoning**
9 ounces **reduced-fat cheese-filled tortelloni**
1 can (15 ounces) **reduced-sodium tomato sauce**
1 package (10 ounces) **frozen spinach, thawed but undrained**
⅛ teaspoon **freshly ground black pepper**
1 teaspoon **sugar** (**optional**)
4 teaspoons **grated Parmesan cheese**

•

In a 2-cup glass measuring cup, combine the onions, garlic and sherry or apple juice. Cover with wax paper and microwave on high power for 2 minutes, or until the onions soften. Set aside.

•

In a large pot, combine the broth and Italian seasoning. Bring to a boil over medium-high heat.

•

Add the tortelloni. Cover and simmer for 5 minutes.

•

Stir in the tomato sauce, spinach, pepper and onion mixture. Cover and simmer for 15 minutes. Taste the soup; if it seems acidic, add the sugar. Serve sprinkled with the Parmesan.

Hands-on time: 10 minutes
Total time: 35 minutes

Per serving: 282 calories
1.8 g. total fat (6% of calories)
0.8 g. saturated fat
4 mg. cholesterol
821 mg. sodium

Chicken and Cranberry Salad with Tangy Dressing
(page 125) ➞

The Salad Bowl

Curried Chicken Salad with Chutney

Use leftover cooked chicken for this tempting salad. If you don't have any, you can easily poach boneless, skinless breast halves in a little broth until just tender; chill before using.

Makes 4 servings

Dressing

¼ cup **mango chutney**
¼ cup **reduced-fat mayonnaise**
2 tablespoons **ketchup**
1½ tablespoons **lemon juice**
3 tablespoons **chopped fresh chives**
1 tablespoon **curry powder**

Salad

2½ cups **chopped cooked chicken breast**
1 cup **chopped celery**
1 **large apple, chopped**
4 cups **mixed leafy greens**

To make the dressing

Chop any large chunks of fruit in the chutney into fine pieces.

In a small bowl, stir together the chutney, mayonnaise, ketchup, lemon juice, chives and curry powder until well-blended.

To make the salad

Combine the chicken, celery and apples in a large bowl. Add the dressing and toss until the salad is well-coated. Cover and refrigerate for at least 15 minutes before serving. Serve the salad on a bed of greens.

Hands-on time: 15 minutes
Total time: 30 minutes

Per serving: 234 calories
6.7 g. total fat (26% of calories)
0.6 g. saturated fat
59 mg. cholesterol
177 mg. sodium

Take It Along

Chicken Salad to Go

Curried Chicken Salad with Chutney is a delicious entrée for a summer outing to the beach or park. Place the greens in a self-sealing plastic bag; combine the chicken, celery and apples with the chutney dressing and pack into a large, tightly sealed container (you can do this up to three hours before serving time). Pack the container in an ice-filled cooler. Wrap the bagged greens in a dish towel and lay over the container. To serve, arrange the greens on paper plates and top with generous scoops of chicken salad.

Mexican Chicken Salad

Salsa provides the basis for a vibrant, juicy dressing for crisp corn and other stick-to-your-ribs ingredients in this Mexican-style meal.

Makes 4 servings

8 ounces **boneless, skinless chicken breast halves, cubed**

¼ teaspoon **salt (optional)**

⅛ teaspoon **freshly ground black pepper**

1¼ cups **mild reduced-sodium salsa**

1 tablespoon **olive oil**

1 tablespoon **honey**

1 teaspoon **chili powder**

1 can (16 ounces) **corn, drained**

1 can (15 ounces) **sodium-free kidney beans, rinsed and drained**

1 **large tomato, cubed**

2 cups **finely shredded lettuce**

¼ cup **chopped fresh chives**

Sweet red pepper rings

Parsley sprigs

•

Sprinkle the chicken with the salt (if using) and black pepper.

•

Coat a large no-stick frying pan with no-stick spray. Place over medium heat. Add the chicken and cook, turning the pieces frequently, for 6 to 8 minutes, or until browned and cooked through.

•

In a large bowl, stir together the salsa, oil, honey and chili powder. Add the corn, beans, tomatoes, lettuce, chives and chicken. Mix well.

•

Serve garnished with the peppers and parsley.

Hands-on time: 15 minutes
Total time: 25 minutes

Per serving: 287 calories
5.7 g. total fat (17% of calories)
0.9 g. saturated fat
23 mg. cholesterol
170 mg. sodium

Couscous and Chicken Salad

Couscous is great in salads, but it drinks up liquid so you can end up using more dressing than you'd like. Here, chicken broth stretches the dressing to carry the essence of the herbs without adding fat.

Makes 4 servings

1½ cups **water**
1 large **clove garlic, minced**
1½ teaspoons **dried marjoram leaves**
1½ teaspoons **dried thyme leaves**
½ teaspoon **salt** (**optional**)
¾ cup **uncooked couscous**
½ cup **defatted reduced-sodium chicken broth**
2 tablespoons **olive oil**
2 tablespoons **lemon juice**
½ cup **finely chopped fresh parsley**
2 drops **hot-pepper sauce**
10 ounces **chopped cooked chicken breast**
2 large **stalks celery, thinly sliced**
1 can (15 ounces) **chick-peas, rinsed and drained**
4 **plum tomatoes, coarsely chopped**

•

In a medium saucepan over high heat, bring the water, garlic, marjoram, thyme and salt (if using) to a boil. Add the couscous, remove from the heat and let stand for 5 minutes, or until the liquid is absorbed.

•

In a large bowl, mix the broth, oil, lemon juice, parsley and hot-pepper sauce. Add the couscous and mix well.

•

Add the chicken, celery, chick-peas and tomatoes. Mix well and let stand at room temperature for 10 minutes.

Hands-on time: 15 minutes
Total time: 30 minutes

Per serving: 388 calories
10.6 g. total fat (24% of calories)
1.6 g. saturated fat
28 mg. cholesterol
415 mg. sodium

Encore!

Herbed Couscous Timbales

Timbales are small side dishes of grains or vegetables usually made in custard cups. Chop the chicken from 2 cups leftover Couscous and Chicken Salad into a fine dice, then mix with the remaining couscous. Pack the mixture into four 4" custard cups that have been lightly oiled. Place the cups in a shallow baking dish and add enough hot water to come halfway up the outside of the cups. Bake at 350° for 25 to 30 minutes. Unmold to serve.

Pan-Grilled Chicken and Pasta Salad

This salad owes much of its rich, mellow flavor to oil-packed sun-dried tomatoes and bottled roasted red peppers, both of which are widely available in supermarkets.

Makes 4 servings

2 teaspoons **olive oil**
⅓ cup **finely chopped onions**
1 pound **boneless, skinless chicken breasts, cut into 2″ × ⅛″ strips**
1 **large tomato, chopped**
1¼ teaspoons **dried marjoram leaves**
½ teaspoon **chili powder**
½ cup **defatted reduced-sodium chicken broth**
¾ cup **canned roasted red peppers, drained and cut into strips**
3 tablespoons **diced oil-packed sun-dried tomatoes**
1½ tablespoons **lemon juice**
¼ teaspoon **salt** (optional)
2 cups **cold cooked vermicelli, cut into 3″ lengths**
Escarole, romaine or curly endive leaves

•

In a large no-stick frying pan, combine the oil, onions and chicken. Cook over high heat, stirring, for 6 to 8 minutes, or until the chicken is browned and cooked through. Transfer the chicken to a bowl.

•

Reduce the heat to medium-high and add the chopped tomatoes, marjoram and chili powder to the pan. Cook for 1 minute. Add the broth, peppers, sun-dried tomatoes, lemon juice and salt (if using).

•

Bring to a boil and cook for 2 minutes. Pour over the chicken and let stand for 10 minutes.

•

Add the vermicelli and toss until evenly incorporated. Serve on a bed of the greens.

Hands-on time: 15 minutes
Total time: 25 minutes

Per serving: 235 calories
5.6 g. total fat (21% of calories)
1 g. saturated fat
46 mg. cholesterol
119 mg. sodium

Chicken and Cranberry Salad with Tangy Dressing

Cranberries, apples and grapes make this salad a perfect fall entrée for lunch or weekend supper. And it looks as good as it tastes.

Makes 4 servings

2 cups **chopped cooked chicken breast**
1 cup **chopped fresh cranberries**
2 cups **chopped apples**
1 cup **halved green seedless grapes**
1 cup **chopped celery**
¼ cup **chopped dried apricots**
¼ cup **raisins**
1 cup **plain nonfat yogurt**
2 tablespoons **nonfat mayonnaise**
2 teaspoons **maple syrup**
4 cups **shredded lettuce**

•

In a large bowl, combine the chicken, cranberries, apples, grapes, celery, apricots and raisins. Toss gently.

•

In a small bowl, mix the yogurt, mayonnaise and maple syrup. Pour over the salad and toss until the ingredients are well-coated. Serve on a bed of the lettuce.

Hands-on time: 10 minutes
Total time: 10 minutes

Per serving: 252 calories
2.3 g. total fat (8% of calories)
0.6 g. saturated fat
44 mg. cholesterol
203 mg. sodium

To Your Health

Apples

Apples have a mouthful of health-giving nutrients that may help reduce cholesterol, prevent cancer, stabilize blood sugar and possibly even lower your risk of developing gallstones. Researchers suspect that the health-promoting effects granted by apples are best gotten by eating the whole fruit, so salads like this are particularly good for you.

Balsamic Chicken Caesar Salad

Balsamic Chicken Caesar Salad

Fragrant balsamic vinegar replaces much of the oil in this updated version of a long-time favorite.

Makes 4 servings

1 tablespoon **olive oil**
¼ cup **plain nonfat yogurt**
2 tablespoons **balsamic vinegar**
3 **large cloves garlic, minced**
2 tablespoons **grated Parmesan cheese**
2 cups **shredded cooked chicken breast**
1 cup **chopped broccoli florets**
1 **sweet red pepper, diced**
1 **head romaine lettuce, torn into bite-size pieces**
1 cup **low-fat croutons**

•

In a large bowl, whisk together the oil, yogurt, vinegar, garlic and Parmesan.

•

Add the chicken, broccoli and peppers. Toss well and let stand for 10 minutes.

•

Add the lettuce and croutons. Toss well.

Hands-on time: 5 minutes
Total time: 15 minutes

Per serving: 205 calories
7.1 g. total fat (31% of calories)
1.6 g. saturated fat
46 mg. cholesterol
170 mg. sodium

Chicken-Cucumber Salad with Orange-Yogurt Dressing

This delicate salad, scented with orange and mustard, looks elegant on a bed of leaf lettuce. If you like, you may replace the fresh orange with 8 ounces of canned mandarin orange segments.

Makes 4 servings

1 pound **boneless, skinless chicken breast halves**
1 cup **sherry or defatted reduced-sodium chicken broth**
1 cup **water**
½ cup **plain nonfat yogurt**
1½ teaspoons **honey mustard**
1 teaspoon **maple syrup**
¼ teaspoon **salt**
¼ teaspoon **freshly ground black pepper**
1 large **orange, peeled and sectioned**
½ large **cucumber, peeled, seeded and diced**
½ cup **raisins**
1 **scallion, chopped**
⅓ cup **chopped fresh parsley**
Lettuce leaves
2 tablespoons **chow mein noodles (optional)**

●

In a large no-stick frying pan, combine the chicken, sherry or broth and water. Bring to a boil over medium-high heat. Reduce the heat and simmer gently, turning the chicken as needed, for 10 minutes, or until the chicken is cooked through.

●

Drain the chicken and discard the poaching liquid. Chop the chicken into bite-size pieces.

●

In a large bowl, combine the yogurt, mustard, maple syrup, salt and pepper. Stir in the oranges, cucumbers, raisins, scallions and parsley. Add the chicken and toss to coat.

●

Serve on a bed of the lettuce leaves. Sprinkle with the chow mein noodles (if using).

Hands-on time: 10 minutes
Total time: 20 minutes

Per serving: 269 calories
2.2 g. total fat (7% of calories)
0.6 g. saturated fat
46 mg. cholesterol
214 mg. sodium

To Your Health

Yogurt

Yogurt is a top source of calcium. One cup of plain nonfat yogurt has about 450 milligrams of calcium, more than half the Recommended Dietary Allowance. Studies suggest that eating lots of high-calcium foods may help prevent osteoporosis—frail bones later in life. Calcium may also play a role in preventing colon cancer and high blood pressure. Yogurt also contains a healthy mixture of other nutrients, especially the all-important B-complex vitamins and potassium.

New-Age Antipasto

Healthy choices at the deli counter combine with raw vegetables and boiled potatoes in this new approach to antipasto salad. Lean but filling!

Makes 4 servings

2 cups **sliced red potatoes**
½ cup **plain nonfat yogurt**
½ cup **nonfat sour cream**
2 tablespoons **nonfat mayonnaise**
1 tablespoon **balsamic vinegar**
1 tablespoon **honey mustard**
Salt (optional)
Freshly ground black pepper
1 cup **sliced fresh mushrooms**
1 cup **julienned lean turkey ham**
1 cup **julienned cooked turkey breast**
Romaine lettuce leaves
Carrot sticks
Celery sticks
1 jar (7 ounces) **roasted red peppers**

●

Place the potatoes in a medium saucepan. Add cold water to cover. Bring to a boil and cook for 8 to 10 minutes, or until the potatoes are just tender. Drain.

●

In a large bowl, whisk together the yogurt, sour cream, mayonnaise, vinegar, mustard, salt (if using) and black pepper. Add the potatoes, mushrooms, ham and turkey. Toss to mix well.

●

Line a platter with the lettuce leaves and mound the salad in the center. Garnish with the carrots, celery and red peppers. Serve at room temperature.

Hands-on time: 10 minutes
Total time: 20 minutes

Per serving: 217 calories
2 g. total fat (8% of calories)
0.6 g. saturated fat
40 mg. cholesterol
484 mg. sodium

Asian Pasta Salad with Pork

Shredded broccoli-slaw mix, one of the newer ready-to-use vegetable products in supermarkets, is the quick-prep secret behind this unusual salad.

Makes 4 servings

Dressing

3 tablespoons	**reduced-sodium soy sauce**
1½ tablespoons	**cider vinegar**
1 tablespoon	**grated fresh ginger**
2 teaspoons	**packed brown sugar**
2 teaspoons	**sesame oil**
¾ teaspoon	**chili powder**

Salad

1 teaspoon	**peanut oil**
8 ounces	**lean boneless pork loin, thinly sliced**
¾ cup	**shredded scallions**
¾ cup	**thinly sliced sweet red pepper strips**
3½ cups	**packaged broccoli-slaw mixture**
2 cups	**cold cooked vermicelli, cut into 3″ lengths**

To make the dressing

In a small bowl, mix the soy sauce, vinegar, ginger, brown sugar, oil and chili powder. Stir until the brown sugar dissolves.

To make the salad

Warm the oil in a large no-stick frying pan over high heat. Add the pork, scallions and peppers. Cook, stirring, for 5 minutes, or until the pork is cooked through.

Stir in the broccoli-slaw mixture and cook for 2 minutes. Remove the pan from the heat and add the dressing. Let stand for 5 minutes.

Transfer the pork mixture to a serving bowl and add the vermicelli. Toss gently, cover and refrigerate for at least 15 minutes before serving.

Hands-on time: 20 minutes
Total time: 40 minutes

Per serving: 239 calories
7.9 g. total fat (28% of calories)
1.8 g. saturated fat
26 mg. cholesterol
440 mg. sodium

Red Potato and Tuna Salad

A new take on an old favorite, this salad suits a summer dinner or picnic perfectly. It can be made up to 24 hours in advance and refrigerated.

Makes 4 servings

3 cups **water**
1 teaspoon **salt** (**optional**)
¼ teaspoon **freshly ground black pepper**
1 tablespoon **dried basil leaves**
1½ pounds **red potatoes, cubed**
2 **large stalks celery, thinly sliced**
1 **large sweet red or green pepper, cubed**
¼ cup **chopped fresh chives**
2 tablespoons **canola oil**
2 tablespoons **defatted reduced-sodium chicken broth**
1½ tablespoons **cider vinegar**
1 tablespoon **Dijon mustard**
1 can (6 ounces) **water-packed tuna**

●

In a large saucepan, combine the water, salt (if using), black pepper and ½ teaspoon of the basil. Bring to a boil over high heat. Add the potatoes, cover and return to a boil. Reduce the heat and simmer for 8 to 10 minutes, or until the potatoes are just tender.

●

In a large bowl, mix the celery, red or green peppers, chives, oil, broth, vinegar, mustard and the remaining 2½ teaspoons basil. Add the tuna (with liquid) and mix, being careful not to break up the tuna too much.

●

Drain the potatoes, rinse with cold water and drain again. Stir into the salad and let marinate at room temperature for 10 minutes before serving.

Hands-on time: 15 minutes
Total time: 30 minutes

Per serving: 274 calories
7.5 g. total fat (24% of calories)
0.6 g. saturated fat
7 mg. cholesterol
235 mg. sodium

To Your Health

Potatoes

Potatoes can help lower your blood pressure, reduce some types of inflammation and decrease your appetite. Not only that, they can also help increase your body's anti-cancer defense systems and boost your resistance to heart attacks. One baked potato offers almost one-quarter of the Recommended Dietary Allowance of potassium—that's more than *any* other food. And since they're low in sodium, potatoes are a terrific choice for people with high blood pressure. Potatoes also contain protease inhibitors, which may prevent cancer cells from blasting their way through the body.

Shrimp, Pepper and Rice Salad

A piquant homemade dressing turns shrimp and rice into an easy warm-weather entrée. Celery and red peppers provide color accents.

Makes 4 servings

Dressing

¼ cup **reduced-fat mayonnaise**
¼ cup **buttermilk**
3 tablespoons **ketchup**
3 tablespoons **chopped fresh chives**
2 tablespoons **chopped fresh dill**
2 teaspoons **Worcestershire sauce**
2 teaspoons **Dijon mustard**
1 teaspoon **sugar**

Salad

2½ cups **cold cooked rice**
1½ cups **coarsely chopped cooked shrimp**
1¼ cups **chopped celery**
1 jar (4 ounces) **chopped red peppers, drained**

To make the dressing
In a small bowl, whisk together the mayonnaise, buttermilk, ketchup, chives, dill, Worcestershire sauce, mustard and sugar.

To make the salad
In a large bowl, combine the rice, shrimp, celery and peppers. Add the dressing and toss until evenly coated. Cover and refrigerate for at least 15 minutes before serving.

Hands-on time: 10 minutes
Total time: 25 minutes

Per serving: 288 calories
5.2 g. total fat (13% of calories)
0.3 g. saturated fat
88 mg. cholesterol
328 mg. sodium

To Your Health

Shrimp
Shrimp, America's favorite shellfish, is a great low-fat source of protein and nerve-protecting vitamin B_{12}. Although shrimp do contain cholesterol, there's far less than originally thought. And shrimp are extra low in saturated fat, which doctors believe plays a larger role in the development of heart disease than cholesterol does.

Individual Seafood Salads in Tomato Baskets

Scooped-out tomatoes make a handsome presentation for a company-special summer salad. To keep the tomatoes from toppling over when filled, cut a small slice off the bottom to give them stability. If you prefer the corn cooked, steam the ears lightly before cutting off the kernels.

Makes 4 servings

8 ounces **fish fillets, such as tuna or salmon**
4 ounces **medium shrimp, peeled and deveined**
1 cup **white wine or fish broth**
3 **ears corn**
⅓ cup **nonfat mayonnaise**
1 tablespoon **honey mustard**
1 tablespoon **plain nonfat yogurt**
½ teaspoon **paprika**
1 **scallion, finely chopped**
¼ cup **chopped fresh basil**
4 **large well-rounded tomatoes**
Lettuce leaves

•

In a saucepan, combine the fish, shrimp and wine or broth. Cook over medium heat for 5 minutes, or until the shrimp turns pink and the fish is cooked through.

•

Drain and place the fish and shrimp in a single layer on a plate. Place in the freezer for 10 minutes to cool the seafood. Then cut into bite-size pieces.

•

Shuck the corn and, using a sharp knife, cut off the kernels. Place in a medium bowl, and stir together with the mayonnaise, mustard, yogurt, paprika, scallions and basil. Add the fish and shrimp. Stir to mix well. If desired, refrigerate until chilled.

•

Cut a ½" slice from the stem end of each tomato. Using a melon baller, scoop out and discard the seeds of each tomato, leaving a ½"-thick shell. Divide the seafood salad evenly among the tomato shells, mounding it slightly on top. Serve on the lettuce leaves.

Hands-on time: 15 minutes
Total time: 30 minutes

Per serving: 245 calories
2.1 g. total fat (7% of calories)
0.4 g. saturated fat
66 mg. cholesterol
395 mg. sodium

Encore!

Seafood Subs

Leftover seafood salad (without the tomato baskets) makes a delicious filling for sub sandwiches. Split 4 whole-wheat buns, toast them lightly, then spread with a thin layer of nonfat mayonnaise or honey mustard. Divide ½ cup shredded lettuce among the sandwiches, then top with leftover seafood salad. Serve the sandwiches with low-fat tomato soup or sliced fresh tomatoes, baked corn tortilla chips and sweet pickles.

———

Salmon and Potato Salad with Dill Dressing

Arranged salads are a nice change of pace from tossed ones. They have plenty of eye appeal and are really no more difficult to prepare.

Makes 4 servings

1 pound **red potatoes, sliced**
½ cup **plain nonfat yogurt**
¼ cup **thinly sliced scallions**
2 teaspoons **minced fresh dill**
5 ounces **spinach leaves or green-leaf lettuce**
1 can (14½ ounces) **red salmon**
1 **cucumber**
12 **pitted black olives, thinly sliced**

•

Place the potatoes in a large saucepan. Add cold water to cover. Bring to a boil and cook for 10 minutes, or until just tender.

•

In a medium bowl, mix the yogurt, scallions and dill.

•

Arrange the spinach or lettuce on a serving platter. Drain and flake the salmon; arrange on the greens.

•

Peel the cucumber and cut it into spears. Arrange next to the salmon.

•

Drain the potatoes and add them to the bowl with the dressing. Toss well to coat. Spoon onto the platter next to the salmon. Sprinkle with the olives.

Hands-on time: 10 minutes
Total time: 20 minutes

Per serving: 324 calories
9.8 g. total fat (27% of calories)
2 g. saturated fat
45 mg. cholesterol
663 mg. sodium

White Bean Salad with Tomatoes and Herbs

Here's a great summer salad entrée—full of crisp vegetables, marinated beans and ripe tomato chunks. It also makes a good side salad for grilled chicken or fish.

Makes 4 servings

2 cans (15½ ounces each) **navy or cannellini beans, rinsed and drained**
2 cups **seeded and chopped tomatoes**
⅓ cup **chopped scallions**
½ cup **chopped celery**
⅓ cup **shredded carrots**
¼ cup **chopped fresh parsley**
1 teaspoon **minced shallots**
¼ cup **white-wine vinegar**
2 tablespoons **olive oil**
1 tablespoon **honey or sugar**
1–2 teaspoons **Dijon mustard**
1 teaspoon **minced fresh thyme**
1 teaspoon **minced fresh rosemary**
Salt (optional)
Freshly ground black pepper
4 cups **shredded leaf lettuce**

•

In a large bowl, toss together the beans, tomatoes, scallions, celery, carrots, parsley and shallots.

•

In a small bowl, whisk together the vinegar, oil, honey or sugar, mustard, thyme, rosemary, salt (if using) and pepper. Pour over the salad mixture and toss gently.

•

Serve on a bed of the lettuce.

Hands-on time: 15 minutes
Total time: 15 minutes

Per serving: 365 calories
8.3 g. total fat (20% of calories)
1.2 g. saturated fat
0 mg. cholesterol
737 mg. sodium

Encore!

Mediterranean Tomato-Bean Torta
This hearty summer sandwich has Mediterranean roots and is very popular in Provence. Start with a 6″ round of hearty peasant bread, halved lengthwise. Scoop the soft interior from the bottom half, leaving a 1″-thick shell. Mound 2 to 3 cups leftover White Bean Salad with Tomatoes and Herbs in the bread shell, then replace the top. Wrap the sandwich in plastic and let stand at room temperature for up to 30 minutes before slicing into thick wedges.

Greek Lemon-Rice Salad

Lemon and rice give this salad a hint of the flavor of avgolemono, the famous Greek lemon-egg soup. The salad is especially good garnished with sliced tomatoes, cucumber spears and crumbled feta cheese.

Makes 4 servings

4 cups **cooked rice**
½ cup **minced scallions**
1 jar (7 ounces) **roasted red peppers, drained and chopped**
⅔ cup **minced celery**
⅔ cup **nonfat mayonnaise**
¼ cup **lemon juice**
2 tablespoons **olive oil**
1 teaspoon **grated lemon rind**
½ teaspoon **salt**
Freshly ground black pepper
Lettuce leaves

•

In a large salad bowl, toss together the rice, scallions, red peppers and celery.

•

In a small bowl, whisk together the mayonnaise, lemon juice, oil, lemon rind, salt and black pepper. Pour over the salad mixture and toss to mix well.

•

Serve on a bed of the lettuce leaves.

Hands-on time: 15 minutes
Total time: 15 minutes

Per serving: 379 calories
7.5 g. total fat (18% of calories)
1.1 g. saturated fat
0 mg. cholesterol
797 mg. sodium

Take It Along

Greek Feast

Celebrate one of the many festivals of the Greek Isles with an outdoor buffet picnic. To keep the salad cool and crisp on the buffet table, line a decorative bowl with lettuce leaves, then place it in a second, larger bowl filled with crushed ice. Mound the Greek Lemon-Rice Salad on the lettuce and smooth the top, garnishing with strips of red pepper and parsley sprigs. Eat within an hour.

Braised Catfish, Sweet Potatoes and Vegetables
(page 164) ➤

Wok, Pot and Skillet

Chicken and Vegetables with Hoisin Sauce

Hoisin sauce, which can be found in the Asian foods section of supermarkets, lends a mild yet mellow and appealing flavor to this bright, beautiful stir-fry.

Makes 4 servings

2 **large cloves garlic, minced**
3½ tablespoons **hoisin sauce**
1½ tablespoons **reduced-sodium soy sauce**
1 tablespoon **minced fresh ginger**
2 teaspoons **cider vinegar**
1 teaspoon **packed brown sugar**
1 pound **boneless, skinless chicken breasts, cubed**
2 teaspoons **peanut oil**
10 **scallions, sliced**
2 cups **mixed small cauliflower and broccoli florets**
1 cup **coarsely chopped sweet red or green peppers**
1½ teaspoons **cornstarch**
⅓ cup **defatted reduced-sodium chicken broth**
2⅔ cups **hot cooked rice**

In a medium bowl, stir together the garlic, hoisin sauce, soy sauce, ginger, vinegar and brown sugar until well-blended. Add the chicken, stir and let marinate for about 10 minutes.

In a large no-stick frying pan, combine the oil, scallions, cauliflower and broccoli and peppers. Cook over high heat, stirring frequently, for 5 minutes, or until the vegetables begin to brown and are crisp-tender. Transfer to a bowl and set aside.

Reduce the heat to medium-high. Add the chicken and marinade to the pan. Cook, stirring occasionally, for 3 to 4 minutes, or until the chicken is almost cooked through.

In a cup, stir the cornstarch into the broth until smooth. Add to the pan. Add the vegetables and cook for 2 minutes, or until the sauce thickens and the chicken is just cooked through.

Serve spooned over the rice.

Hands-on time: 15 minutes
Total time: 25 minutes

Per serving: 335 calories
4.7 g. total fat (13% of calories)
1.1 g. saturated fat
46 mg. cholesterol
427 mg. sodium

Chicken Stir-Fry with Oriental Vegetables

For variety, you can use just about any type of frozen vegetable combination in this recipe. Just be sure to select an all-vegetable mixture without rice or seasonings.

Makes 4 servings

1 tablespoon **ketchup**
2 teaspoons **cider vinegar**
1½ teaspoons **minced fresh ginger**
1 **large clove garlic, minced**
½ teaspoon **sugar**
2½ tablespoons **reduced-sodium soy sauce**
1 pound **boneless, skinless chicken breasts, cubed**
⅓ cup **defatted reduced-sodium chicken broth**
2½ teaspoons **cornstarch**
½ teaspoon **sesame oil**
2 teaspoons **peanut oil**
1 bag (1 pound) **frozen oriental vegetable combo, rinsed with hot water and drained**
2⅔ cups **hot cooked rice**

In a large bowl, stir together the ketchup, vinegar, ginger, garlic, sugar and 1 tablespoon of the soy sauce. Add the chicken and mix well. Let marinate for 5 minutes.

In a cup, stir together the broth, cornstarch, sesame oil and the remaining 1½ tablespoons soy sauce.

In a large no-stick frying pan, warm the peanut oil over high heat until hot but not smoking. Add the chicken and marinade. Cook, stirring constantly, for 3 minutes.

Add the mixed vegetables and cook, stirring, for 3 minutes, or until heated through.

Stir the broth mixture into the pan and cook just until the sauce thickens.

Serve over the rice.

Hands-on time: 10 minutes
Total time: 20 minutes

Per serving: 334 calories
5.3 g. total fat (14% of calories)
1.3 g. saturated fat
46 mg. cholesterol
472 mg. sodium

Beef and Broccoli Stir-Fry

Here's the beef—in a classic Chinese stir-fry with broccoli, water chestnuts and red peppers. Chopsticks, anyone?

Makes 4 servings

1½ teaspoons **cornstarch**
⅓ cup + 2 tablespoons **water**
2 tablespoons **reduced-sodium soy sauce**
2 tablespoons **sherry or apple juice**
1 tablespoon **ketchup**
1 teaspoon **packed brown sugar**
1 teaspoon **rice vinegar**
½ teaspoon **ground ginger**
2–3 drops **hot-chili oil**
¼ teaspoon **freshly ground black pepper**
8–10 ounces **beef round steak, thinly sliced and cut into 2″ strips**
2 teaspoons **peanut oil**
1 **large onion, coarsely chopped**
2 cups **broccoli florets**
1 can (8 ounces) **sliced water chestnuts, drained**
1 **large sweet red pepper, diced**
3 cups **hot cooked rice**

•

In a small bowl, stir together the cornstarch and ⅓ cup of the water until smooth. Add the soy sauce, sherry or apple juice, ketchup, brown sugar, vinegar, ginger and hot-chili oil. Mix well.

•

Sprinkle the black pepper evenly over the beef. Coat a large no-stick frying pan with no-stick spray. Place over medium heat and cook the beef, stirring, for 4 to 5 minutes, or until browned. Transfer the beef and pan juices to a bowl.

•

In the same pan, combine the peanut oil, onions, broccoli and the remaining 2 tablespoons water. Cook over medium heat, stirring frequently, for 5 to 6 minutes, or until crisp-tender.

•

Stir in the water chestnuts, soy sauce mixture and beef and pan juices. Cook over medium heat for 2 to 3 minutes.

•

Stir in the red peppers and cook for 2 minutes, or until the beef is cooked through. Serve with the rice.

Hands-on time: 15 minutes
Total time: 30 minutes

Per serving: 359 calories
5.5 g. total fat (14% of calories)
1.4 g. saturated fat
36 mg. cholesterol
350 mg. sodium

To Your Health

Broccoli

Broccoli just may be the number one anti-cancer vegetable, say researchers, for several reasons. It belongs to the cancer-preventing cabbage family, and it is rich in carotene, vitamin C and calcium—all of which can help protect against cancer. Broccoli is also a great source of fiber.

Stir-Fry Know-How

Stir-frying is the ultimate quick-cook method. You can easily whip up a satisfying meal at the last minute, and you can mix and match ingredients to take advantage of what's on hand.

Lest you think stir-fries signify just Asian meals, this technique works equally well for Mediterranean, Mexican and other dishes. And although a wok is often the pan of choice, a large frying pan is just as effective.

To get the best results for your effort, make sure to cut the food into uniform, bite-size pieces. Thin strips or small cubes are appropriate for meats and poultry. Vegetables can be sliced (straight or on an angle), diced, julienned or shredded. You can use more than one cut for vegetables in the same dish. In fact, a variety of cuts and ingredients heightens the visual appeal of the dish. As is logical, start stir-frying the longer-cooking items first and add the more tender ones as you go along.

Almost-Endless Choices

The following are simply suggestions for the various components of colorful, tasty dishes. Feel free to pick and choose according to your preference and what's in the pantry.

Protein
- Beef *(lean cuts such as flank steak and round steak, cut into strips)*
- Chicken breasts *(boneless and skinless, cut into strips or cubes)*
- Crab *(flaked or lump pieces)*
- Lamb *(lean cuts such as leg and loin, cut into strips or cubes)*
- Lobster meat *(cooked and cut into cubes)*
- Pork *(lean cuts such as the tenderloin, cut into strips or cubes)*
- Scallops *(whole or cut into bite-size pieces)*
- Shrimp *(peeled and deveined)*
- Tempeh *(cubed or cut into strips)*
- Tofu *(cubed or cut into strips)*

Vegetables
- Asparagus
- Bean sprouts
- Bok choy or Chinese cabbage
- Broccoli
- Carrots
- Cauliflower
- Celery
- Corn *(baby ear)*
- Cucumbers
- Eggplant
- Green beans
- Leeks
- Mushrooms
- Onions *(red and yellow)*
- Peppers *(such as red, yellow, orange or green)*
- Potatoes
- Scallions
- Snow peas or sugar snap peas
- Spinach
- String beans
- Swiss chard
- Yellow squash
- Zucchini

Staples
- Broth *(chicken, beef or vegetable; preferably reduced-sodium)*
- Cornstarch
- Oil *(such as canola, olive or peanut)*
- Pasta or noodles, cooked
- Rice, cooked

Branching Out

The preceding basics fit most any type of stir-fry you care to make. The ones that follow give a definite ethnic spin to your creations.

For Asian Dishes

- Bamboo shoots
- Black bean sauce
- Cashews
- Chili paste
- Chili peppers (dried red)
- Garlic
- Ginger
- Hoisin sauce
- Hot-chili oil
- Oyster sauce
- Peanuts
- Plum sauce
- Sesame oil
- Sesame seeds (lightly toasted)
- Sherry (dry)
- Water chestnuts

For Mediterranean Dishes

- Almonds
- Basil
- Beans (white)
- Chick-peas
- Couscous
- Garlic
- Hazelnuts
- Lemon juice and grated rind
- Lentils (red or green)
- Mint
- Olives (black)
- Orange juice and grated rind
- Oregano
- Pine nuts
- Roasted red or yellow peppers
- Rosemary
- Thyme
- Tomatoes

For Mexican Dishes

- Avocados
- Beans (black or red)
- Cilantro
- Cinnamon
- Cumin
- Garlic
- Lime juice
- Tomatillos
- Tomatoes

Keep It Light

Stir-fries can be among the healthiest one-dish meals you can prepare. The biggest pitfall you need to avoid is using too much oil to cook the ingredients. Here are some ways to ensure that your stir-fries really are lean.

Use a no-stick frying pan or wok.

Stir-fry vegetables in a little broth instead of oil. You can flavor the broth with garlic, ginger or herbs.

Precook long-cooking vegetables by microwaving, steaming or blanching them. Or use frozen vegetables that you've thawed.

Microwave meat or poultry until nearly cooked through. Finish it in a little oil.

Flavor sauces with aromatic spices and herbs or fruit juice. Or add just a touch of a very assertive oil such as hot-chili oil or sesame oil. (An alternative is to omit the oil and get similar flavor from hot-pepper flakes or toasted sesame seeds, for instance.)

When making an old favorite recipe, cut the oil in half and proceed as usual. Add oil only as necessary if the ingredients stick to the pan.

Sweet-and-Sour Pork Chop Skillet

This is an elegant way to dress up pork chops without too much effort. A simple tossed green salad would go well with this dish.

Makes 4 servings

> 4 **lean boneless center-cut loin pork chops (4 ounces each)**
> ¼ teaspoon **peanut oil**
> 1 **medium onion, thinly sliced**
> 1 **large stalk celery, sliced**
> 1 **large sweet red pepper, cut into strips**
> 1 **apple, chopped**
> ¼ cup **apricot preserves**
> 2 tablespoons **cider vinegar**
> 2 tablespoons **reduced-sodium soy sauce**
> 1 teaspoon **minced fresh ginger**
> 3 cups **hot cooked rice**

Coat a large no-stick frying pan with no-stick spray. Add the pork chops and cook over medium-high heat, turning the chops once or twice, for 5 minutes, or until browned. Remove from the pan.

Add the oil to the pan and heat until hot but not smoking. Add the onions, celery, peppers and apples. Cook, stirring constantly, for 3 minutes. If needed, add a little water to prevent burning.

In a small bowl, stir together the preserves, vinegar, soy sauce and ginger until smooth. Add to the pan.

Return the pork to the pan. Reduce the heat slightly and continue cooking, turning the chops once or twice, for 10 minutes, or until cooked through. If the pan looks dry, add 1 or 2 tablespoons water, as needed.

Serve over the rice.

Hands-on time: 10 minutes
Total time: 25 minutes

Per serving: 403 calories
8.1 g. total fat (18% of calories)
2.6 g. saturated fat
51 mg. cholesterol
317 mg. sodium

Encore!

Chinese Pork-and-Noodle Toss

For a fast variation on this skillet entrée, cube 2 of the cooked pork chops, discarding the bone and gristle. Combine enough leftover vegetables and sauce with the pork to equal 3 cups; heat in a microwave or saucepan. Cook 6 ounces rice-stick noodles or vermicelli and drain well. Toss with the pork mixture. Season with additional soy sauce and minced parsley or cilantro.

Ground Turkey and Rice Skillet Dinner

Ground turkey breast is just as convenient as hamburger but lower in fat. It's a great way to update a traditional ground beef skillet dinner.

Makes 4 servings

1½ teaspoons **olive oil**
12 ounces **ground turkey breast**
1 cup **chopped scallions**
¾ cup **chopped celery**
¾ cup **chopped sweet red or green peppers**
1½ cups **defatted reduced-sodium chicken broth**
1½ tablespoons **reduced-sodium soy sauce**
1 teaspoon **chili powder**
½ teaspoon **dried thyme leaves**
½ teaspoon **dried marjoram leaves**
¼ teaspoon **dried oregano leaves**
1¼ cups **quick-cooking white or brown rice**

●

Coat a large frying pan with no-stick spray. Add the oil and place over medium-high heat. Crumble the turkey into the pan. Cook, breaking up the meat with a wooden spoon, for 4 to 5 minutes, or until lightly browned.

●

Add the scallions, celery and peppers. Cook, stirring, for 5 minutes, or until the scallions soften. Stir in the broth, soy sauce, chili powder, thyme, marjoram and oregano.

●

Bring to a simmer and cook for 10 minutes, or until the mixture has cooked down slightly.

●

Stir in the rice. Cover and cook for 5 minutes. Remove from the heat and let stand for 5 minutes longer, or until the liquid is absorbed. Fluff with a fork and serve.

Hands-on time: 10 minutes
Total time: 30 minutes

Per serving: 338 calories
4 g. total fat (11% of calories)
0.9 g. saturated fat
37 mg. cholesterol
438 mg. sodium

Beef, Kasha and Noodle Varnishkas

Varnishkas traditionally go with pot roast and gravy. This speedy version uses thin sliced beef; buckwheat is cooked in beef broth for added flavor.

Makes 4 servings

3 cups **uncooked bow-tie noodles**
2 **medium onions, thinly sliced**
12 ounces **extra-lean beef, thinly sliced and cut into bite-size pieces**
1 **clove garlic, minced**
1 **egg**
1 cup **medium buckwheat groats**
2 cups **defatted reduced-sodium beef broth**
¼ teaspoon **freshly ground black pepper**

Cook the noodles in a large pot of boiling water until just tender. Drain.

Coat a large no-stick frying pan with no-stick spray. Add the onions and sauté over medium heat for 5 minutes, or until softened.

Add the beef and garlic to the pan. Cook, stirring, for 5 minutes, or until the beef is lightly browned. If needed, add 1 to 2 tablespoons water to prevent sticking.

In a small bowl, lightly beat the egg with a fork. Add the buckwheat and mix well. Add to the pan and cook, stirring, for 3 to 4 minutes, or until the egg dries and the buckwheat groats separate.

Add the broth and pepper. Bring to a boil over high heat. Reduce the heat to medium, cover and simmer for 8 to 10 minutes, or until the liquid has been absorbed.

Add the noodles to the pan. Mix well and heat through.

Hands-on time: 10 minutes
Total time: 40 minutes

Per serving: 412 calories
9 g. total fat (19% of calories)
0.3 g. saturated fat
128 mg. cholesterol
374 mg. sodium

To Your Health

Buckwheat

Kasha is another name for the hulled, crushed kernels of buckwheat. Like wheat, buckwheat makes excellent breads and cereals. But it doesn't contain the gluten that gives some people problems. In addition, buckwheat offers special benefits to those with diabetes. Buckwheat's special mix of starch and fiber is absorbed very slowly by the body, which can improve glucose (sugar) tolerance in some people with adult-onset diabetes.

Beef and Noodle Paprikash

This quick entrée has all the full flavor of a traditional paprikash dish—without the classic amount of fat. Extra-lean ground beef and nonfat yogurt are two of its slimming secrets.

Makes 4 servings

8 ounces **extra-lean ground beef**
1 **large onion, chopped**
1 **small stalk celery, chopped**
1 **small apple, chopped**
1⅔ cups **sliced mushrooms**
2 cups **defatted reduced-sodium beef broth**
½ teaspoon **dried thyme leaves**
¼ teaspoon **caraway seeds**
2 cups **uncooked medium yolk-free egg noodles**
1 tablespoon **paprika**
3 tablespoons **tomato paste**
2 tablespoons **plain nonfat yogurt**

•

Coat a large frying pan with no-stick spray. Crumble the beef into the pan. Add the onions, celery, apples and mushrooms. Cook over medium-high heat, breaking up the mixture with a wooden spoon, for 4 to 5 minutes, or until the meat is lightly browned.

•

Stir in the broth, thyme, caraway seeds and noodles. Bring to a boil.

•

Reduce the heat, cover and simmer for 5 to 8 minutes, or until the noodles are just tender.

•

Stir in the paprika and tomato paste. Cover and simmer for 5 minutes.

•

Remove from the heat, stir in the yogurt and serve.

Hands-on time: 10 minutes
Total time: 25 minutes

Per serving: 275 calories
7.9 g. total fat (26% of calories)
2.8 g. saturated fat
35 mg. cholesterol
294 mg. sodium

Chicken Stew with Cider and Herbs

Although this stew is great any time of year, it's especially welcome in the autumn, when cider is at its freshest. It's a really hearty one-dish meal that needs no extra accompaniment.

Makes 4 servings

1 teaspoon **olive oil**

1 **frying chicken (3–3½ pounds),
cut into serving pieces and skinned**

½ cup + 3 tablespoons **water**

2 **large onions, thinly sliced**

2 cups **sliced mushrooms**

½ teaspoon **dried thyme leaves**

2 **bay leaves**

½ teaspoon **ground nutmeg**

8 **whole pitted prunes**

1 teaspoon **minced garlic**

2 cups **cider**

2 tablespoons **cornstarch**

4 cups **hot cooked rice or noodles**

●

Preheat the oven to 400°.

●

Lightly coat a Dutch oven with no-stick spray. Add the oil and place over medium-high heat. Add the chicken and cook, turning, for 8 to 10 minutes, or until browned on all sides. Transfer to a plate.

●

Add ½ cup of the water to the pot and scrape the bottom with a wooden spoon to loosen any browned bits. Bring the water to a simmer and add the onions. Cover and simmer for 10 minutes, or until the onions soften.

●

Add the mushrooms, thyme, bay leaves, nutmeg, prunes and garlic. Cover and cook for 10 minutes, or until the vegetables are tender.

●

Add the chicken and cider to the pot. Cover and bake for 25 minutes, or until the chicken is cooked through.

●

Transfer the chicken to a serving platter and cover loosely with foil to keep warm. Remove and discard the bay leaves.

●

In a cup, stir the cornstarch into the remaining 3 tablespoons water until smooth. Add to the liquid in the pot. Stir over medium heat until thickened. Serve over the rice or noodles.

Encore!

French Chicken-and-Rice Casserole

Bone enough leftover chicken to equal 3 cups of bite-size pieces. Mix with 1 cup of the stew sauce, 2 cups cooked rice, 10 ounces undiluted canned low-fat cream of mushroom soup and ½ cup minced parsley. Place in an oiled casserole and top with toasted bread crumbs. Bake at 400° for 25 to 30 minutes, or until bubbly.

———

Hands-on time: 25 minutes
Total time: 1¼ hours

Per serving: 829 calories
15.6 g. total fat (17% of calories)
4.1 g. saturated fat
171 mg. cholesterol
173 mg. sodium

Hunter's Pot Roast with Vegetables

Hunter's Pot Roast with Vegetables

Browning beef under the broiler lets you get away without using fat for that step. In addition, roasting the vegetables before adding them to the stew contributes an extra layer of flavor.

Makes 4 servings

2½ tablespoons **unbleached flour**
1 pound **lean beef top round, cubed**
2¼ cups **defatted reduced-sodium beef broth**
3 **large onions, quartered**
4 **large carrots, cut into ½″ lengths**
4 **large all-purpose potatoes, cut into 1″ chunks**
1 tablespoon **olive oil**
¼ cup **red wine or water**
2 teaspoons **paprika**
1 teaspoon **dried thyme leaves**
½ teaspoon **dried marjoram leaves**
⅛ teaspoon **freshly ground black pepper**
1½ cups **small mushrooms**
¼ cup **tomato paste**
⅓ cup **hot water**
Salt (optional)

•

Preheat the broiler. Coat a large shallow baking pan with no-stick spray.

•

Put the flour in a self-sealing plastic bag and add the beef. Close the bag and shake to coat the beef. Spread the beef (and any excess flour) evenly in the prepared pan.

•

Broil 5″ from the heat, stirring frequently, for 5 to 7 minutes, or until the beef is lightly browned on all sides. Transfer the meat to a Dutch oven.

•

Add ½ cup of the broth to the baking pan and scrape up the browned bits with a wooden spoon. Transfer the liquid to the Dutch oven.

•

Turn off the broiler and set the oven temperature to 400°.

•

Place the onions, carrots and potatoes in the same baking pan. Drizzle with the oil and toss to mix well. Spread in an even layer. Bake, stirring occasionally, for 30 minutes.

(continued)

Encore!

Pot Roast Sandwiches

Split and toast 2 large rye or whole-wheat buns or hard rolls, then spread with Dijon mustard. Strain 1 cup leftover beef from Hunter's Pot Roast with Vegetables and divide between the 2 bottom rolls. Top with roasted vegetables as desired, then sprinkle each roll with 1 tablespoon shredded mozzarella. Broil until the cheese melts and the meat is heated through. Add the roll tops.

While the vegetables are baking, add the wine or water, paprika, thyme, marjoram, pepper and the remaining 1¾ cups broth to the Dutch oven. Bring to a boil over medium-high heat. Reduce the heat, cover and simmer for 30 minutes.

Add the roasted vegetables and the mushrooms to the beef mixture. Cover and simmer, stirring occasionally, for 20 minutes.

In a cup, mix the tomato paste and hot water until smooth. Add to the beef mixture and cook for 5 minutes.

Skim off and discard any fat from the stew, season to taste with the salt (if using) and serve.

Hands-on time: 20 minutes
Total time: 1¼ hours

Per serving: 448 calories
9.6 g. total fat (19% of calories)
2.5 g. saturated fat
72 mg. cholesterol
365 mg. sodium

Irish Stew

This lightened version of Irish stew takes its traditional sweet flavor from onions caramelized in balsamic vinegar and brown sugar.

Makes 4 servings

¼ cup **unbleached flour**
½ teaspoon **salt**
¼ teaspoon **dry mustard**
1 pound **cubed lean stew meat or sirloin**
1 teaspoon **olive oil**
¼ cup **balsamic vinegar**
1½ cups **diced onions**
1 cup **cubed red potatoes**
⅔ cup **diced carrots**
2 cups **defatted reduced-sodium beef broth**
1 tablespoon **packed brown sugar**
1 tablespoon **cornstarch**
2 tablespoons **water**
4 cups **hot cooked yolk-free egg noodles**

In a self-sealing plastic bag, combine the flour, salt and mustard. Add the beef, close the bag and shake until coated. Transfer the beef to a colander and shake gently to remove excess flour.

Lightly coat a Dutch oven with no-stick spray. Add the oil and place over medium-high heat. Add the beef. Cook, stirring frequently, for 5 to 8 minutes, or until the beef is lightly browned. Transfer to a plate.

Add the vinegar to the pot and bring to a simmer, scraping the bottom of the pan with a wooden spoon. Add the onions, potatoes, carrots and ¼ cup of the broth to the pot. Cook, stirring frequently, for 5 minutes, or until the vegetables soften slightly.

Add the brown sugar, beef and the remaining 1¾ cups broth to the pot. Cover, reduce the heat to medium and cook for 20 to 25 minutes, or until the vegetables are tender.

In a cup, mix the cornstarch and water until smooth. Add to the pot and cook, stirring, for 4 to 5 minutes, or until the sauce thickens.

Serve over the noodles.

Hands-on time: 15 minutes
Total time: 40 minutes

Per serving: 497 calories
10.4 g. total fat (19% of calories)
3 g. saturated fat
114 mg. cholesterol
544 mg. sodium

Take It Along

A Movable Irish Feast
Heat 1 cup Irish Stew to boiling, then mix in ½ cup cooked noodles. Transfer to a 2-cup soup Thermos, seal and take to work, the park or anywhere you want to celebrate Saint Paddy's Day. Eat with Irish soda bread or thick-cut light rye bread.

Fish, Potato and Vegetable Stew

Don't worry about leftovers. This delicate, chunky fish stew gets even better after the flavors have had a chance to mellow in the refrigerator for a day or two.

Makes 4 servings

1 tablespoon **butter or margarine**
2 **medium onions, quartered**
1 **large stalk celery, thinly sliced**
3 **large carrots, thinly sliced**
1⅓ cups **defatted reduced-sodium chicken broth**
3 **large potatoes, cut into ¾" cubes**
¾ teaspoon **dried marjoram leaves**
¾ teaspoon **dry mustard**
½ teaspoon **dried tarragon leaves**
⅛ teaspoon **curry powder**
½ cup **2% low-fat milk**
1 pound **cod, haddock or other mild white fish fillets, cut into 2" chunks**
Salt (optional)
Freshly ground black pepper

In a Dutch oven, combine the butter or margarine, onions, celery and carrots. Cook over medium-high heat, stirring frequently, for 5 minutes, or until the onions soften.

Stir in the broth, potatoes, marjoram, mustard, tarragon and curry powder. Bring to a boil. Reduce the heat and simmer, stirring occasionally, for 15 to 18 minutes, or until most of the liquid evaporates and the vegetables are just tender.

Add the milk, fish, salt (if using) and pepper. Simmer for 3 minutes, or until the fish pieces flake easily when touched with a fork.

Hands-on time: 10 minutes
Total time: 35 minutes

Per serving: 277 calories
4.5 g. total fat (15% of calories)
2.3 g. saturated fat
59 mg. cholesterol
297 mg. sodium

Sage Chicken and Rice

Sage in the coating mixture and the slight nip of Dijon mustard in the sauce enliven these tender stuffed chicken rolls.

Makes 4 servings

2½ cups **defatted reduced-sodium chicken broth**
1 cup **uncooked basmati rice**
2 cups **small broccoli florets**
4 **boneless, skinless chicken breast halves**
(**4 ounces each**)
1 **egg, lightly beaten**
¾ cup **unbleached flour**
1 teaspoon **dried sage leaves**
¼ teaspoon **freshly ground black pepper**
¼ teaspoon **salt**
2 tablespoons **butter or margarine**
2 teaspoons **canola oil**
4 **scallions, sliced**
2 tablespoons **water**
¼ cup **white wine or**
defatted reduced-sodium chicken broth
1 teaspoon **Dijon mustard**

●

In a medium saucepan, bring 2¼ cups of the broth to a boil over high heat. Add the rice and broccoli. Reduce the heat to medium-low, cover and cook for 20 to 25 minutes, or until the water is absorbed. Fluff with a fork and keep warm.

●

Place the chicken breasts between sheets of wax paper. Pound with a meat mallet to an even ¾″ thickness. Place the egg in a shallow bowl. Beat lightly with a fork. In another shallow bowl, mix the flour, sage, pepper and salt. Dip the chicken breasts into the egg and then into the flour mixture to coat evenly.

●

Melt the butter or margarine in a large no-stick frying pan over medium heat. Add the chicken and cook, turning, for 8 to 10 minutes, or until browned on both sides. Transfer to a warm platter.

●

Add the oil and scallions to the pan. Cook for 3 minutes, or until the scallions soften. Add the water, wine or broth, mustard and the remaining ¼ cup broth. Reduce the heat to low and simmer for 5 minutes. Pour over the chicken and serve with the rice.

Hands-on time: 30 minutes
Total time: 1¼ hours

Per serving: 480 calories
11.3 g. total fat (21% of calories)
4.5 g. saturated fat
134 mg. cholesterol
447 mg. sodium

Garlic French Chicken

You might call this coq au vin lightened for today's palate. And unlike the classic dish, it won't overstress a busy cook.

Makes 4 servings

1 **frying chicken** (**3 pounds**),
    cut into serving pieces and skinned
1 teaspoon **dried thyme leaves**
½ teaspoon **celery seeds**
¼ teaspoon **ground cumin**
½ teaspoon **salt**
½ teaspoon **freshly ground black pepper**
2 **medium onions, cut into eighths**
3 **carrots, halved lengthwise and**
    cut into 2″ pieces
8–10 **cloves garlic, chopped**
¼ cup **balsamic vinegar**
1 cup **red wine or**
    defatted reduced-sodium chicken broth
2 tablespoons **cornstarch**
3 tablespoons **water**
4 cups **hot cooked noodles or rice**

Preheat the oven to 400°.

Coat a large shallow baking pan with no-stick spray. Arrange the chicken pieces in a single layer in the pan.

In a small bowl, stir together the thyme, celery seeds, cumin, salt and pepper. Rub the spice mixture into the chicken. Surround the chicken with the onions, carrots and garlic. Pour the vinegar and wine or broth over the chicken and vegetables.

Bake for 1 hour. Turn the chicken and baste the vegetables with the cooking juices. Bake for 15 to 20 minutes, or until the chicken is cooked through. Transfer the chicken and vegetables to a platter and cover loosely with foil to keep warm.

In a cup, mix the cornstarch and water until smooth. Pour the pan juices into a small saucepan. Add the cornstarch mixture. Stir over medium heat until thickened. Serve the chicken and vegetables over the noodles or rice. Spoon on the sauce.

Hands-on time: 5 minutes
Total time: 1½ hours

Per serving: 761 calories
14.2 g. total fat (17% of calories)
3.9 g. saturated fat
171 mg. cholesterol
464 mg. sodium

Curried Turkey, Vegetables and Fruit

A blend of spices and herbs, plus raisins and honey, lends this quick curry a hint of sweetness and a slightly exotic flavor and aroma.

Makes 4 servings

1½ teaspoons **butter or margarine**
12 ounces **ground turkey breast**
2 **onions, chopped**
1 cup **coarsely diced mixed sweet red and green peppers**
1½ cups **defatted reduced-sodium chicken broth**
1 tablespoon **honey**
½ cup **raisins**
1 teaspoon **curry powder**
½ teaspoon **dried thyme leaves**
½ teaspoon **ground ginger**
½ teaspoon **ground cinnamon**
¼ teaspoon **ground cloves**
⅛ teaspoon **ground nutmeg**
2 **large bay leaves**
Pinch of saffron (optional)
2½ cups **hot cooked rice**

•

In a large no-stick frying pan, melt the butter or margarine over medium-high heat. Crumble the turkey into the pan. Cook, breaking up the meat with a wooden spoon, for 4 to 5 minutes, or until lightly browned.

•

Add the onions and peppers. Cook, stirring frequently, for 5 minutes, or until the onions soften. Add the broth, honey, raisins, curry powder, thyme, ginger, cinnamon, cloves, nutmeg, bay leaves and saffron (if using). Stir until blended.

•

Bring to a simmer and cook for 10 minutes, or until the mixture cooks down slightly.

•

Remove and discard the bay leaves. Stir in the rice and cook for 5 minutes, or until piping hot.

Hands-on time: 10 minutes
Total time: 25 minutes

Per serving: 371 calories
3.9 g. total fat (9% of calories)
1.6 g. saturated fat
41 mg. cholesterol
233 mg. sodium

Szechuan Shrimp

Here's a classic Chinese recipe adapted to beat the clock—shrimp and vegetables enlivened with a little Szechuan heat.

Makes 4 servings

2 tablespoons **reduced-sodium soy sauce**

1 tablespoon **rice vinegar**

1½ tablespoons **sugar**

¼ cup **water**

1 teaspoon **cornstarch**

3 tablespoons **sherry or apple juice**

2 teaspoons **sesame oil**

2–3 drops **hot-chili oil**

2 teaspoons **chopped fresh ginger**

2 **large cloves garlic, minced**

¼ cup **thinly sliced scallions**

1 **large carrot, shredded**

1 **large stalk celery, chopped**

12 ounces **peeled and deveined medium shrimp**

3 cups **hot cooked rice**

In a small bowl, combine the soy sauce, vinegar, sugar, water and cornstarch. Stir until smooth. Set aside.

In a large no-stick frying pan, combine the sherry or apple juice, sesame oil and hot-chili oil. Add the ginger, garlic, scallions, carrots and celery. Cook, stirring, for 2 to 3 minutes.

Add the shrimp and cook for 3 to 4 minutes, or until the shrimp turn pink.

Stir the cornstarch mixture and add it to the pan. Cook, stirring, until the mixture thickens.

Serve over the rice.

Hands-on time: 10 minutes
Total time: 20 minutes

Per serving: 308 calories
3.4 g. total fat (10% of calories)
0.6 g. saturated fat
131 mg. cholesterol
432 mg. sodium

Encore!

Shrimp-Stuffed Potatoes

Bake 2 large russet potatoes. When cool enough to handle, cut off the top third of each and scoop out the flesh, leaving ½"-thick shells. (Reserve the flesh for another use.) Spoon leftover Szechuan Shrimp into the shells and bake at 350° for 15 minutes. Top with chopped scallions and a dash of soy sauce.

———

Shrimp in Garlic Sauce with Tomatoes

There's something irresistible about the combination of garlic, tomatoes and shrimp. Although this dish claims no ethnic heritage, it's reminiscent of food from the south of France.

Makes 4 servings

1 teaspoon **olive oil**

¼ cup **white wine or**
   defatted reduced-sodium chicken broth

2 **large sweet red peppers, thinly sliced**

2–3 teaspoons **minced garlic**

2 teaspoons **honey**

1½ teaspoons **lemon juice**

1 **large ripe tomato, coarsely chopped**

1 pound **peeled and deveined medium shrimp**

½ teaspoon **chopped fresh mint**

1 tablespoon **minced fresh parsley**

Salt (optional)

Freshly ground black pepper

4 cups **hot cooked rice**

•

In a large no-stick frying pan, combine the oil and wine or broth. Place over medium-high heat until hot. Add the red peppers and garlic. Cook, stirring frequently, for 10 minutes, or until the peppers soften.

•

Add the honey, lemon juice, tomatoes, shrimp, mint and parsley. Cook for 3 minutes, or until the shrimp turn pink and are heated through. Season with the salt (if using) and black pepper.

•

Serve over the rice.

Hands-on time: 10 minutes
Total time: 25 minutes

Per serving: 401 calories
2.8 g. total fat (7% of calories)
0.6 g. saturated fat
174 mg. cholesterol
208 mg. sodium

Braised Catfish, Sweet Potatoes and Vegetables

For this casserole, we bake tender catfish fillets with layers of colorful vegetables. If you're looking for an especially light dinner, omit the rice.

Makes 4 servings

2 teaspoons **sesame oil**
1 **large sweet potato, thinly sliced**
4 **catfish fillets (4 ounces each)**
1 package (10 ounces) **frozen spinach, thawed**
1 package (10 ounces) **frozen stir-fry vegetables, thawed**
2 cups **defatted reduced-sodium chicken broth**
1 tablespoon **reduced-sodium soy sauce**
2 cups **toasted croutons**
3 cups **hot cooked rice**

●

Preheat the oven to 400°.

●

Coat an 8″ × 12″ baking dish with the oil. Cover the bottom with the sweet potatoes. Top with the catfish. Spread the spinach on top of the fish. Sprinkle with the stir-fry vegetables.

●

In a small saucepan, combine the broth and soy sauce. Bring to a boil. Pour over the vegetables and catfish. Sprinkle with the croutons.

●

Bake for 25 minutes, or until bubbling hot and lightly browned. Let stand for 5 minutes before serving.

●

Serve the fish and vegetables over the rice.

Hands-on time: 10 minutes
Total time: 45 minutes

Per serving: 596 calories
7.7 g. total fat (12% of calories)
1.6 g. saturated fat
65 mg. cholesterol
689 mg. sodium

Pork Lo Mein

Crisp snow peas and peppers marry well with pork and a pungent sauce for a low-fat version of that Chinese favorite, lo mein.

Makes 4 servings

5 ounces **uncooked lo mein noodles or thin spaghetti, broken in half**
6 ounces **pork loin, thinly sliced and cut into thin strips**
1 **large onion, chopped**
2 **large cloves garlic, minced**
2 teaspoons **sesame oil**
⅔ cup **defatted reduced-sodium chicken broth**
3 tablespoons **reduced-sodium soy sauce**
1½ teaspoons **ground ginger**
2–3 drops **hot-chili oil (optional)**
¼ cup **sherry or apple juice**
1½ cups **snow peas**
1 **sweet red pepper, diced**
⅓ cup **sliced scallions**
2 teaspoons **rice vinegar**

●

Cook the noodles or spaghetti in a large pot of boiling water until just tender. Drain and set aside.

●

Coat a large no-stick frying pan with no-stick spray. Place over medium heat. Add the pork and cook, stirring, for 6 to 7 minutes, or until the pork is lightly browned. Transfer to a bowl.

●

Add the onions, garlic, sesame oil, 3 tablespoons of the broth and 2 tablespoons of the soy sauce to the pan. Cook over medium heat, stirring frequently, for 7 to 8 minutes.

●

Add the ginger, hot-chili oil (if using), 3 tablespoons of the sherry or apple juice and the remaining broth to the pan. Stir in the pork. Cover and simmer for 4 to 5 minutes, or until the pork is cooked.

●

Add the snow peas, red peppers and scallions. Cook, stirring frequently, for 5 minutes, or until the vegetables soften.

●

Add the vinegar, the remaining 1 tablespoon soy sauce and the remaining 1 tablespoon sherry or apple juice. Stir to mix well.

●

Stir in the noodles or spaghetti. Mix well and heat through.

Hands-on time: 10 minutes
Total time: 30 minutes

Per serving: 316 calories
4.3 g. total fat (12% of calories)
0.9 g. saturated fat
30 mg. cholesterol
701 mg. sodium

Thai Curried Vegetables

This is worth a trip to an Asian market for the few authentic ingredients needed if your supermarket doesn't carry them. A good low-fat substitute for the coconut milk, according to healthy cooking expert Jeanne Jones, is additional evaporated skim milk flavored with coconut extract.

Makes 4 servings

6 ounces	**uncooked thin spaghetti or rice noodles, broken into 3″ lengths**
3 cups	**small broccoli florets**
⅓ cup	**defatted reduced-sodium chicken broth**
2 cups	**chopped onions**
½ cup	**thinly sliced carrots**
1	**sweet red pepper, seeded and diced**
2	**small red potatoes, cubed**
1½ tablespoons	**minced fresh ginger**
1 tablespoon	**chopped garlic**
2 tablespoons	**Thai red curry paste**
7 ounces	**reduced-fat coconut milk**
7 ounces	**evaporated skim milk**
1–2 tablespoons	**fish sauce or reduced-sodium soy sauce**

Cook the spaghetti or noodles and broccoli in a large pot of boiling water until the pasta is just tender. Drain and set aside.

Heat the broth in a large no-stick frying pan over medium-high heat. Add the onions and cook, stirring frequently, for 5 minutes. Add the carrots, peppers, potatoes, ginger and garlic. Cook, stirring frequently, for 5 minutes, or until the vegetables are tender.

In a large pot, combine the curry paste, coconut milk and evaporated skim milk. Bring to a boil over medium-high heat. Cook for 5 minutes, stirring occasionally.

Add the vegetables, fish sauce or soy sauce, pasta and broccoli to the pot with the curry sauce. Cook for 5 minutes.

Hands-on time: 10 minutes
Total time: 30 minutes

Per serving: 290 calories
3.3 g. total fat (9% of calories)
0.1 g. saturated fat
2 mg. cholesterol
265 mg. sodium

Take It Along

Thai Takeout
Take a taste of Thailand to a potluck dinner. Reheat Thai Curried Vegetables over gentle heat to prevent the delicate fish sauce from turning bitter. Jazz up the curry by taking along containers of raisins and chopped dried apricots, green apples and cilantro.

Singapore Noodles

We've adapted an Asian favorite to save both time and calories. Look for rice-stick noodles (sometimes just called rice noodles) in the ethnic section of your grocery store.

Makes 4 servings

3½ ounces **uncooked rice-stick noodles**
6 ounces **boneless, skinless chicken breasts, cubed**
2 teaspoons **sesame oil**
1 **medium onion, chopped**
½ cup **chopped scallions**
1 **large carrot, shredded**
1 cup **defatted reduced-sodium chicken broth**
3 tablespoons **reduced-sodium soy sauce**
1½ teaspoons **curry powder**
1 teaspoon **sugar**
¾ teaspoon **ground ginger**
⅛ teaspoon **salt (optional)**
⅛ teaspoon **freshly ground black pepper**
6 ounces **cooked medium shrimp**
1 can (8 ounces) **sliced water chestnuts, drained**

Cook the noodles in a large pot of boiling water for 3 minutes, or until tender. Drain, rinse and drain again. Using a knife or scissors, cut the long strands into about 3″ lengths. Set aside.

Coat a large no-stick frying pan with no-stick spray. Place over medium heat and add the chicken. Cook, stirring, for 5 to 6 minutes, or until lightly browned. Transfer to a small bowl and set aside.

Place the oil, onions, scallions, carrots, 2 tablespoons of the broth and 1 tablespoon of the soy sauce in the pan. Cook over medium heat, stirring frequently, for 5 minutes.

Stir in the curry powder, sugar, ginger, salt (if using), pepper, the remaining broth and the remaining 2 tablespoons soy sauce. Add the shrimp, water chestnuts and chicken. Cook for 2 minutes.

Add the noodles and cook for 2 minutes, or until heated through.

Hands-on time: 15 minutes
Total time: 30 minutes

Per serving: 278 calories
3.9 g. total fat (12% of calories)
0.7 g. saturated fat
100 mg. cholesterol
776 mg. sodium

Baked Vegetable-and-Cheese Potatoes (page 188) ➔

Vegetarian
Feasts

Indian Chick-Pea and Potato Dinner

This wonderfully savory dish from India is a filling vegetarian main course. To make it even more hearty, add rice. This also works well as a side dish.

Makes 4 servings

4 teaspoons **butter or margarine**
3 **large potatoes, diced**
1 package (10 ounces) **frozen chopped spinach, thawed**
2 **large onions, chopped**
1 **clove garlic, chopped**
1 tablespoon **minced fresh ginger**
2 cans (15 ounces each) **chick-peas, rinsed and drained**
1¾ teaspoons **ground coriander**
1¾ teaspoons **curry powder**
¼ teaspoon **ground cloves**
¼ teaspoon **ground cardamom**
1 can (14½ ounces) **stewed tomatoes, drained and pureed**
3 tablespoons **chopped fresh cilantro (optional)**

Preheat the oven to 375°.

Melt 2 teaspoons of the butter or margarine in a Dutch oven over medium-high heat. Add the potatoes. Cook, stirring, for 3 to 4 minutes, or until the potatoes just begin to soften.

Stir in the spinach and cook for 2 minutes longer, or until the spinach is heated through. Remove from the pot and set aside.

Place the onions, garlic and ginger in a food processor and coarsely puree. Add the puree and the remaining 2 teaspoons butter or margarine to the pot. Cook over high heat, stirring, for 5 minutes, or until most of the liquid evaporates.

Puree half of the chick-peas in the food processor; add to the pot. Stir in the remaining whole chick-peas, coriander, curry powder, cloves and cardamom. Cook, stirring, for 2 to 3 minutes.

Transfer half of the mixture to an 8″ × 12″ baking dish and smooth it into an even layer. Top with half of the potato-spinach mixture. Top with half of the tomatoes. Repeat layers.

Cover and bake for 45 minutes, or until the potatoes are tender when pierced with a fork. Garnish with the cilantro (if using).

Hands-on time: 20 minutes
Total time: 1 hour

Per serving: 412 calories
8.3 g. total fat (17% of calories)
3 g. saturated fat
10 mg. cholesterol
962 mg. sodium

Curried Lentil-and-Onion Stew

The russet colors of curried onions and sweet potatoes make this a great autumn entrée. Keep it tender but not mushy by slightly undercooking the lentils.

Makes 4 servings

1 teaspoon **olive oil**
1½ cups **coarsely chopped onions**
2 cups **peeled and chopped tomatoes**
2 cups **cooked, peeled and chopped sweet potatoes**
2 teaspoons **curry powder**
1 cup **green lentils, rinsed and drained**
½ cup **dry sherry or apple juice**
2½ cups **reduced-sodium vegetable broth or water**
4 ounces **uncooked spaghetti**
2 teaspoons **reduced-sodium soy sauce**
¼ cup **chopped fresh parsley**

●

Lightly coat a Dutch oven with no-stick spray. Add the oil and set over medium-high heat. Add the onions and cook, stirring frequently, for 3 minutes, or until the onions soften.

●

Add the tomatoes, sweet potatoes, curry powder and lentils. Cook, stirring frequently, for 2 minutes. Add the sherry or apple juice and cook for 1 minute. Add the broth or water and bring to a boil.

●

Reduce the heat to medium, cover and simmer for 30 minutes, or until the lentils are tender but not mushy.

●

While the vegetables are cooking, cook the spaghetti in a large pot of boiling water until just tender. Drain and add to the pot. Stir in the soy sauce and parsley.

Hands-on time: 10 minutes
Total time: 40 minutes

Per serving: 563 calories
3.3 g. total fat (5% of calories)
0.4 g. saturated fat
0 mg. cholesterol
805 mg. sodium

Javanese Tempeh Curry

Javanese Tempeh Curry

You'll love the spicy complexity of this curry. Tempeh—sold in natural food stores—is an Indonesian soy food that adds protein and texture. For variety, you could substitute tofu.

Makes 4 servings

2½ cups **apple juice**
1½ cups **thinly sliced onions**
1½ cups **sliced mushrooms**
½ cup **diced red potatoes**
1 teaspoon **yellow mustard seeds**
1 package (8 ounces) **tempeh, cubed**
¾ teaspoon **caraway seeds**
1½ teaspoons **turmeric**
1 teaspoon **ground red pepper**
5 **large cloves garlic, minced**
1 tablespoon **grated fresh ginger**
¾ teaspoon **ground cumin**
2 cups **peeled, seeded and diced butternut squash**
2 cups **peeled and diced eggplant**
1 cup **frozen peas**
Salt (optional)
Freshly ground black pepper
4 cups **hot cooked rice**
½ cup **mango chutney**

•

In a Dutch oven, combine the apple juice, onions, mushrooms, potatoes, mustard seeds, tempeh, caraway seeds, turmeric, red pepper, garlic, ginger and cumin. Cover and simmer over medium-high heat for 10 minutes, or until the potatoes are tender.

•

Add the squash and eggplant. Cook for 10 minutes, or until the vegetables are very soft.

•

Add the peas and season with the salt (if using) and black pepper. Serve over the rice with the chutney on the side.

Hands-on time: 15 minutes
Total time: 35 minutes

Per serving: 671 calories
6.2 g. total fat (8% of calories)
0.9 g. saturated fat
0 mg. cholesterol
65 mg. sodium

Mexican Red Rice and Beans

Here's a soul-satisfying dish that proves you can enjoy Mexican-style cooking with little fat and less effort. It's easy on the budget, too.

Makes 4 servings

2 teaspoons **olive oil**

1 cup **chopped onions**

1 **clove garlic, minced**

2 tablespoons + 1½ cups **water**

1 cup **uncooked white rice**

1 can (8 ounces) **reduced-sodium tomato sauce**

1 **small green pepper, chopped**

½ teaspoon **chili powder**

½ teaspoon **dried oregano leaves**

½ teaspoon **ground cumin**

¼ teaspoon **salt (optional)**

2–3 drops **hot-pepper sauce**

1 can (16 ounces) **reduced-sodium kidney beans, rinsed and drained**

3 **plum tomatoes, chopped**

●

In a large saucepan, combine the oil, onions, garlic and 2 tablespoons of the water. Cook over medium heat, stirring frequently, for 6 to 7 minutes, or until the onions soften.

●

Add the rice, tomato sauce, green peppers, chili powder, oregano, cumin, salt (if using), hot-pepper sauce and the remaining 1½ cups water.

●

Stir, bring to a boil, cover and simmer for 20 minutes, or until the rice is tender and the liquid is absorbed.

●

Stir in the beans and tomatoes. Cook over low heat for 2 minutes, or until heated through.

Hands-on time: 10 minutes
Total time: 30 minutes

Per serving: 354 calories
3.5 g. total fat (9% of calories)
0.4 g. saturated fat
0 mg. cholesterol
37 mg. sodium

Encore!

Red River Burritos

Wrap 4 flour tortillas in a damp paper towel and microwave them on high power for 1 minute to soften. Reheat 2 cups leftover Mexican Red Rice and Beans and divide among the tortillas; roll tightly. Arrange the burritos, seam side down, in a baking dish, top with ⅓ cup shredded low-fat Cheddar cheese and broil for 2 minutes to melt the cheese. Top each burrito with a spoonful of salsa, a dollop of nonfat yogurt and some chopped cilantro for color.

Polenta with Caramelized Onions and Mushrooms

Polenta, made of coarsely ground cornmeal, can be served soft or firmed up. Here it's soft, topped with a sweet ragout of caramelized onions and mushrooms. To make it firm, pour it into a shallow pan and let stand until set. Unmold and cut with a knife.

Makes 4 servings

1 teaspoon **olive oil**

2 **large onions, thinly sliced**

¼ cup **reduced-sodium vegetable broth or water**

3 cups **sliced mushrooms**

2 **cloves garlic, minced**

¼ cup **balsamic vinegar**

½ cup **chopped fresh parsley**

5 cups **water**

1¼ cups **quick-cooking polenta**

½ cup **shredded reduced-fat Cheddar cheese**

2 tablespoons **grated Parmesan cheese**

Lightly coat a Dutch oven with no-stick spray. Add the oil and place over medium-high heat. When the oil is hot, add the onions and broth or water.

Reduce the heat to medium-low. Cover and cook, stirring frequently, for 15 minutes, or until the onions are very soft.

Add the mushrooms and garlic. Raise the heat to medium. Cook, stirring frequently, for 10 minutes, or until the onions are golden and the mushrooms are lightly browned.

Add the vinegar and parsley; cook for 1 minute, or until the liquid is reduced by half.

Bring the water to a boil in a medium saucepan. Gradually whisk in the polenta. Cook, stirring, for 5 minutes, or until the water is absorbed. Add the Cheddar and Parmesan and stir well.

Serve the polenta topped with the onion and mushroom mixture.

Hands-on time: 10 minutes
Total time: 40 minutes

Per serving: 263 calories
5.9 g. total fat (20% of calories)
2.2 g. saturated fat
8 mg. cholesterol
380 mg. sodium

To Your Health

Parsley

Fresh parsley is a good source of disease-fighting vitamins A and C, plus the blood-building nutrients folate and iron. If you don't have fresh parsley, use dried parsley; even just a tablespoon provides a very healthy dose of trace elements because the nutrients are concentrated. Gram for gram, dried parsley provides two to three times more copper, iron, magnesium and boron than almost any other food.

Bean and Vegetable Enchilada Bake

In this Mexican favorite, vegetables and beans are layered with tortillas and topped with melted Cheddar. To vary, use cubed zucchini for the cauliflower.

Makes 4 servings

1 cup **chopped onions**

2 **cloves garlic, minced**

2 teaspoons **olive oil**

1 **small green pepper, chopped**

2 cups **chopped cauliflower florets**

¾ cup **mild picante sauce**

1 can (8 ounces) **reduced-sodium tomato sauce**

1½ teaspoons **ground cumin**

1 teaspoon **chili powder**

1 cup **reduced-sodium kidney beans, rinsed and drained**

6 **corn tortillas (6″ diameter)**

¾ cup **shredded reduced-fat Cheddar cheese**

¼ cup **nonfat sour cream**

1 **medium tomato, chopped**

•

Preheat the oven to 375°.

•

In a large no-stick frying pan, combine the onions, garlic and oil. Cook over medium heat, stirring frequently, for 5 to 6 minutes, or until the onions soften. Add a little water if necessary.

•

Add the peppers, cauliflower, picante sauce, tomato sauce, cumin, chili powder and beans. Simmer for 5 minutes.

•

Spread half of the vegetable mixture in the bottom of an 8″ × 12″ baking dish. Top with the tortillas, laying them as evenly as possible over the vegetable mixture. Sprinkle evenly with ½ cup of the Cheddar.

•

Add the remaining vegetable mixture, spreading it out with the back of a large spoon. Cover with aluminum foil and bake for 25 to 30 minutes, or until heated through.

•

Remove and discard the foil. Sprinkle with the remaining ¼ cup Cheddar and bake for 5 minutes, or until the cheese is partially melted. Serve with the sour cream and tomatoes.

Hands-on time: 10 minutes
Total time: 40 minutes

Per serving: 305 calories
8.5 g. total fat (24% of calories)
2.1 g. saturated fat
9 mg. cholesterol
745 mg. sodium

Italian Bean-and-Potato Salad

Beans add plenty of protein to this main-dish salad. The balsamic vinegar lends a smoky-sweet flavor that blends well with the potatoes and beans.

Makes 4 servings

1 **large potato**
2 tablespoons **olive oil**
2 tablespoons **balsamic vinegar**
¼ teaspoon **salt**
Freshly ground black pepper
2 cans (15½ ounces each) **navy or cannellini beans, rinsed and drained**
½ **large cucumber, peeled,**
    halved lengthwise and thinly sliced
3 **scallions, chopped**
1 **large sweet red or yellow pepper,**
    seeded and chopped
¼ cup **chopped fresh basil**
¼ cup **chopped fresh parsley**
Lettuce leaves
1 **large tomato, sliced into 16 thin wedges**

•

Place the potato in a medium saucepan. Add cold water to cover. Bring to a boil and cook for 15 minutes, or until easily pierced with a sharp knife. Drain, cool slightly, quarter and thinly slice.

•

In a large salad bowl, whisk together the oil, vinegar, salt and black pepper. Add the beans, potatoes, cucumbers and scallions and toss well.

•

Cover and marinate at room temperature for 30 minutes.

•

Add the red or yellow peppers, basil and parsley. Marinate for 15 minutes longer, tossing occasionally. Serve on a bed of lettuce with the tomato wedges.

Hands-on time: 15 minutes
Total time: 1¼ hours

Per serving: 363 calories
7.9 g. total fat (20% of calories)
1 g. saturated fat
0 mg. cholesterol
979 mg. sodium

Take It Along

Salad in an Edible Bowl
Marinated vegetable salads are great to take to work or even to parties since they can stand at room temperature longer than poultry, fish, meat or egg salads. For an untraditional Italian lunch, transport your salad in an edible bowl: Slice the top third off a large, crusty hard roll and scoop out the soft center. Spoon 1 cup Italian Bean and Potato Salad into the bread bowl and replace the top. Wrap in plastic wrap.

___

Egg Fried Rice

A light, colorful, hurry-up meal, this dish is most convenient and tastes best if prepared with rice that was cooked a day ahead and refrigerated.

Makes 4 servings

1 teaspoon **sesame oil**
2 **eggs**
3 **egg whites**
⅛ teaspoon **freshly ground black pepper**
1 teaspoon + 1½ tablespoons **reduced-sodium soy sauce**
1 tablespoon **peanut oil**
8 **scallions**
1 **small stalk celery, coarsely chopped**
⅓ cup **chopped sweet red peppers (optional)**
1 **large clove garlic**
1 cup **frozen green peas, rinsed with hot water and drained**
2½ cups **cold cooked rice**
1½ teaspoons **minced fresh ginger**

Warm the sesame oil in a large no-stick frying pan over medium heat.

In a small bowl, beat the eggs, egg whites, black pepper and 1 teaspoon of the soy sauce with a fork until well-blended. Pour into the pan. Cook, occasionally tipping the pan from side to side to distribute the eggs evenly, for 1 to 2 minutes, or until just cooked through. (Do not stir.)

Slide the eggs from the pan onto a cutting board. When slightly cooled, finely chop and set aside.

Using the same frying pan, combine the peanut oil, scallions, celery, red peppers (if using) and garlic. Cook over medium-high heat, stirring frequently, for 4 minutes, or until the scallions soften.

Stir in the peas, rice, ginger and the remaining 1½ tablespoons soy sauce. Cook, stirring, for 3 minutes. Add the chopped eggs. Cook, stirring, for 1 to 2 minutes, or until evenly mixed and heated through.

Hands-on time: 10 minutes
Total time: 20 minutes

Per serving: 301 calories
7.5 g. total fat (23% of calories)
1.6 g. saturated fat
107 mg. cholesterol
494 mg. sodium

Stir-Fried Tofu and Vegetables

Tofu adds protein to this speedy skillet dinner. Bok choy, with its silvery-white stalks and blue-green leaves, is as vitamin-rich as it is beautiful.

Makes 4 servings

2½ tablespoons **reduced-sodium teriyaki sauce**
2 tablespoons **sherry or apple juice**
3–4 drops **hot-chili oil**
6–8 ounces **firm tofu, cubed**
2 teaspoons **sesame oil**
¾ cup **reduced-sodium vegetable broth**
¼ cup **sliced scallions**
1 **clove garlic, minced**
3 cups **sliced bok choy**
1 **large carrot, shredded**
1 **small sweet red pepper, diced**
1 can (8 ounces) **sliced water chestnuts, drained**
1 teaspoon **rice vinegar**
½ teaspoon **ground ginger**
Salt (optional)
3 cups **hot cooked rice**

In a medium bowl, whisk together the teriyaki sauce, sherry or apple juice and hot-chili oil. Add the tofu, stir to coat and marinate at room temperature for 10 minutes, stirring occasionally.

In a large no-stick frying pan, combine the sesame oil and 2 tablespoons of the broth. Using a slotted spoon, transfer the tofu to the pan. (Set aside the marinade.) Cook over medium heat, stirring frequently, for 2 to 3 minutes.

Add the scallions, garlic, bok choy and carrots. Cook, stirring frequently, for 1 to 2 minutes, or until the vegetables begin to soften.

Add the reserved marinade and the remaining broth. Cook for 5 minutes.

Add the peppers, water chestnuts, vinegar, ginger and salt (if using). Cook, stirring, for 2 minutes, or until heated through.

Serve over the rice.

Hands-on time: 10 minutes
Total time: 30 minutes

Per serving: 502 calories
7.5 g. total fat (13% of calories)
1.1 g. saturated fat
0 mg. cholesterol
308 mg. sodium

Baked Vegetable-and-Cheese Potatoes

Super spuds! Baked potatoes make easy entrées when scooped out and stuffed with vegetables. Here, blue cheese and nippy radishes and scallions add flavor punch.

Makes 4 servings

4 **large baking potatoes**
½ cup **nonfat sour cream**
2 tablespoons **crumbled blue cheese**
2 **scallions, chopped**
2 tablespoons **chopped radishes**
2 tablespoons **chopped green peppers**
2 tablespoons **minced fresh parsley**

Preheat the oven to 400°.

Pierce the potatoes with a fork and bake them for 45 minutes, or until fork-tender. Let cool slightly and then slice the top inch off each potato horizontally. Scoop the potato flesh into a bowl, leaving a 1"-thick shell.

Preheat the broiler.

Mix the potato flesh with the sour cream, blue cheese, scallions, radishes, peppers and parsley. Mound the mixture into the potato shells. Broil about 5" from the heat until the filling turns golden and is heated through.

Hands-on time: 15 minutes
Total time: 1 hour

Per serving: 269 calories
1.2 g. total fat (4% of calories)
0.7 g. saturated fat
3 mg. cholesterol
106 mg. sodium

Take It Along

Hot Potato!
Nothing is as satisfying for a winter lunch as a hot potato, especially one filled with vegetables and cheese. Wrap an extra stuffed potato in plastic and carry it to work. Microwave on high power for three minutes. Round out the meal with a Thermos of hot tomato soup and some low-fat croutons or breadsticks.

Chicken Potpie with Thyme Biscuits
(page 191)

Blue-Plate Specials

Roast Chicken Stuffed with Garlic

There's nothing like a crispy yet very moist roast chicken and melt-in-your-mouth vegetables! Try spreading the mellow roasted garlic on French bread.

Makes 4 servings

2 **large whole garlic bulbs**
1 **roasting chicken (3–3½ pounds),**
   skinned, rinsed and patted dry
2 teaspoons **olive oil**
1 **large onion, quartered**
2 **large carrots, quartered lengthwise**
2 **large sweet red peppers,**
   quartered lengthwise

●

Preheat the oven to 475°.

●

Cut ¼" off the top of one of the garlic bulbs. Break it apart and insert the cloves in the cavity of the chicken.

●

Coat a Dutch oven with no-stick spray. Place over medium-high heat and add 1 teaspoon of the oil. When the oil is hot but not smoking, place the chicken, breast side down, in the pot and sear for 3 minutes, or until lightly browned.

●

Lightly mist the chicken with no-stick spray and turn it over. Sear for 3 minutes on the other side.

●

Break apart the other bulb of garlic and tuck the unpeeled cloves around the chicken in the pot.

●

Lay the onions, carrots and red peppers in a shallow baking dish. Brush them with the remaining 1 teaspoon oil.

●

Place both the Dutch oven and the baking dish in the oven. Bake for 25 minutes, or until the vegetables are tender. Remove the baking dish containing the vegetables from the oven. Keep warm.

●

Continue roasting the chicken for 15 minutes. Turn it over and roast for another 15 minutes. Reduce the heat to 400°. Roast, basting with the pan juices every 5 minutes, until the juices run clear when the thigh is pierced with a fork. Quarter the chicken and serve with the garlic and vegetables.

Hands-on time: 15 minutes
Total time: 1¼ hours

Per serving: 424 calories
15.7 g. total fat (34% of calories)
4 g. saturated fat
171 mg. cholesterol
177 mg. sodium

Encore!

Roast Cranberry-Chicken Sandwiches

Here's a sandwich reminiscent of Thanksgiving but extra-flavorful because it's seasoned with roasted garlic. Toast 4 thick slices of homestyle bread and lightly spread with a combination of nonfat mayonnaise, cranberry sauce and mustard. Slice leftover roast chicken and mound it on the bread. Squeeze the roasted garlic onto the chicken and top with shredded lettuce or cabbage, then the remaining piece of bread. Great with oven-roasted potatoes.

Chicken Potpie with Thyme Biscuits

Dried thyme gives a homey Thanksgiving stuffing flavor to these biscuits, which are extra easy because they're whipped up from a mix.

Makes 4 servings

2½ cups **defatted reduced-sodium chicken broth**
1 **bay leaf**
1 cup **baby carrots**
½ cup **sliced celery**
½ cup **frozen small whole onions**
½ cup **frozen sugar snap peas**
¼ cup **unbleached flour**
¼ teaspoon **poultry seasoning**
⅓ cup **skim milk**
1¾ cups **cubed cooked chicken breast**
1¼ cups **biscuit mix**
½ teaspoon **dried thyme leaves**
⅓ cup **skim milk**

Preheat the oven to 425°.

In a medium saucepan, bring the broth and bay leaf to a boil over medium-high heat. Add the carrots and celery. Cook for 5 minutes.

Add the onions and cook for 2 minutes. Add the peas. Cook for 2 minutes, or until the vegetables are tender.

Strain the liquid into a 4-cup glass measuring cup. If needed, add more broth or some water to bring the level to 2 cups. Transfer the vegetables to a medium bowl and set aside. Remove and discard the bay leaf. Return the liquid to the saucepan.

In a small bowl, whisk together the flour, poultry seasoning and milk. Whisk the flour mixture into the broth. Cook, whisking, over medium heat for 2 minutes, or until thickened. Stir in the chicken and reserved vegetables. Transfer the mixture to a shallow 2-quart casserole.

In a small bowl, stir together the biscuit mix and thyme. Stir in the milk to form a soft dough. Drop 4 mounds of dough on top of the chicken and vegetables.

Bake for 10 to 12 minutes, or until the biscuits are browned and the chicken mixture is bubbling.

Hands-on time: 10 minutes
Total time: 30 minutes

Per serving: 354 calories
10 g. total fat (26% of calories)
1.4 g. saturated fat
53 mg. cholesterol
826 mg. sodium

Spaghetti and Meatballs

Meatballs made of lean ground turkey and a sauce full of herbs and fresh vegetables—this is a healthy version of an old favorite your family will love.

Makes 4 servings

8 ounces **ground turkey breast**
⅓ cup **fresh bread crumbs**
2 tablespoons **minced garlic**
2 tablespoons **canned chopped mild green chili peppers**
1 tablespoon **reduced-sodium Worcestershire sauce (optional)**
½ teaspoon **freshly ground black pepper**
Pinch of dried thyme leaves
Pinch of ground red pepper
1 can (12 ounces) **plum tomatoes, chopped (with juice)**
⅓ cup **red wine or**
defatted reduced-sodium chicken broth
⅓ cup **minced onions**
2 tablespoons **tomato paste**
2 tablespoons **minced fresh parsley**
1 teaspoon **dried basil leaves**
1 teaspoon **dried oregano leaves**
Pinch of grated nutmeg
8 ounces **uncooked spaghetti**

In a medium bowl, combine the turkey, bread crumbs, garlic, chili peppers, Worcestershire sauce (if using), black pepper, thyme and red pepper. Mix thoroughly and form into 1″ balls.

Coat a large no-stick frying pan with no-stick spray. Place over medium-high heat. Add the meatballs and cook, stirring, for 3 minutes, or until browned on all sides.

Add the tomatoes (with juice), wine or broth, onions, tomato paste, parsley, basil, oregano and nutmeg. Simmer over medium-low heat for 1 hour.

Cook the spaghetti in a large pot of boiling water until just tender. Drain. Serve topped with the meatballs and sauce.

Hands-on time: 15 minutes
Total time: 1¼ hours

Per serving: 345 calories
6 g. total fat (15% of calories)
1.3 g. saturated fat
21 mg. cholesterol
284 mg. sodium

Take It Along

Just Like Mom Makes

Pack yourself a satisfying supper for late-night work or studying. Spoon ½ cup leftover spaghetti into a microwave-safe serving dish, top with meatballs and sauce, then sprinkle with Parmesan. Cover and microwave on high for 4 minutes. Serve with sliced Italian bread, lightly misted with water, dusted with garlic powder and toasted until golden.

Hamburger Stroganoff

Here, a familiar beef-and-mushroom dish is prettied up with red peppers, perked up with horseradish and enriched with nonfat sour cream.

Makes 4 servings

9 ounces **extra-lean ground beef**
1 cup **chopped onions**
8 ounces **mushrooms, sliced**
2 **cloves garlic, minced**
1¼ teaspoons **dried thyme leaves**
2 cups **defatted reduced-sodium beef broth**
1 **sweet red pepper, chopped**
1 tablespoon **Dijon mustard**
2 teaspoons **prepared horseradish**
¼ teaspoon **freshly ground black pepper**
¼ teaspoon **salt** (**optional**)
1 cup **nonfat sour cream**
3 cups **hot cooked rice**

•

Coat a large no-stick frying pan with no-stick spray. Crumble the beef into the pan. Cook over medium-high heat, breaking up the meat with a wooden spoon, for 5 minutes, or until lightly browned.

•

Line a platter with several thicknesses of paper towels. Transfer the beef to the platter and drain well.

•

Wipe out the pan with a paper towel. Add the onions, mushrooms, garlic and thyme. Cook over medium-high heat, stirring frequently, for 5 minutes, or until the onions soften.

•

Add the broth, red peppers, mustard, horseradish, black pepper and salt (if using). Simmer, stirring occasionally, for 20 minutes, or until the sauce thickens slightly.

•

Reduce the heat and add the sour cream. Heat for 2 minutes. Serve over the rice.

Hands-on time: 20 minutes
Total time: 45 minutes

Per serving: 203 calories
3.6 g. total fat (16% of calories)
1.1 g. saturated fat
40 mg. cholesterol
427 mg. sodium

Hungarian Goulash

For an authentic goulash, use Hungarian paprika. Tomatoes, sour cream and caraway are often optional ingredients in a goulash; here we use caraway, but you could enrich the dish with the other items.

Makes 4 servings

2 teaspoons **canola oil**
¾ pound **beef eye of round steak, thinly sliced**
⅛ teaspoon **freshly ground black pepper**
2 cups **thinly sliced onions**
1 **small clove garlic, minced**
1 tablespoon **paprika**
1¼ cups **water or defatted reduced-sodium beef broth**
1 tablespoon **unbleached flour**
8 ounces **uncooked egg noodles**
1 teaspoon **caraway seeds**
¼ cup **nonfat sour cream** (**optional**)

•

Coat a large frying pan with no-stick spray. Add the oil and place over medium-high heat. Add the beef and sprinkle with the pepper. Cook, stirring, for 5 minutes, or until browned. Transfer to a plate.

•

Add the onions to the pan. Cook for 2 minutes. Add the garlic and paprika. Cook, stirring constantly, for 1 minute. Add 1 cup of the water or broth and bring to a boil over high heat.

•

Return the beef to the pan. Reduce the heat to low, cover and simmer for 25 minutes, or until the beef is tender.

•

In a small bowl, whisk together the flour and the remaining ¼ cup water or broth. Stir into the frying pan. Cook for 3 to 4 minutes, or until the sauce thickens.

•

While the beef is cooking, cook the noodles in a large pot of boiling water until just tender. Drain. Serve topped with the beef mixture. Sprinkle with the caraway seeds and top with the sour cream (if using).

Hands-on time: 10 minutes
Total time: 40 minutes

Per serving: 406 calories
8.7 g. total fat (20% of calories)
1.7 g. saturated fat
109 mg. cholesterol
62 mg. sodium

Oven-Baked Fish and Chips

This famous English dish is usually quite high in fat. You can make it fast and lean—but still crisp and satisfying—by baking, not deep frying.

Makes 4 servings

2 **large baking potatoes**
¼ cup **unbleached flour**
1 teaspoon **baking powder**
½ teaspoon **poultry seasoning**
1 **egg, lightly beaten**
¼ cup **skim milk**
8 **haddock, cod or flounder fillets**
(**4 ounces each**)

Preheat the oven to 475°. Line a baking sheet with aluminum foil and coat with no-stick spray.

Pierce the potatoes several times with a sharp knife and set on paper towels on a microwave-safe dish. Microwave on high power for 8 minutes, or until the potatoes are soft.

Set aside until cool enough to handle. Cut each potato into 8 lengthwise slices. Arrange in a single layer on half of the baking sheet. Mist the tops lightly with no-stick spray.

In a small bowl, whisk together the flour, baking powder and poultry seasoning. Stir in the egg and milk to make a batter the consistency of pancake batter. If needed, add more milk.

Pat the fish fillets dry with paper towels. Dip the fish into the batter to coat lightly and set the pieces on the baking sheet, not touching each other.

Bake for 20 minutes, or until the potatoes and fish are crisp and lightly browned and the interior of the fish flakes when tested with a fork.

Hands-on time: 10 minutes
Total time: 40 minutes

Per serving: 298 calories
2.8 g. total fat (9% of calories)
0.7 g. saturated fat
143 mg. cholesterol
237 mg. sodium

Tuna-Noodle Casserole

A family-pleasing dinner that's never really gone out of style! This low-fat version uses a quick homemade "cream" sauce that contains fresh mushrooms.

Makes 4 servings

6 ounces **uncooked wide egg noodles**
¼ cup **sherry or**
defatted reduced-sodium chicken broth
1 teaspoon **olive oil**
8 ounces **mushrooms, sliced**
¼ cup **unbleached flour**
2 cups **skim milk**
1 can (7 ounces) **water-packed solid white tuna, drained**
¼ cup **chopped parsley**
Salt (optional)
Freshly ground black pepper
¼ cup **toasted bread crumbs**

Take It Along

Using Your Noodle

Here's a kid's favorite hot lunch. Heat a small amount of Tuna Noodle Casserole in the micro-wave on high power for 3 minutes, then spoon into a 1-cup soup Thermos. Pack along a bag of whole baby carrots, radishes or sliced apples and a container of low-fat fig bars or raisins.

Preheat the oven to 450°. Lightly coat a 2-quart casserole with no-stick spray.

Cook the noodles in a large pot of boiling water until just tender. Drain and set aside.

In a large no-stick frying pan, combine the sherry or broth and oil. Bring to a boil over medium-high heat. Add the mushrooms. Cook, stirring frequently, for 6 minutes, or until the liquid evaporates.

Reduce the heat to medium. Add the flour. Cook, stirring, for 2 minutes (the mixture will be dry). Slowly stir in the milk.

Raise the heat to medium-high. Whisking constantly, bring the sauce to a boil and cook until thickened. Remove from the heat.

Stir in the tuna and parsley and sprinkle with the salt (if using) and pepper. Stir in the noodles.

Spoon into the prepared casserole dish. Top with the bread crumbs. Bake for 25 minutes, or until the top browns slightly.

Hands-on time: 15 minutes
Total time: 45 minutes

Per serving: 357 calories
4.7 g. total fat (12% of calories)
0.7 g. saturated fat
60 mg. cholesterol
308 mg. sodium

Sweet-and-Sour Cabbage

You'll love the great taste of stuffed cabbage—and get it in a fraction of the usual time! This version chops the cabbage and combines all the stuffing ingredients in one pot.

Makes 4 servings

8 ounces **extra-lean ground beef**
1 **small head cabbage, chopped**
2 cans (14½ ounces each) **sodium-free stewed tomatoes**
1 cup **water**
1 **small onion, sliced**
¼ cup **raisins**
¼ teaspoon **freshly ground black pepper**
2 tablespoons **lemon juice**
2 tablespoons **honey**
3 cups **hot cooked rice**

●

Coat a Dutch oven with no-stick spray. Crumble the beef into the pot. Cook over medium-high heat, breaking up the meat with a wooden spoon, for 4 to 5 minutes, or until lightly browned.

●

Line a platter with several thicknesses of paper towels. Transfer the beef to the platter and drain well.

●

Wipe out the pot with a paper towel. Return the beef to the pot. Add the cabbage, tomatoes, water, onions, raisins and pepper. Bring to a boil over high heat.

●

Reduce the heat to medium-high, cover and cook for 15 minutes, or until the cabbage softens.

●

Add the lemon juice and honey. Cook for 10 minutes, or until the cabbage is tender.

●

Serve over the rice.

Hands-on time: 10 minutes
Total time: 35 minutes

Per serving: 305 calories
10 g. total fat (28% of calories)
4 g. saturated fat
38 mg. cholesterol
153 mg. sodium

To Your Health

Cabbage

Cabbage is an honored member of the crucifer family, praised for its ability to protect against certain types of cancer. Cabbage is also a rich source of vitamin C, which plays a role against cancer and boosts immunity in general. In addition, cabbage contributes a respectable amount of fiber to the diet.

Macaroni and Cheese with Vegetables

A steaming pot of macaroni and cheese makes a great vegetarian main dish. This version is especially appealing because of the colorful mix of vegetables that's stirred in.

Makes 4 servings

1½ cups **uncooked small pasta shells**
1 cup **chopped onions**
1 **clove garlic, minced**
1 package (10 ounces) **frozen peas and carrots**
2 cups **small broccoli or cauliflower florets**
2 tablespoons **1% low-fat milk**
1 cup **1% low-fat cottage cheese**
½ teaspoon **dry mustard**
¼ teaspoon **freshly ground black pepper**
⅛ teaspoon **salt** (**optional**)
1½ cups **shredded reduced-fat sharp Cheddar cheese**

Bring a large pot of water to a boil. Add the pasta, onions and garlic. Cook for 3 minutes.

Add the peas and carrots and broccoli or cauliflower. Cook for 5 minutes, or until the pasta is just tender. Drain and return to the pot.

In a medium bowl, stir together the milk, cottage cheese, mustard, pepper and salt (if using). Add to the pasta mixture.

Stir in the Cheddar. Cook over low heat, stirring constantly, for 2 minutes, or until the cheese melts and the mixture is hot. Let stand for 5 minutes before serving.

Hands-on time: 15 minutes
Total time: 30 minutes

Per serving: 375 calories
8.3 g. total fat (20% of calories)
4.2 g. saturated fat
57 mg. cholesterol
912 mg. sodium

Take It Along

Comfort Food for Cabin Fever

Who says late-night snacks have to be high-fat and unhealthy? Macaroni and Cheese with Vegetables is not just for kids! It's a great take-along snack for times when you know you'll be working late and want to avoid the vending machines. Pack a 1-cup micro-wave-safe container with leftover pasta, sauce and vegetables. Microwave on high power for 4 minutes, stirring once, then let stand for 1 minute.

Braised Pork and Sauerkraut with Apples

For many Germans and Scandinavians, pork and sauerkraut is the perfect comfort food for chilly evenings. To lower the usual salt content, we use only a little sauerkraut and extend it with fresh cabbage.

Makes 4 servings

¼ cup **unbleached flour**
¼ teaspoon **freshly ground black pepper**
2 tablespoons **paprika**
1 pound **boneless pork tenderloin, cubed**
2 cups **defatted reduced-sodium chicken broth**
1 **large onion, sliced**
2 cups **sliced green cabbage**
1 **green pepper, diced**
2 **medium apples, chopped**
½ cup **canned sauerkraut, rinsed and drained**
1 cup **nonfat sour cream**

•

Preheat the oven to 350°.

•

Combine the flour, black pepper and 1 tablespoon of the paprika in a self-sealing plastic bag. Add the pork, close the bag and shake to coat the pieces well.

•

Coat a Dutch oven with no-stick spray. Place over medium-high heat. Working in batches, brown the pork in the pot, stirring frequently. Transfer the pork to a plate.

•

Add 1 cup of the broth to the pot and bring to a boil over high heat; scrape with a wooden spoon to loosen any browned bits.

•

Add the onions. Cook, stirring frequently, for 3 minutes. Add the cabbage and green peppers. Cook for 3 minutes, or until the vegetables soften.

•

Stir in the apples, sauerkraut, the remaining 1 cup broth and the remaining 1 tablespoon paprika.

•

Cover and bake for 1 hour, or until the pork is tender. Just before serving, stir in the sour cream.

Hands-on time: 15 minutes
Total time: 1½ hours

Per serving: 327 calories
5.1 g. total fat (14% of calories)
1.6 g. saturated fat
81 mg. cholesterol
580 mg. sodium

Pork and Cabbage Supper

Traditional cooks make extra of this savory dish to freeze for later in the month. Store in 1- to 2-cup portions in self-sealing plastic freezer bags. Press out any excess air and stack the bags. Thaw overnight in the refrigerator, then transfer to a no-stick frying pan. Stir in ¼ teaspoon cornstarch per serving to prevent the sauce

The Potato Bar

Potatoes are a great source of potassium and other nutrients. They make an almost instant low-fat meal when served with any of the toppings below.

If you have the time, you can bake potatoes in a conventional oven at 400° for about 1 hour. Serve them straight from the oven or reheat them later.

A quicker alternative is to microwave the potatoes. Scrub 4 large baking potatoes (about 2 pounds) and pierce them with a fork in several places. Arrange in a square pattern or spoke pattern on a paper towel placed on the floor of the microwave. Microwave on high power for 5 minutes, then turn the potatoes and microwave on high power for 7 to 10 minutes longer, or until the potatoes are tender. Cover with paper towels and let the potatoes stand for 3 minutes to finish cooking.

Easy Potato Toppings

Each of the following recipes makes enough for four baked potatoes. Split the hot potatoes and top them with your choice of sauce.

Creamy Shrimp Topping

Sauté ½ cup sliced mushrooms, ¼ cup diced sweet red peppers and 2 chopped scallions in a large no-stick frying pan with ¼ cup fat-free chicken broth. **Add** ½ cup frozen cooked shrimp; cook for 1 minute. **Remove** from the heat and stir in ¼ cup shredded part-skim mozzarella cheese and 2 tablespoons nonfat yogurt.

Summer Garden Topping

Sauté ⅓ cup diced yellow squash, ⅓ cup diced zucchini, ⅓ cup diced red onions and ⅓ cup diced sweet red peppers in ¼ cup fat-free chicken broth. **Add** 2 cloves garlic (minced) and ¼ cup chopped parsley; cook for 1 minute. **Remove** from the heat and stir in ⅓ cup reduced-calorie cream cheese. **Season** with chopped fresh herbs or salt and pepper.

Southwestern Salsa Topping

Stir together ½ cup nonfat yogurt, ½ cup low-fat sour cream, ½ cup mild prepared salsa and ¼ cup chopped scallions.

Pesto Topping

Remove half of the potato flesh from the baked potatoes and mix with ½ cup reduced-fat pesto sauce, ¼ cup grated Parmesan cheese and ½ teaspoon minced garlic. **Spoon** back into the potatoes and broil until golden.

Tonnato

Combine 8 ounces drained canned water-packed tuna, ½ cup nonfat mayonnaise, 2 tablespoons drained capers, 2 tablespoons Dijon mustard, 2 teaspoons lime juice and chopped fresh herbs to taste.

Pesto Focaccia
(page 221) ——▶

Bread
Makes a Meal

Vegetable Pizza

Pan-grilled vegetables make a scrumptious pizza topping. For variety, you could replace the peppers and zucchini with other vegetables, such as fennel and eggplant.

Makes 4 servings

2 teaspoons **olive oil**
1 **medium onion, chopped**
1 **large clove garlic, diced**
1½ cups **diced zucchini**
1 **sweet red or green pepper, diced**
½ teaspoon **dried Italian seasoning**
¼ teaspoon **salt** (**optional**)
⅛ teaspoon **freshly ground black pepper**
⅔ cup **reduced-sodium pizza sauce**
1 **large unbaked Neapolitan-style pizza crust**
1 cup **shredded reduced-fat mozzarella cheese**

Preheat the oven to 450°.

In a large no-stick frying pan, combine the oil, onions, garlic, zucchini, red or green peppers, Italian seasoning, salt (if using) and black pepper. Cook over medium-high heat, stirring frequently, for 6 to 7 minutes, or until the vegetables begin to char.

Spread the pizza sauce over the pizza crust, leaving a ¼" border. Spoon the vegetables evenly over the sauce and sprinkle with the mozzarella.

Bake for 7 to 9 minutes, or until the edges brown. Cut into wedges to serve.

Hands-on time: 15 minutes
Total time: 30 minutes

Per serving: 303 calories
7.7 g. total fat (23% of calories)
0.3 g. saturated fat
10 mg. cholesterol
606 mg. sodium

Sneaky Snacks for Teenagers

If your teens are always clamoring for snacks, surprise them with homemade pizza from the freezer. Slice cooled leftover Vegetable Pizza into wedges, then slide them into self-sealing plastic freezer bags, pressing out any excess air. Freeze for up to 3 months. Reheat slices by removing them from the bags and popping them frozen into the microwave; cook on high power for 5 to 6 minutes, or until heated through.

French Bread Pizza

Pizza with terrific fresh toppings—mushrooms, peppers, tomato and basil—is very simple when the crust is a halved loaf of French bread.

Makes 4 servings

1 loaf **French baguette bread**
⅔ cup **shredded part-skim mozzarella cheese**
½ cup **reduced-sodium pizza sauce**
1 large **tomato, sliced**
⅓ cup **sliced mushrooms**
1 small **green pepper, sliced**
2 tablespoons **grated Parmesan cheese**
1–2 tablespoons **chopped fresh basil leaves** (**optional**)

Preheat the oven to 425°.

Slice the baguette in half lengthwise and then slice it in half again vertically. Lay the pieces, cut side up, on a baking sheet and sprinkle with ⅓ cup of the mozzarella. Bake for 8 to 10 minutes, or until the cheese melts.

Turn off the oven and preheat the broiler.

Top each piece of bread with pizza sauce, tomatoes, mushrooms, peppers, Parmesan, basil (if using) and the remaining ⅓ cup mozzarella.

Broil 5″ from the heat for 3 to 4 minutes, or until heated through and bubbling.

Hands-on time: 10 minutes
Total time: 20 minutes

Per serving: 394 calories
7.8 g. total fat (18% of calories)
2.7 g. saturated fat
10 mg. cholesterol
833 mg. sodium

Take It Along

Picnic Pizzazz
Surprise guests and family at your next picnic with French Bread Pizza—great straight from the cooler as an appetizer (cut into strips for finger food) or reheated on the grill or portable hibachi. After baking at home, cut the pizza into slices, wrap and place in the cooler (for grilling, use heavy-duty aluminum foil). At the picnic, grill the foil packets over low coals for 15 minutes to heat the pizza through.

Grilled Onion-and-Potato Pizza

Pizza gets a delicious smoky flavor when cooked on a charcoal grill. Making it is a snap with store-bought frozen dough. Here, potatoes and herbs make an unusual topping.

Makes 4 servings

2 tablespoons **olive oil**
1 **large onion, thinly sliced**
2 cups **sliced mushrooms**
¾ teaspoon **minced fresh rosemary**
½ teaspoon **minced fresh sage**
1 **potato**
  Cornmeal
1 **uncooked frozen pizza crust
  (10″–12″ round), thawed**
¼ cup **grated Parmesan**

Preheat the grill.

Coat a large no-stick frying pan with no-stick spray. Add 1 tablespoon of the oil and place over medium-high heat. Add the onions, mushrooms, rosemary and sage. Cook, stirring frequently, for 15 minutes, or until the onions are very soft and golden. Remove from the heat and set aside.

Slice the potato as thinly as possible (almost translucent).

Lightly coat a large baking sheet with no-stick spray and dust it with cornmeal. Shake off the excess.

Working on a lightly floured counter, flatten the dough to form a 12″ round about ¹⁄₁₆″ thick. Lay it on the baking sheet.

Carefully slide the dough from the baking sheet onto the grill and grill for 1 minute, or until the dough puffs slightly and grill marks appear. Transfer, grilled side up, back onto the baking sheet.

Brush the grilled side with the remaining 1 tablespoon oil and arrange the potato slices over it without overlapping them. Top with the cooked vegetables and sprinkle with the Parmesan.

Return the pizza to the grill and continue to cook, rotating frequently to prevent scorching, until the cheese melts and the potatoes soften. Cut into wedges to serve.

Hands-on time: 20 minutes
Total time: 25 minutes

Per serving: 325 calories
11.1 g. total fat (31% of calories)
2.1 g. saturated fat
5 mg. cholesterol
465 mg. sodium

Southwestern Pizza

Why should Italians have all the fun? Try this nontraditional "cowboy pizza" for a quick and pleasing dinner.

Makes 4 servings

6 ounces **ground turkey breast**
1 medium **onion, chopped**
1 large **clove garlic, minced**
1 small **sweet red, yellow or green pepper, diced**
1 can (8 ounces) **reduced-sodium tomato sauce**
½ cup **reduced-sodium kidney beans, rinsed, drained and slightly mashed**
2 teaspoons **chili powder**
2–3 drops **hot-pepper sauce** (**optional**)
1 large **unbaked Neapolitan-style pizza crust**
½ cup **shredded reduced-fat Cheddar cheese**

Preheat the oven to 450°.

Coat a large no-stick frying pan with no-stick spray. Crumble the turkey into the pan. Add the onions, garlic and red, yellow or green peppers. Cook over medium heat, breaking up the meat with a wooden spoon, for 7 to 8 minutes, or until the turkey lightly browns and the onions soften.

Add the tomato sauce, beans, chili powder and hot-pepper sauce (if using). Simmer for 5 minutes.

Spread the sauce evenly over the pizza crust, leaving a ¼" border. Sprinkle with the Cheddar.

Bake for 7 to 9 minutes, or until the edges brown. Cut into wedges to serve.

Hands-on time: 10 minutes
Total time: 35 minutes

Per serving: 324 calories
5.5 g. total fat (15% of calories)
1.5 g. saturated fat
24 mg. cholesterol
594 mg. sodium

Take It Along

Road Food

For the first lunch on the annual summer camping trip, pack a special treat: pizza. Bake South-western Pizza at home, cool and cut into half-slices (for easier handling on the road). Wrap well in plastic. For travel, store in the cooler, where they'll keep safely for five to six hours as long as the cooler is set in a shady spot in the car. Take along doubled paper plates, napkins and small cartons of juice.

Chicken and Cheese Mini Calzones

These quick calzones use frozen bread dough. Defrost it in a greased bowl overnight in the fridge or follow the microwave thawing instructions on the package.

Makes 8

½ cup **chopped onions**
½ cup **nonfat ricotta cheese**
½ cup **reduced-fat spreadable cheese flavored with garlic and herbs**
⅛ teaspoon **freshly ground black pepper**
1½ cups **chopped cooked chicken breast**
1 **loaf** (**1 pound**) **frozen white bread dough, thawed**
1 cup **chunky tomato sauce, warmed**

•

Preheat the oven to 375°. Coat a baking sheet with no-stick spray.

•

Coat a large frying pan with no-stick spray. Add the onions. Cook for 3 minutes, or until softened. Remove from the heat and stir in the ricotta, garlic-and-herb cheese and pepper. Add the chicken and mix well. Set aside.

•

Divide the dough into 8 equal portions. On a lightly floured surface, roll or pat each portion into a 5″ round. Spread ¼ cup of the chicken mixture on each round, leaving a ¼″ border. Moisten the edges of each crust with a little water and fold each into a half-moon shape. Press the edges together with the tines of a fork to seal.

•

Place the calzones on the baking sheet and bake for 15 to 20 minutes, or until golden. Serve with the tomato sauce.

Hands-on time: 10 minutes
Total time: 30 minutes

Per calzone: 216 calories
4.8 g. total fat (19% of calories)
1.8 g. saturated fat
30 mg. cholesterol
396 mg. sodium

Greek Chicken Pita Sandwiches

You'll like these easy sandwiches for lunch boxes or a quick Sunday supper. The combination of yogurt, lemon and oregano gives these pitas their Greek flavor.

Makes 4 servings

2 cups **shredded cooked chicken breast**
1 cup **peeled, seeded and diced cucumbers**
1 **scallion, chopped**
1 **small green or sweet red pepper, diced**
½ cup **plain nonfat yogurt**
⅓ cup **chopped fresh parsley**
1 tablespoon **lemon juice**
1½ teaspoons **honey mustard**
1 teaspoon **maple syrup or honey**
¼ teaspoon **dried oregano leaves**
¼ teaspoon **salt**
¼ teaspoon **freshly ground black pepper**
4 **whole-wheat pita breads**
Lettuce leaves

In a medium bowl, combine the chicken, cucumbers, scallions, green or red peppers, yogurt, parsley, lemon juice, mustard, maple syrup or honey, oregano, salt and black pepper. Mix well.

Wrap the pitas in plastic wrap and microwave on high power for 1 minute. Split each pita in half crosswise. Stuff the halves with the lettuce leaves. Spoon the chicken mixture into the pita pockets.

Hands-on time: 10 minutes
Total time: 10 minutes

Per serving: 227 calories
2.5 g. total fat (10% of calories)
0.5 g. saturated fat
44 mg. cholesterol
421 mg. sodium

Who wouldn't gobble up these hot open-face turkey sandwiches? The Newburg-style gravy has traditional flavor but considerably less fat than the original sauce. Serve cranberry sauce on the side and some crunchy crudités.

Makes 4 servings

¼ cup **defatted reduced-sodium chicken broth**
2 tablespoons **sherry or apple juice**
2 tablespoons **unbleached flour**
1½ cups **skim milk**
½ cup **shredded reduced-fat Cheddar cheese**
4 **thick slices whole-wheat or white bread, toasted**
8 ounces **cooked sliced turkey breast**
2 tablespoons **chopped fresh parsley**

●

In a large no-stick frying pan, bring the broth and sherry or apple juice to a boil over medium-high heat.

●

Reduce the heat to medium. Stir in the flour and cook, stirring, for 2 minutes.

●

Whisk in the milk in a thin stream. Continue whisking until the sauce is thick and smooth. Remove from the heat and stir in the Cheddar until smooth.

●

Arrange the toast on plates and top with the turkey and sauce. Sprinkle with the parsley.

Hands-on time: 10 minutes
Total time: 15 minutes

Per serving: 232 calories
3.8 g. total fat (15% of calories)
1.5 g. saturated fat
54 mg. cholesterol
468 mg. sodium

Barbecued Turkey Sandwiches

You don't even have to fire up the barbie for these wonderful low-fat sandwiches. A zippy sauce and munchy vegetables add lots of character to the mild turkey cutlets.

Makes 4 servings

12 ounces **turkey breast cutlets,**
cut into 4 sandwich-size pieces
¼ teaspoon **dried thyme leaves**
¼ teaspoon **salt (optional)**
⅛ teaspoon **freshly ground black pepper**
2 teaspoons **canola oil**
1 **medium onion, chopped**
1 **medium green pepper, chopped**
1 **clove garlic, minced**
4 tablespoons **defatted reduced-sodium chicken broth**
1 can (8 ounces) **reduced-sodium tomato sauce**
2 teaspoons **sugar**
1½ teaspoons **Worcestershire sauce**
1 teaspoon **cider vinegar**
½ teaspoon **mustard**
½ teaspoon **chili powder**
4 **rolls or hamburger buns**

Sprinkle the turkey with the thyme, salt (if using) and black pepper.

Coat a large no-stick frying pan with no-stick spray. Add the turkey. Cook over medium heat, turning once, for 4 minutes, or until cooked through. Transfer to a plate and set aside.

In the same pan, combine the oil, onions, green peppers, garlic and 1 tablespoon of the broth. Cook over medium heat, stirring frequently, for 5 to 6 minutes, or until the onions soften.

Stir in the tomato sauce, sugar, Worcestershire sauce, vinegar, mustard, chili powder and the remaining 3 tablespoons broth. Cook over low heat, stirring frequently, for 5 to 6 minutes, or until the sauce thickens slightly.

Add the turkey to the pan and stir gently to coat. Cook for 1 to 2 minutes, or until heated through.

Toast the rolls or buns. Fill with the turkey and sauce.

Hands-on time: 10 minutes
Total time: 25 minutes

Per serving: 270 calories
6.2 g. total fat (21% of calories)
1.2 g. saturated fat
37 mg. cholesterol
377 mg. sodium

Italian Sausage Sandwiches

This skinny version of the sausage sandwich is easy and ready on short order, thanks to bulk sausage and canned sauce. Choose an Italian bread that's low in sodium.

Makes 4 servings

8 ounces **reduced-fat ground pork and turkey bulk sausage**
1 **large onion, coarsely chopped**
2 **small sweet red or green peppers, chopped**
1½ cups **coarsely chopped mushrooms**
1 cup **reduced-sodium pizza sauce**
4 **small loaves Italian bread (each about 4½″ long)**
Red onion slices (optional)

Coat a large no-stick frying pan with no-stick spray. Crumble the sausage into the pan. Cook over medium-high heat, breaking up the meat with a wooden spoon, for 4 to 5 minutes, or until lightly browned.

Line a platter with several thicknesses of paper towels. Transfer the sausage to the platter and drain well.

Wipe out the pan with a paper towel. Return the sausage to the pan. Add the chopped onions, peppers and mushrooms. Cook over medium-high heat, stirring, for 5 minutes, or until the vegetables soften and begin to brown.

Add the pizza sauce and simmer, stirring occasionally, for 3 to 4 minutes, or until heated through.

Slice each loaf of bread in half horizontally. Divide the filling among the sandwiches. Top with the onion slices (if using).

Hands-on time: 10 minutes
Total time: 20 minutes

Per serving: 210 calories
4.9 g. total fat (21% of calories)
1.4 g. saturated fat
36 mg. cholesterol
671 mg. sodium

Texas Barbecue Pork and Bean Sandwiches

Zingy barbecue sauce. lean slivers of pork, spicy beans and homestyle bread make this a Texas boy's dream sandwich. Offer low-fat coleslaw with it.

Makes 4 servings

4 **lean boneless center-cut loin pork chops**
(**4 ounces each**)
⅓ cup **reduced-sodium barbecue sauce**
1 can (16 ounces) **pinto or black beans, drained and rinsed**
¼ cup **chopped red onions**
3 tablespoons **chopped fresh cilantro**
1 **clove garlic, minced**
1 tablespoon **chili powder** (**optional**)
1 teaspoon **ground cumin**
Salt (**optional**)
Freshly ground black pepper
8 **thick slices potato bread or other**
homestyle white bread

●

Place the pork chops in a shallow dish, top with the barbecue sauce and turn several times to coat. Cover and refrigerate for at least 30 minutes.

●

Preheat the broiler.

●

In a medium saucepan, heat the beans, onions, cilantro, garlic, chili powder (if using) and cumin; mash the beans slightly as they cook. Season to taste with the salt (if using) and pepper.

●

Broil the pork chops 5″ from the heat, turning once, for 4 minutes, or until cooked through. Cut into thin strips.

●

Spoon the bean mixture onto 4 slices of the bread. Top with the pork and the remaining 4 slices bread to make sandwiches. Serve hot.

Hands-on time: 15 minutes
Total time: 45 minutes

Per serving: 403 calories
14.6 g. total fat (30% of calories)
3.4 g. saturated fat
59 mg. cholesterol
670 mg. sodium

Philly Cheesesteak with Peppers and Onions

Philly Cheesesteak with Peppers and Onions

Yo! Philly cheesesteak *is* on the menu! We've filled a roll with lean grilled steak, low-fat cheese, peppers and onions for authentic flavor. For quick last-minute preparation, grill the steak the night before.

Makes 4 servings

> 1 cup **thinly sliced onions**
> 1 **large green pepper, sliced**
> 2 **cloves garlic, minced**
> ¼ cup **defatted reduced-sodium chicken broth**
> 1 **long loaf Italian-style bread, halved lengthwise, cut into 4 sections and toasted**
> 1 pound **lean steak, trimmed, grilled and cut into thin slices**
> ½ cup **shredded part-skim mozzarella cheese**

Preheat the broiler.

In a large no-stick frying pan, cook the onions, peppers and garlic in the broth over medium heat, stirring frequently, for 15 to 20 minutes, or until very soft.

Divide the vegetables among the 4 bottom sections of bread, top with the steak and sprinkle with the mozzarella.

Lay the open sandwiches on a baking sheet or broiler pan. Broil 5" from the heat for 2 to 3 minutes, or until the cheese melts and the steak is warmed through. Top with the remaining bread.

Hands-on time: 10 minutes
Total time: 25 minutes

Per serving: 544 calories
7.7 g. total fat (13% of calories)
3.3 g. saturated fat
80 mg. cholesterol
724 mg. sodium

ToYourHealth

Onions
The sulfur compounds that give onions such distinctive tear-jerking abilities are the same ones that may also lower your chances of cancer and heart attack. A number of studies support the idea that onions help protect against stomach and colon cancer. Onions also have a dramatic effect on the body's ability to dissolve blood clots that can develop, lodge in an artery and cause a heart attack.

English Muffin Brunch Sandwiches

Here's our version of a famous fast-food sandwich. It's just as tasty and lower in fat than the drive-through version. To lessen your salt intake, buy reduced-sodium muffins or substitute reduced-sodium bread.

Makes 4 servings

4	**plain or sourdough English muffins, split and toasted**
3 tablespoons	**shredded reduced-fat sharp Cheddar cheese**
4	**slices Canadian bacon (1 ounce each)**
2	**scallions, finely chopped**
2	**eggs**
3	**egg whites**
1 tablespoon	**skim milk**
¼ teaspoon	**salt (optional)**
	Freshly ground black pepper

Preheat the oven to 200°.

Line a baking sheet with aluminum foil. Lay the muffin halves, cut side up, on the sheet. Sprinkle with the Cheddar. Place in the oven until needed.

Coat a large no-stick frying pan with no-stick spray. Add the bacon and scallions. Cook over medium-high heat for 2 to 3 minutes, or until the bacon is lightly browned.

Remove the bacon. Drain on paper towels and set aside. Leave the scallions in the pan.

In a bowl, beat the eggs, egg whites, milk, salt (if using) and pepper with a fork until blended. Add to the pan and scramble over medium heat for 4 to 5 minutes, or until just cooked through.

Remove the muffins from the oven. Top the muffin bottoms with the scrambled eggs and bacon slices. Add the muffin tops to form sandwiches.

Hands-on time: 10 minutes
Total time: 20 minutes

Per serving: 251 calories
6.8 g. total fat (25% of calories)
2 g. saturated fat
125 mg. cholesterol
946 mg. sodium

Pesto Focaccia

Focaccia is an Italian flatbread sold in many supermarkets. For a really crispy crust, place a pizza stone or baking tiles on the lowest rack of a cold oven and preheat for 30 minutes. The low-fat pesto sauce used here is also good on pasta and other sandwiches.

Makes 4 servings

1 cup **packed fresh basil leaves**
½ cup **chopped spinach leaves**
¼ cup **chopped fresh parsley**
1½ tablespoons **grated Parmesan cheese**
1 tablespoon **olive oil**
2 **cloves garlic, minced**
3 tablespoons **plain nonfat yogurt**
3 tablespoons **fresh bread crumbs**
1 **plain focaccia (14″ round)**
½ cup **shredded part-skim mozzarella cheese**
1 pound **plum tomatoes, sliced**

Preheat the oven to 500°.

In a food processor, combine the basil, spinach, parsley and Parmesan; chop coarsely. Add the oil, garlic, yogurt and bread crumbs. Blend to a pastelike consistency.

Spread half of the basil mixture on the focaccia. Top with ¼ cup of the mozzarella. Arrange the tomatoes on top. Sprinkle with the remaining ¼ cup mozzarella.

Place on a baking sheet. Bake for 10 to 15 minutes, or until the rim of the crust is lightly browned and the topping is hot. Remove the pizza from the oven and top with the remaining basil mixture. Cut into wedges to serve.

Hands-on time: 10 minutes
Total time: 25 minutes

Per serving: 453 calories
7 g. total fat (14% of calories)
2.4 g. saturated fat
10 mg. cholesterol
744 mg. sodium

Grilled Vegetable Sandwiches

Another fast focaccia sandwich, this features savory grill-roasted vegetables. It's perfect for a summer lunch with a side salad and fruit dessert.

Makes 4 servings

2 **large sweet red peppers, quartered**
2 **large green peppers, quartered**
2 tablespoons **olive oil**
2 **onions, thinly sliced**
2 cups **sliced mushrooms**
2 **large cloves garlic, minced**
¼ teaspoon **fennel seeds**
Salt (optional)
Freshly ground black pepper
4 squares (4") **thick focaccia bread**

●

Preheat the grill or broiler.

●

Lightly coat the red peppers and green peppers with no-stick spray and grill or broil them, turning frequently, for 5 to 6 minutes, or until lightly browned. Cool slightly and cut into strips.

●

Coat a large no-stick frying pan with no-stick spray. Add the oil, onions, mushrooms, garlic and fennel seeds. Cook over medium heat for 10 minutes, or until the vegetables soften and turn golden.

●

Add the pepper slices. Cook for 2 to 3 minutes, or until heated through. Season with the salt (if using) and black pepper.

●

Split the focaccia squares horizontally and fill with the vegetable mixture.

Hands-on time: 5 minutes
Total time: 20 minutes

Per serving: 282 calories
7.1 g. total fat (23% of calories)
1 g. saturated fat
0 mg. cholesterol
293 mg. sodium

Torta Niçoise

From Mediterranean shores comes easy, elegant fare: a hollowed-out loaf of bread stuffed with salad, allowed to marinate, then cut into wedges.

Makes 4 servings

1 **round loaf Italian bread**
1 **large tomato, thinly sliced**
1 **large cucumber, thinly sliced**
1 **small red onion, thinly sliced into rings**
1 can (7 ounces) **water-packed tuna, drained and flaked**
1 jar (7 ounces) **roasted red peppers, drained**
Salt (**optional**)
Freshly ground black pepper
⅓ cup **balsamic vinegar**
¼ cup **plain nonfat yogurt**
2 tablespoons **lemon juice**
1 tablespoon **honey mustard**
1 tablespoon **olive oil**
1 tablespoon **minced garlic**

●

Slice off the top of the bread horizontally and reserve the sliced-off piece. Using your fingers, pull out the soft interior of the loaf, leaving about a ½"-thick shell; use the interior for another purpose.

●

Arrange the tomatoes, cucumbers and onions in overlapping circles inside the loaf. Top with the tuna and red peppers. Season with the salt (if using) and black pepper.

●

In a small bowl, whisk together the vinegar, yogurt, lemon juice, mustard, oil and garlic. Drizzle over the vegetables and replace the top on the loaf.

●

Wrap the loaf tightly in plastic wrap and refrigerate for at least 30 minutes. Serve cut into wedges.

Hands-on time: 15 minutes
Total time: 45 minutes

Per serving: 487 calories
4.8 g. total fat (9% of calories)
0.8 g. saturated fat
18 mg. cholesterol
786 mg. sodium

Take It Along

Fourth of July Fireworks Picnic

An elegant sandwich to set alongside the turkey hot dogs at your next fireworks-viewing picnic is this Torta Niçoise. You can make it in the morning and tightly wrap the assembled sandwich in several layers of plastic. Refrigerate it for up to eight hours. Pack into an ice-filled cooler. At the picnic, unwrap the sandwich and cut into small wedges, using toothpicks to hold the smaller pieces together.

Vegetable Kabobs with Herb Butter
(page 237)

No-Pot Cooking

Fragrant Asian Chicken and Vegetables

Curry powder and other spices give chicken and vegetables an exotic taste.

Makes 4 servings

2½ tablespoons **apricot or peach preserves**
2½ tablespoons **reduced-sodium soy sauce**
1 tablespoon **rice vinegar**
2½ teaspoons **curry powder**
2 teaspoons **peanut oil**
1¾ teaspoons **chili powder**
¼ teaspoon **ground cinnamon**
⅛ teaspoon **freshly ground black pepper**
4 **boneless, skinless chicken breast halves (4 ounces each)**
4 **potatoes, cut into ½" cubes**
3 **large onions, thinly sliced**
3 **large carrots, thinly sliced**

Preheat the oven to 425°.

Lay four 12″ × 18″ pieces of aluminum foil or parchment paper on the work surface and lightly coat with no-stick spray.

In a large bowl, combine the preserves, soy sauce, vinegar, curry powder, oil, chili powder, cinnamon and pepper. Add the chicken, potatoes, onions and carrots and stir gently to coat.

Place a piece of chicken on each piece of foil or paper and top evenly with the vegetables.

Fold the long sides of the foil or paper together, making several folds to encase the food snugly. Fold the ends closed, like a package, to enclose securely.

Lay the packets, seam side up, on a baking sheet. Bake for 30 to 35 minutes, or until the chicken and vegetables are tender when pierced with a fork. Be careful of escaping steam when opening the packets.

Hands-on time: 15 minutes
Total time: 45 minutes

Per serving: 335 calories
4.9 g. total fat (13% of calories)
1 g. saturated fat
46 mg. cholesterol
411 mg. sodium

Encore!

Chicken Stir-Fry

Thinly slice enough leftover chicken to equal 1 cup. Heat ½ cup chicken broth in a wok or frying pan and stir-fry the chicken for 2 minutes. Remove from the pan. Add ¼ cup apple juice and 3 cups mixed chopped vegetables to the pan. Stir-fry for 2 minutes, then cover and steam for 2 minutes, or until the vegetables are crisp-tender. Add the chicken, 2 cups cooked rice and 2 tablespoons oyster sauce. Stir-fry for 1 minute to heat through.

Chicken in Raspberry Vinegar

The fruity tang of raspberry vinegar, now a staple in most supermarkets, marries beautifully with chicken in this simple baked entrée.

Makes 4 servings

½ cup **raspberry vinegar**
½ cup **sliced scallions**
¼ cup **honey or packed brown sugar**
2 tablespoons **reduced-sodium soy sauce**
4 **boneless, skinless chicken breast halves
(4 ounces each)**
4 cups **cooked rice**
1 cup **small broccoli florets**
1 cup **peeled and halved pearl onions**
1 cup **thinly sliced carrots**

Preheat the oven to 400°.

Lay four 12″ × 18″ pieces of aluminum foil or parchment paper on the work surface and lightly coat with no-stick spray.

In a shallow pan, mix the vinegar, scallions, honey or brown sugar and soy sauce. Add the chicken and turn to coat both sides. Cover with plastic wrap and marinate for 15 minutes (or place in the refrigerator and marinate for up to 1 hour).

Place 1 cup of the rice in the center of each piece of foil or paper; spread evenly into a thin rectangle about the size of a chicken breast. Top each with the chicken, then with broccoli, onions and carrots. Drizzle with the marinade.

Fold the long sides of the foil or paper together, making several folds to encase the food snugly. Fold the ends closed, like a package, to enclose securely.

Lay the packets, seam side up, on a baking sheet. Bake for 30 to 35 minutes, or until the chicken is tender when pierced with a fork. Be careful of escaping steam when opening the packets.

Hands-on time: 5 minutes
Total time: 50 minutes

Per serving: 462 calories
2.7 g. total fat (5% of calories)
0.7 g. saturated fat
46 mg. cholesterol
326 mg. sodium

Steak and Vegetables

Thin slices of lean beef mix with sassy Dijon, steak sauce, sweet peppers and tomatoes. For variety, serve over noodles instead of rice.

Makes 4 servings

1 **lean steak** (**1 pound**), **trimmed**
2 tablespoons **Dijon mustard**
2 teaspoons **reduced-sodium steak sauce**
1 **small green pepper, thinly sliced**
2 **tomatoes, sliced**
¼ cup **sherry or apple juice**
2 tablespoons **water**
1 tablespoon **cornstarch**
4 cups **hot cooked rice**
2 tablespoons **chopped fresh parsley**

●

Preheat the oven to 350°.

●

Line a large baking sheet with a 12″ × 18″ piece of aluminum foil. Lightly coat the foil with no-stick spray.

●

Cut the steak lengthwise into 4 equal strips and then cut each strip in half horizontally. Place the pieces between 2 sheets of plastic wrap. Using a meat mallet, pound to make 8 very thin pieces.

●

Place 4 of the pieces on the foil and spread with the mustard and steak sauce. Arrange the peppers and tomatoes over the steak and then top with the remaining steak. Spoon the sherry or apple juice over the meat.

●

Fold the long sides of the foil together, making several folds to encase the food snugly. Fold the ends closed, like a package, to enclose securely. Bake, seam side up, for 30 to 35 minutes, or until the meat is tender and cooked through. Be careful of escaping steam when opening the packet.

●

In a small saucepan, mix the water and cornstarch. Spoon the cooking juices from the packet into the pan. Mix well. Cook, stirring, over medium-high heat for 2 to 3 minutes, or until the sauce thickens.

●

Serve the steak and vegetables with the rice. Spoon the sauce over each serving and sprinkle with the parsley.

Hands-on time: 15 minutes
Total time: 45 minutes

Per serving: 568 calories
9.1 g. total fat (15% of calories)
2.9 g. saturated fat
108 mg. cholesterol
217 mg. sodium

Saturday Night Steak Supper
Reserve half of the Steak and Vegetables to freeze for an easy dinner next Saturday night before the movies. Package 2 cups cooked rice or noodles in a large microwave-safe container. Thinly slice the leftover steak and place on top. Cover with the leftover sauce and vegetables. Cover well and freeze for up to 2 weeks. Thaw overnight in the refrigerator, then microwave on high power for 5 to 8 minutes. Serve with a green salad and hot French bread rolls.

Pork Chop Dinner

What could be easier than this oven barbecue? Slip the pork chop and vegetable packets into the oven; come back later to tender entrées ready to serve.

Makes 4 servings

½ cup **ketchup**
2 tablespoons **packed brown sugar**
1 tablespoon **reduced-sodium soy sauce**
2 teaspoons **canola oil**
1 teaspoon **chili powder**
¼ teaspoon **ground allspice**
¼ teaspoon **freshly ground black pepper**
4 **boneless center-cut loin pork chops (4 ounces each), trimmed**
3 **large potatoes, cut into ½″ cubes**
3 **large onions, thinly sliced**
1 **large stalk celery, thinly sliced**
2 **large carrots, thinly sliced**

Preheat the oven to 425°.

Lay four 12″ × 18″ pieces of aluminum foil or parchment paper on the work surface. Lightly coat with no-stick spray.

In a large bowl, combine the ketchup, brown sugar, soy sauce, oil, chili powder, allspice and pepper. Add the pork, potatoes, onions, celery and carrots and toss until coated.

Place 1 pork chop on each piece of foil or paper and divide the vegetables and sauce evenly over the pork.

Fold the long sides of the foil or paper together, making several folds to encase the food snugly. Fold the ends closed, like a package, to enclose securely.

Lay the packets, seam side up, on a baking sheet. Bake for 30 to 35 minutes, or until the pork and vegetables are tender when pierced with a fork. Be careful of escaping steam when opening the packets.

Hands-on time: 10 minutes
Total time: 40 minutes

Per serving: 411 calories
12.2 g. total fat (26% of calories)
3.5 g. saturated fat
59 mg. cholesterol
529 mg. sodium

Easy Freeze

Twice the Food— Half the Fuss

While you're cooking, why not plan ahead? Make an extra batch of this Pork Chop Dinner, wrap each uncooked serving in its foil packet, then slide the packets into self-sealing plastic bags and freeze for an impromptu company dinner later in the month. Defrost the packets in the refrigerator overnight. Bake at 425° for 40 minutes, or until the meat and vegetables are done.

Baked Cod in Spanish Sauce

A piquant fresh tomato sauce with lemon, garlic and paprika jazzes up fresh cod fillets served over rice.

Makes 4 servings

¼ cup **lemon juice**
3 **cloves garlic, minced**
1 teaspoon **paprika**
4 **cod fillets** (4 ounces each and about ¾" thick)
4 cups **cooked rice**
Salt (optional)
Freshly ground black pepper
1½ cups **coarsely chopped tomatoes**
⅓ cup **chopped scallions**
1 tablespoon **red-wine vinegar**

•

Preheat the oven to 400°.

•

Lay four 12" × 18" pieces of aluminum foil or parchment paper on the work surface and lightly coat with no-stick spray.

•

In a shallow pan, mix the lemon juice, garlic and paprika. Add the cod and turn to coat both sides. Cover with plastic wrap and let stand for 15 minutes (or refrigerate for no longer than 2 hours).

•

Place 1 cup of the rice in the center of each piece of foil or paper; spread evenly into a thin rectangle about the size of a cod fillet.

•

Using a metal spatula or slotted spoon, lift the fish from the marinade and place on top of the rice. Sprinkle with the salt (if using) and pepper.

•

Add the tomatoes, scallions and vinegar to the marinade and stir. Spoon over the cod.

•

Fold the long sides of the foil or paper together, making several folds to encase the food snugly. Fold the ends closed, like a package, to enclose securely.

•

Lay the packets, seam side up, on a baking sheet. Bake for 15 to 20 minutes, or until the fish flakes when tested with a fork. Be careful of escaping steam when opening the packets.

Hands-on time: 10 minutes
Total time: 35 minutes

Per serving: 374 calories
1.6 g. total fat (4% of calories)
0.3 g. saturated fat
45 mg. cholesterol
74 mg. sodium

Fish and Vegetables in Spicy Orange Sauce

Most any mild, white, firm-fleshed fish will work in this speedy entrée. As with other *en papillote* dishes, parchment is traditional, but foil works fine.

Makes 4 servings

4 cups **cooked rice**
4 **orange roughy, haddock, cod or red snapper fillets (4 ounces each)**
1 **small sweet red pepper, cut into rings**
1 **small green pepper, cut into rings**
⅓ cup **orange juice**
¼ cup **chopped drained mandarin orange sections**
4 **large cloves garlic, minced**
2 teaspoons **honey mustard**
1 teaspoon **honey or packed brown sugar**
1 teaspoon **olive oil**
½ teaspoon **grated orange rind**
¼ teaspoon **ground red pepper (optional)**
¼ teaspoon **freshly ground black pepper**

Preheat the oven to 400°.

Lay four 12″ × 18″ pieces of aluminum foil or parchment paper on the work surface and lightly coat with no-stick spray.

Place 1 cup of the rice in the center of each piece of foil or paper; spread evenly into a thin rectangle about the size of a fish fillet. Top with the fillets and then with alternating rings of red and green peppers.

In a small bowl, combine the orange juice, orange sections, garlic, mustard, honey or brown sugar, oil, orange rind, ground red pepper (if using) and black pepper. Spoon over the fish.

Fold the long sides of the foil or paper together, making several folds to encase the food snugly. Fold the ends closed, like a package, to enclose securely.

Lay the packets, seam side up, on a baking sheet. Bake for 12 to 15 minutes, or until the fish is opaque and flakes when tested with a fork. Be careful of escaping steam when opening the packets.

Hands-on time: 10 minutes
Total time: 25 minutes

Per serving: 396 calories
2.5 g. total fat (6% of calories)
0.4 g. saturated fat
45 mg. cholesterol
86 mg. sodium

To Your Health

Oranges

Citrus fruits are packed with natural substances that may prevent cancer, reduce allergy symptoms and help protect the heart, say researchers. Most notably, oranges and other citrus fruits are loaded with vitamin C, a nutrient known for its ability to neutralize potentially cancer-causing agents in the body.

Herbed Fish and Vegetables

Good catch! An entire fish dinner in a packet, basted with lemon-herb dressing, makes a lean meal. And cleanup is a snap.

Makes 4 servings

1½ tablespoons **lemon juice**
1 teaspoon **dried thyme leaves**
½ teaspoon **onion salt**
¼ teaspoon **ground allspice**
⅛ teaspoon **freshly ground black pepper**
Pinch of ground red pepper (optional)
4 **swordfish, halibut or other firm white fish fillets (4 ounces each)**
4 **medium potatoes, cut into ½" cubes**
4 **onions, quartered**
2 **stalks celery, thinly sliced**
1 **large green pepper, cubed**
4 teaspoons **butter or margarine**

Preheat the oven to 425°.

Lay four 12″ × 18″ pieces of aluminum foil or parchment paper on the work surface and lightly coat with no-stick spray.

In a medium bowl, combine the lemon juice, thyme, onion salt, allspice, black pepper and red pepper (if using). Add the fish, potatoes, onions, celery and green peppers. Toss to coat.

Place a fish fillet in the center of each piece of foil or paper. Divide the vegetables evenly among them. Top with the butter or margarine.

Fold the long sides of foil or paper together, making several folds to encase the food snugly. Fold the ends closed, like a package, to enclose securely.

Lay the packets, seam side up, on a baking sheet. Bake for 25 to 30 minutes, or until the fish and vegetables are tender when tested with a fork. Be careful of escaping steam when opening the packets.

Hands-on time: 10 minutes
Total time: 40 minutes

Per serving: 373 calories
8.8 g. total fat (21% of calories)
3.7 g. saturated fat
55 mg. cholesterol
369 mg. sodium

Baked Fish with Fennel

A fragrant fennel-garlic marinade permeates the fish as it bakes. If you like, you can make this recipe with small whole trout that have been cleaned.

Makes 4 servings

4 cups **cooked rice**
4 **trout fillets** (**4 ounces each**)
2 cups **julienned carrots**
⅓ cup **lemon juice**
½ teaspoon **ground fennel seeds**
¼ teaspoon **freshly ground black pepper**
4 **large cloves garlic, minced**
Pinch of dried thyme leaves

Preheat the oven to 400°.

Lay four 12″ × 18″ pieces of aluminum foil or parchment paper on the work surface and lightly coat with no-stick spray.

Place 1 cup of the rice in the center of each piece of foil or paper; spread evenly into a thin rectangle about the size of a trout fillet. Top with the trout and carrots.

In a small bowl, combine the lemon juice, fennel seeds, pepper, garlic and thyme. Drizzle over the trout and carrots.

Fold the long sides of the foil or paper together, making several folds to encase the food snugly. Fold the ends closed, like a package, to enclose securely.

Lay the packets, seam side up, on a baking sheet. Bake for 12 minutes, or until the fish is opaque and flakes when tested with a fork. Be careful of escaping steam when opening the packets.

Hands-on time: 10 minutes
Total time: 25 minutes

Per serving: 410 calories
4.5 g. total fat (10% of calories)
0.8 g. saturated fat
65 mg. cholesterol
35 mg. sodium

Encore!

Savory Fish Salad

Cool any leftover trout and flake the fillets. Mix each cup of fish with 2 tablespoons nonfat yogurt, 2 tablespoons nonfat mayonnaise and chopped fresh herbs. Line salad plates with crisp greens and sprinkle with lemon juice or balsamic vinegar. Mound the trout salad in the center and garnish with sliced cucumbers, tomatoes, radishes or red peppers.

Vegetable Kabobs with Herb Butter

An enticing entrée for a summer lunch or supper, these kabobs are basted with fresh rosemary butter. You can prepare these packets on the grill; cover and cook for about 35 minutes.

Makes 4 servings

1 **small yellow summer squash, quartered lengthwise**
1 **small zucchini, quartered lengthwise**
1 **small Japanese eggplant, quartered lengthwise**
3 **medium new red potatoes, thinly sliced**
1 **sweet red pepper, quartered**
1 **green pepper, quartered**
8 **cloves garlic, halved**
4 **shallots, halved lengthwise**
1 tablespoon **melted butter or margarine**
2 teaspoons **minced fresh rosemary**
½ teaspoon **salt**
½ teaspoon **freshly ground black pepper**
4 cups **hot cooked rice**

Preheat the oven to 450°.

Place a 12″ × 18″ double thickness of aluminum foil on the work surface. Lightly coat with no-stick spray.

Thread the vegetables on 4 long metal skewers, alternating the squash, zucchini, eggplant, potatoes, red peppers and green peppers with garlic and shallots. Lay the skewers on the foil.

In a small bowl, combine the butter or margarine, rosemary, salt and black pepper. Brush half the mixture lightly over the vegetables. Turn the kabobs and brush the other side.

Fold the long sides of the foil together, making several folds to encase the food snugly. Fold the ends closed to enclose securely (the end of the skewers might protrude).

Place the packet on a baking sheet. Bake for 35 minutes, or until the potatoes are soft. Be careful of escaping steam when opening the packet. Serve with the rice.

Hands-on time: 15 minutes
Total time: 50 minutes

Per serving: 382 calories
3.9 g. total fat (9% of calories)
1.1 g. saturated fat
3 mg. cholesterol
307 mg. sodium

Chicken and Artichoke Risotto
(page 241)

Microwave
to Order

Ede's Chicken Enchiladas

Easy enchiladas from your microwave—green chilies, chicken and vegetables are wrapped in corn tortillas and cloaked in a vibrant tomato sauce.

Makes 4 servings

⅓ cup **defatted reduced-sodium chicken broth**
2 cups **chopped onions**
2 cups **shredded cooked chicken breast**
1 cup **shredded carrots**
1 can (4 ounces) **chopped mild green chili peppers, drained**
½ teaspoon **ground coriander**
¼ teaspoon **ground cumin**
2 cups **enchilada sauce**
8 **corn tortillas** (**6″ diameter**)
½ cup **shredded part-skim mozzarella cheese**
¼ cup **plain nonfat yogurt**
¼ cup **nonfat sour cream**
2 tablespoons **chopped fresh cilantro**

In a large no-stick frying pan, bring the broth to a simmer over medium-high heat. Add the onions, cover and cook for 5 minutes, or until softened.

Add the chicken, carrots, peppers, coriander, cumin and 1 cup of the enchilada sauce. Cover and cook for 5 minutes.

Coat an 8″ × 8″ microwave-safe baking dish with no-stick spray.

Stack the tortillas and wrap them in plastic wrap. Place on a plate and microwave on high power for 30 seconds to soften. Unwrap and lay the tortillas on the work surface. Spoon several tablespoons of the chicken mixture down the center of each tortilla. Roll up.

Arrange the tortillas, seam side down, in the prepared baking dish. Spoon the remaining 1 cup enchilada sauce over the tortillas. Sprinkle with the mozzarella. Cover with wax paper or a lid and microwave on high power for 2 minutes, or until the cheese melts and the filling is bubbling.

In a small bowl, combine the yogurt, sour cream and cilantro.

Remove the baking dish from the microwave and dot with the sour cream mixture. Microwave, uncovered, for 1 minute, or until just heated through.

Hands-on time: 15 minutes
Total time: 30 minutes

Per serving: 366 calories
6.1 g. total fat (15% of calories)
0.6 g. saturated fat
49 mg. cholesterol
1,210 mg. sodium

Easy TV Dinners
Make your own Tex-Mex TV dinners to freeze and reheat later. Let the chicken enchiladas cool, then portion out 2 enchiladas per serving and pack in microwave-safe TV-dinner trays. Add ½ cup cooked rice and ¼ cup steamed carrots, greens or broccoli to each tray. Cover with a tight-fitting lid. Freeze for up to 3 weeks. Uncover and microwave on high power for 8 to 10 minutes, rotating the tray halfway through the cooking time.

Chicken and Artichoke Risotto

Creamy-textured risotto is amazingly easy when prepared in the microwave—no heavy-duty stirring required.

Makes 4 servings

Risotto

¾ cup **uncooked Arborio rice**
2 teaspoons **olive oil**
2⅔ cups **defatted reduced-sodium chicken broth**
½ teaspoon **dried tarragon leaves**
¼ teaspoon **freshly ground black pepper**

Chicken and Vegetables

8 ounces **boneless, skinless chicken breasts, cubed**
1 **medium onion, chopped**
2 teaspoons **olive oil**
8 tablespoons **defatted reduced-sodium chicken broth**
1 jar (14¾ ounces) **water-packed artichoke heart quarters, drained**
1 teaspoon **dried tarragon leaves**
1 **small sweet red pepper, diced**

•

To make the risotto

In a 2½-quart microwave-safe casserole, combine the rice and oil. Microwave on high power for 1 minute. Stir in the broth, tarragon and black pepper. Cover with wax paper or a lid and microwave for a total of 8 minutes; stop and stir after 4 minutes.

•

Stir. Microwave, uncovered, for 11 to 13 minutes, or until the rice is tender. Allow to stand for 5 minutes.

To make the chicken and vegetables

Coat a large no-stick frying pan with no-stick spray. Add the chicken and cook over medium heat, stirring frequently, for 4 to 5 minutes, or until lightly browned. Transfer the chicken to a plate.

•

Add the onions, oil and 2 tablespoons of the broth to the pan. Cook over medium heat, stirring frequently, for 5 to 6 minutes.

•

Return the chicken to the pan and add the artichokes, tarragon and the remaining 6 tablespoons broth. Bring to a boil. Cover and simmer for 10 minutes, or until the chicken is cooked through.

•

Add the red peppers, cover and cook for 5 minutes, or until the peppers are crisp-tender. Stir the chicken mixture into the risotto.

Hands-on time: 10 minutes
Total time: 1 hour

Per serving: 292 calories
6.1 g. total fat (18% of calories)
1 g. saturated fat
23 mg. cholesterol
494 mg. sodium

Encore!

Chicken and Artichoke Timbales

Pack leftover risotto into lightly oiled custard cups, bake, then unmold onto dinner plates for an elegant side dish or first course. Use ½ to ¾ cup risotto per cup, press firmly to fill, then dust the top with Parmesan. Set the cups in a baking dish and add about 1″ hot water to the dish. Bake at 350° for 30 minutes. Cool slightly or completely before unmolding.

———

Turkey Quesadillas

More fun than a fiesta, these double-decker tortilla wedges are filled with turkey, chilies and cheese. Top them off with some super salsa.

Makes 4 servings

2 **medium tomatoes, diced**
1 cup **corn kernels**
2 tablespoons **chopped fresh cilantro**
½ teaspoon **ground cumin**
Juice of 1 lime
¼ teaspoon **salt**
Freshly ground black pepper
8 **flour tortillas** (**8″ diameter**)
1½ cups **shredded reduced-fat Monterey Jack cheese**
1 cup **shredded cooked turkey breast**
1 can (4 ounces) **diced mild green chili peppers, drained**
2 **scallions, chopped**
1 jar (7 ounces) **roasted red peppers, drained**

•

In a medium bowl, stir together the tomatoes, corn, cilantro, cumin, lime juice, salt and black pepper. Cover and refrigerate for at least 30 minutes.

•

Sprinkle 4 of the tortillas with the Monterey Jack. Top evenly with the turkey, chili peppers, scallions and red peppers. Top with the remaining 4 tortillas.

•

Lay each quesadilla on a microwave-safe plate and microwave on high power for 1 minute, or until the cheese melts. Cut into wedges and top with the tomato mixture.

Hands-on time: 10 minutes
Total time: 40 minutes

Per serving: 420 calories
13.2 g. total fat (27% of calories)
4.6 g. saturated fat
53 mg. cholesterol
633 mg. sodium

California Appetizers
Using kitchen shears, cut any leftover quesadillas into small triangles. Cover a baking sheet with foil, arrange the quesadillas in a single layer and freeze until firm. Transfer to self-sealing plastic freezer bags. To reheat, place frozen triangles on a no-stick baking sheet and bake at 400° for 15 minutes, or until lightly browned and crisp.

Put some bayou flavor on the table with this hearty one-pot dinner. This dish makes good use of frozen black-eyed peas, which are a nice convenience.

Makes 4 servings

1 package (10 ounces) **frozen black-eyed peas, rinsed under hot water and drained**
¾ cup **defatted reduced-sodium chicken broth**
2 teaspoons **olive oil**
12 ounces **ground turkey breast**
1 **large onion, chopped**
1 cup **coarsely chopped celery**
1 jar (4 ounces) **roasted red peppers, drained and chopped**
2 teaspoons **chili powder**
1¼ teaspoons **dried thyme leaves**
¾ teaspoon **dried oregano leaves**
¾ teaspoon **ground allspice**
1 can (8 ounces) **tomato sauce**
⅓ cup **finely diced lean smoked ham**
¼ cup **uncooked quick-cooking rice**
1 teaspoon **sugar**
¼ teaspoon **garlic salt (optional)**

●

In a round 2-quart microwave-safe casserole, combine the peas and broth. Cover with wax paper or a lid and microwave on high power for a total of 12 minutes; stop and stir every 4 minutes. Transfer to a large bowl.

●

In the same casserole, combine the oil, turkey and onions. Break up the turkey with a spoon. Cover and microwave on high power for a total of 3 minutes; stop and stir after 1½ minutes.

●

Add the celery, peppers, chili powder, thyme, oregano, allspice and the reserved peas and liquid. Cover and microwave for a total of 8 minutes, or until the peas are just tender; stop and stir after 4 minutes.

●

Stir in the tomato sauce, ham, rice, sugar and garlic salt (if using). Cover and microwave for 5 minutes, or until heated through. Let stand, covered, for 5 minutes. Fluff with a fork before serving.

Hands-on time: 15 minutes
Total time: 35 minutes

Per serving: 287 calories
5.5 g. total fat (13% of calories)
1.2 g. saturated fat
41 mg. cholesterol
647 mg. sodium

To Your Health

Black-Eyed Peas
Sometimes known as black-eyed beans, cow-peas or even black-eyed suzies, these tiny cream-colored beans have a distinctive black mark. They are particularly popular served with rice in the South. Half a cup has more than eight grams of dietary fiber (an impressive amount), 89 percent of the Recommended Dietary Allowance (RDA) for blood-building folate and 22 percent of the RDA for iron.

Southwestern Casserole

Here's a Tex-Mex roundup of black beans, corn, some chuckwagon spices and other good things—all prepared in the microwave in 30 minutes.

Makes 4 servings

1 cup **chopped onions**
1 **clove garlic, minced**
1 **small sweet red pepper, diced**
2 cans (15 ounces each) **reduced-sodium tomato sauce**
1 can (15 ounces) **black beans, rinsed and drained**
¾ cup **corn kernels**
1 tablespoon **canned chopped mild green chili peppers**
1 teaspoon **chili powder**
½ teaspoon **dried oregano leaves**
¼ teaspoon **salt** (**optional**)
¼ teaspoon **freshly ground black pepper**
1 cup **crumbled fat-free corn chips**
1 cup **shredded reduced-fat sharp Cheddar cheese**

In a 2½-quart microwave-safe casserole, combine the onions, garlic and red peppers. Cover with wax paper or a lid and microwave on high power for 3 to 4 minutes, or until the onions soften.

Add the tomato sauce, beans, corn, chili peppers, chili powder, oregano, salt (if using) and black pepper; stir well. Transfer 2 cups of the mixture to a bowl and set aside.

Spread the chips in an even layer over the mixture remaining in the casserole. Sprinkle with ½ cup of the Cheddar. Top with the reserved bean mixture, spreading it with the back of a large spoon.

Cover with wax paper or a lid and microwave for a total of 10 minutes; stop and give the casserole a quarter turn after 5 minutes.

Sprinkle with the remaining ½ cup Cheddar. Cover and microwave for 1 to 2 minutes, or until the cheese has melted. Allow the casserole to stand, covered, for 5 minutes before serving.

Hands-on time: 10 minutes
Total time: 30 minutes

Per serving: 386 calories
6.5 g. total fat (14% of calories)
2.4 g. saturated fat
12 mg. cholesterol
933 mg. sodium

Microwave Hot-Cha-Cha Beef

Ring the dinner bell! Here's pinto beans con carne—with beef and spicy south-of-the-border fixings. For variety, kidney beans are fine, too.

Makes 4 servings

1 teaspoon **olive oil**
1 **small onion, chopped**
1 **large clove garlic, minced**
8 ounces **extra-lean ground beef**
2 cups **frozen corn kernels, rinsed**
with hot water and drained
1 cup **defatted reduced-sodium beef broth**
½ cup **salsa**
2–4 tablespoons **canned chopped mild green chili peppers**
1 cup **uncooked quick-cooking rice**
1 cup **canned pinto beans, rinsed and drained**
1¼ teaspoons **chili powder**
½ teaspoon **dried thyme leaves**
Salt (optional)

●

In a 2-quart round microwave-safe casserole, combine the oil, onions and garlic. Crumble the beef into the casserole and stir lightly.

●

Cover with wax paper or a lid and microwave on high power for a total of 2½ minutes; stop and stir well after 1 minute to break up the beef.

●

Add the corn, broth, salsa and chili peppers. Cover and microwave for 5 to 6 minutes, or until the liquid comes to a boil.

●

Stir in the rice, beans, chili powder and thyme. Cover and microwave for a total of 5 minutes, or until the rice is tender; stop and stir after 2½ minutes.

●

Let stand, covered, for about 5 minutes. Season with the salt (if using). Fluff with a fork before serving.

Hands-on time: 12 minutes
Total time: 25 minutes

Per serving: 324 calories
9.3 g. total fat (25% of calories)
2.9 g. saturated fat
35 mg. cholesterol
496 mg. sodium

Microwave Beef-and-Vegetable Stew

No long, slow cooking here! Ground turkey combines with ground beef in this ultrafast low-fat stew.

Makes 4 servings

1 cup **finely chopped onions**

2 **cloves garlic, minced**

6 ounces **extra-lean ground beef**

4 ounces **ground turkey breast**

1 can (15 ounces) **reduced-sodium tomato sauce**

2 teaspoons **sugar**

2 teaspoons **cider vinegar**

1 teaspoon **dried thyme leaves**

1 teaspoon **dried basil leaves**

1 **bay leaf**

Freshly ground black pepper

½ cup **defatted reduced-sodium beef broth**

1½ cups **frozen mixed vegetables (corn, peas, lima beans, carrots, green beans), thawed**

½ cup **uncooked quick-cooking rice**

¼ teaspoon **salt (optional)**

●

In a 2½-quart microwave-safe casserole, combine the onions and garlic. Crumble the beef and turkey into the casserole. Cover with wax paper or a lid and microwave on high power for a total of 8 minutes; stop and stir, breaking up the meat, every 2 minutes. Break up any remaining large pieces of meat.

●

Stir in the tomato sauce, sugar, vinegar, thyme, basil, bay leaf and pepper. Add the broth, mixed vegetables and rice. Mix well.

●

Cover and microwave for a total of 12 minutes, or until the rice is tender; stop and stir every 4 minutes.

●

Remove and discard the bay leaf. Season with the salt (if using).

Hands-on time: 10 minutes
Total time: 30 minutes

Per serving: 282 calories
2.9 g. total fat (9% of calories)
1 g. saturated fat
39 mg. cholesterol
148 mg. sodium

Microwave Potato, Cheddar and Ham Casserole

That all-American comfort food, scalloped potatoes, makes a meal when spruced up with diced ham and a melted cheese topping.

Makes 4 servings

1 cup **defatted reduced-sodium chicken broth**
1 cup **shredded reduced-fat sharp Cheddar cheese**
3 tablespoons **unbleached flour**
1¾ teaspoons **dry mustard**
¾ teaspoon **dried marjoram leaves**
⅛ teaspoon **freshly ground black pepper**
1½ teaspoons **butter or margarine**
1 cup **chopped onions**
¾ cup **finely chopped celery**
½ cup **2% low-fat milk**
4½ cups **thinly sliced potatoes**
¾ cup **lean diced smoked ham**

•

Place the broth in a 2-cup glass measuring cup and microwave on high power for 1½ minutes, or until hot. Pour into a blender.

•

Set aside 2 tablespoons of the Cheddar. With the motor running, add the remaining Cheddar to the blender. Add the flour, mustard, marjoram and pepper. Blend until smooth.

•

In a round 2-quart microwave-safe casserole, combine the butter or margarine, onions and celery. Cover with wax paper or a lid and microwave on high power for 2 minutes.

•

Stir in the cheese mixture, stirring vigorously until blended and smooth. Stir in the milk and then the potatoes.

•

Cover and microwave on high power for a total of 10 minutes; stop and stir after 5 minutes.

•

Stir in the ham. Cover and microwave for a total of 10 minutes, or until the potatoes are just tender; stop and stir after 5 minutes.

•

Sprinkle with the remaining 2 tablespoons Cheddar. Let stand for 3 to 4 minutes, or until the cheese melts.

Hands-on time: 15 minutes
Total time: 40 minutes

Per serving: 310 calories
7.7 g. total fat (22% of calories)
4.1 g. saturated fat
26 mg. cholesterol
877 mg. sodium

Encore!

Ham and Cheddar Frittata
In a large ovenproof frying sauté half a medium onion in ½ cup chicken broth for 10 minutes. Add 2 cups chopped mixed vegetables and sauté for 2 minutes. Stir in 2 cups chopped leftover Microwave Potato, Cheddar and Ham Casserole; remove from the heat. Lightly beat 4 egg whites, 2 eggs, ⅓ cup shredded low-fat Cheddar and chopped herbs or salt and pepper. Pour into the pan and bake at 375° for 25 to 30 minutes, or until the frittata is slightly puffed and set.

———

Shrimp Risotto

Shrimp Risotto

Shrimp and zucchini make this variation of microwave risotto quite colorful.

Makes 4 servings

Risotto

¾ cup	**uncooked Arborio rice**
2 teaspoons	**olive oil**
2⅔ cups	**defatted reduced-sodium chicken broth**
½ teaspoon	**dried thyme leaves**
1	**large bay leaf**
¼ teaspoon	**freshly ground black pepper**

Shrimp

12 ounces	**medium shrimp, peeled and deveined**
⅓ cup	**defatted reduced-sodium chicken broth**
1 cup	**diced zucchini**
2	**cloves garlic, minced**
½ teaspoon	**dried basil leaves**

To make the risotto

In a 2½-quart microwave-safe casserole, combine the rice and oil. Microwave on high power for 1 minute.

Stir in the broth, thyme, bay leaf and pepper. Cover with wax paper or a lid and microwave for a total of 8 minutes; stop and stir after 4 minutes.

Stir. Microwave, uncovered, for 11 to 13 minutes, or until most of the liquid is absorbed and the rice is tender. Allow to stand for 5 minutes. Remove and discard the bay leaf.

To prepare the shrimp

In a large no-stick frying pan, combine the shrimp, broth, zucchini, garlic and basil. Cook over medium heat, stirring frequently, for 3 to 4 minutes, or until the shrimp turn pink.

Add to the risotto and stir gently to mix.

Hands-on time: 5 minutes
Total time: 30 minutes

Per serving: 233 calories
3.3 g. total fat (13% of calories)
0.6 g. saturated fat
131 mg. cholesterol
505 mg. sodium

Heavenly Leftovers
Spoon cooled Shrimp Risotto into self-sealing plastic freezer bags. Freeze for up to 6 weeks. Thaw overnight in the refrigerator and reheat in the microwave on high power for 4 minutes, stirring halfway through the cooking time. Let stand for 2 minutes to finish heating evenly.

Sole with Vegetables and Sliced Almonds

Sole amandine is usually swimming in butter. This slimmed-down version gets flavor and color from the vegetables and a sprinkling of almonds on top.

Makes 4 servings

¼ cup **white wine or**
defatted reduced-sodium chicken broth
2 **scallions, minced**
1 **sweet red pepper, thinly sliced**
1 cup **thinly sliced mushrooms**
¼ cup **lemon juice**
2 teaspoons **chopped fresh chives**
2 teaspoons **minced fresh parsley**
5 **almonds, coarsely chopped**
4 **sole or flounder fillets (5 ounces each)**

Bring the wine or broth to a boil in a no-stick frying pan over medium-high heat. Add the scallions, peppers and mushrooms. Cook, stirring frequently, for 7 minutes, or until the liquid evaporates.

Add the lemon juice, chives, parsley and almonds. Remove from the heat.

Oil a rectangular microwave-safe casserole large enough to hold the fillets in a single layer. Add the fillets. Spoon the vegetables on top.

Cover with vented plastic wrap or a lid. Microwave on high power for 4 to 5 minutes, or until the fish flakes when tested with a fork. Let stand, covered, for 2 minutes before serving.

Hands-on time: 5 minutes
Total time: 17 minutes

Per serving: 162 calories
3.7 g. total fat (21% of calories)
0.6 g. saturated fat
66 mg. cholesterol
106 mg. sodium

Rice with Creamy Spinach, Salmon and Dill

Fragrant rice is tossed with a creamy sauce of spinach, salmon and fresh dill. Microwaving quickly heats the dish through and lets the flavors blend.

Makes 4 servings

¼ cup **defatted reduced-sodium chicken broth**
2 **small onions, chopped**
1 **scallion, chopped**
2 **cloves garlic, minced**
1 pound **spinach, washed and stems removed**
4 cups **hot cooked basmati or other white rice**
1 can (7½ ounces) **red salmon, drained and flaked**
2 teaspoons **chopped fresh dill**
Freshly ground black pepper
1 cup **1% low-fat cottage cheese**
¼ cup **grated Parmesan cheese**

•

Bring the broth to a boil in a no-stick frying pan over medium-high heat. Add the onions, scallions and garlic. Cook, stirring frequently, for 3 minutes. Add the spinach and cook for 5 to 6 minutes, or until the spinach is wilted.

•

Remove the pan from the heat. Stir in the rice, salmon, dill and pepper.

•

Puree the cottage cheese and Parmesan in a blender until smooth. Stir into the rice mixture.

•

Coat a shallow rectangular microwave-safe casserole with no-stick spray. Add the rice mixture. Cover with vented plastic or a lid. Microwave on high power for 4 minutes, or until heated through. Let stand, covered, for 2 minutes before serving.

Hands-on time: 7 minutes
Total time: 20 minutes

Per serving: 456 calories
6.2 g. total fat (12% of calories)
2.5 g. saturated fat
28 mg. cholesterol
725 mg. sodium

Encore!

Scandinavian Fish Chowder

In a large saucepan, sauté ¼ cup diced celery, ¼ cup diced red peppers, ¼ cup diced red onions and 1 teaspoon garlic in ¼ cup apple juice or dry sherry for 10 minutes. Add 2 cups chicken broth and bring to a boil. Stir in 2 cups leftover Rice with Creamy Spinach, Salmon and Dill; heat through but do not boil. Remove from the heat and stir in ⅓ cup low-fat sour cream.

——

Polenta with Ratatouille

Polenta with Ratatouille

Polenta—cooked cornmeal—is a cinch in the microwave. Here we top it with ratatouille, that delicious vegetable mélange from southern France.

Makes 4 servings

2 cups **1% low-fat milk**
2 cups **water**
1¼ cups **coarse cornmeal**
½ teaspoon **salt** (**optional**)
2 teaspoons **olive oil**
1 cup **chopped onions**
1 tablespoon **minced garlic**
2 cups **diced green peppers**
2 cups **diced eggplant**
2 cups **diced tomatoes**
¼ cup **minced fresh basil**
1 teaspoon **dried oregano leaves**
Freshly ground black pepper
¼ cup **shredded reduced-fat Monterey Jack cheese**

•

In a rectangular 3-quart microwave-safe casserole, mix the milk and water. Whisk in the cornmeal and salt (if using).

•

Cover with vented plastic. Microwave on high power for a total of 12 minutes, or until most of the liquid is absorbed; stop and stir after 6 minutes.

•

Let stand, covered, for 5 minutes.

•

Coat a large no-stick frying pan with no-stick spray. Add the oil and place over medium-high heat. Add the onions, garlic and green peppers. Cook, stirring frequently, for 5 minutes, or until the onions and peppers begin to soften.

•

Add the eggplant, tomatoes, basil, oregano and black pepper. Cook, stirring occasionally, for 10 minutes, or until the eggplant is tender.

•

Spoon the vegetables over the cornmeal. Sprinkle with the Monterey Jack. Microwave for 1 minute, or until the cheese melts.

Hands-on time: 7 minutes
Total time: 35 minutes

Per serving: 304 calories
8.1 g. total fat (23% of calories)
2.8 g. saturated fat
14 mg. cholesterol
376 mg. sodium

Butter Bean Casserole

Mellow butter beans and tomato sauce form the basis of this vegetarian dish. If rutabaga isn't available, use turnip; either is a great foil for the beans.

Makes 4 servings

½ cup **peeled and shredded rutabaga**
1 **large onion, chopped**
1 **large stalk celery, thinly sliced**
1 **medium potato, cubed**
1 **clove garlic, minced**
1 can (15 ounces) **reduced-sodium tomato sauce**
1 can (15 ounces) **butter beans, rinsed and drained**
1 teaspoon **dried basil leaves**
¼ teaspoon **dried oregano leaves**
Pinch of ground celery seed
¼ teaspoon **salt** (**optional**)
⅛ teaspoon **freshly ground black pepper**

•

In a round 2½-quart microwave-safe casserole, combine the rutabagas, onions, celery, potatoes and garlic. Cover with wax paper or a lid and microwave on high power for 8 minutes, or until the vegetables soften; stop and stir after 4 minutes.

•

Add the tomato sauce, beans, basil, oregano, celery seed, salt (if using) and pepper. Mix well. Cover and microwave for 4 to 5 minutes, or until heated through. Let stand for 2 to 3 minutes before serving.

Hands-on time: 10 minutes
Total time: 23 minutes

Per serving: 201 calories
0.4 g. total fat (2% of calories)
0 g. saturated fat
0 mg. cholesterol
531 mg. sodium

Stuffed Eggplant

These eggplant boats will win raves for a pretty presentation as well as their combination of tastes and textures. A low-fat peanut sauce adds pizzazz.

Makes 4 servings

2 **Japanese eggplants, about 1 pound each**
1 cup **diced onions**
1 cup **shredded carrots**
1 **sweet red pepper, diced**
1 cup **chopped bok choy**
2 tablespoons **defatted reduced-sodium chicken broth**
2 cups **diagonally sliced snow peas**
1 cup **hot cooked basmati or brown rice**
2 tablespoons **reduced-sodium soy sauce**
1 tablespoon **hoisin sauce**
2 teaspoons **creamy peanut butter**
1 teaspoon **grated fresh ginger**
1 **clove garlic, minced**

•

Halve each eggplant, remove the tops and, using a melon baller, scoop out the flesh, leaving ¼"-thick shells.

•

Chop the eggplant flesh and set aside.

•

Put the shells in boiling salted water and cook for 2 to 3 minutes to soften. Invert and drain on paper towels.

•

In a rectangular microwave-safe casserole, combine the onions, carrots, peppers, bok choy, broth and chopped eggplant. Cover with vented plastic or a lid and microwave on high power for 5 minutes, or until the peppers soften.

•

Add the snow peas, rice, soy sauce, hoisin sauce, peanut butter, ginger and garlic. Mix well and mound into the eggplant shells.

•

Rinse out the casserole. Arrange the eggplant shells side by side in the casserole. Cover and microwave for 2 minutes, or until the vegetables and rice are heated through.

Hands-on time: 10 minutes
Total time: 20 minutes

Per serving: 199 calories
2.1 g. total fat (9% of calories)
0.4 g. saturated fat
0 mg. cholesterol
354 mg. sodium

To Your Health

Eggplant

Eggplant is filling but not fattening, as long as you don't cook it in a lot of oil, which it soaks up like a sponge. Eggplant is very low in calories, fat and sodium, with fair amounts of fiber, potassium and folate. Some studies have suggested that eggplant can help lower cholesterol and possibly protect against the development of plaque in your arteries.

Vegetable Lasagna

Reduced-fat dairy products take the guilt out of cheese lasagna. No-boil noodles and the microwave take out the fuss.

Makes 4 servings

1 cup **nonfat ricotta cheese**
1 cup **part-skim ricotta cheese**
½ cup **fat-free egg substitute**
¼ cup **grated Parmesan cheese**
¼ cup **chopped fresh parsley**
2 cups **tomato sauce**
1 cup **water**
15 **no-boil lasagna noodles**
1 package (10 ounces) **frozen chopped spinach, thawed and squeezed dry**
1 cup **shredded part-skim mozzarella cheese**

In a medium bowl, mix the nonfat ricotta, part-skim ricotta, egg substitute, Parmesan and parsley.

In a 4-cup glass measuring cup, mix the tomato sauce and water. Microwave on high power for 3 to 5 minutes, or until hot but not boiling.

Pour 1 cup of the sauce into an 8″ × 12″ microwave-safe casserole. Place 5 of the noodles, overlapping if necessary, in the casserole. Cover with half of the cheese mixture.

Repeat with 5 more noodles and 1 cup of the sauce.

Mix the spinach with the remaining cheese mixture. Spread over the noodles and sauce. Sprinkle with the mozzarella.

Top with the remaining 5 noodles and the remaining 1 cup sauce.

Cover with vented plastic or a lid. Microwave on 80% power for a total of 21 minutes; stop and give the casserole a quarter turn every 7 minutes.

Uncover and let stand for 10 minutes before serving.

Hands-on time: 10 minutes
Total time: 38 minutes

Per serving: 608 calories
12.8 g. total fat (19% of calories)
7.3 g. saturated fat
40 mg. cholesterol
911 mg. sodium

Potato-Vegetable Frittata with Cheddar
(page 286) ➤

Warm from the Oven

Turkey-Vegetable Potpie

Under a low-fat but flaky crust nestle tender turkey and vegetables in a savory sauce. Take a bow and don't tell anyone how easy it was!

Makes 4 servings

Filling

3 tablespoons **unbleached flour**
¼ teaspoon **salt**
¼ teaspoon **dried thyme leaves**
1 pound **turkey tenderloin, cubed**
2 cups **defatted reduced-sodium chicken broth**
1 cup **thinly sliced celery**
½ cup **diced carrots**
2 **scallions, chopped**
1 jar (4 ounces) **roasted red peppers, drained and thinly sliced**
¼ cup **minced fresh parsley**
1 teaspoon **reduced-sodium soy sauce**
¼ teaspoon **poultry seasoning**

Crust

1¾ cups **unbleached flour**
½ teaspoon **salt (optional)**
2 teaspoons **baking powder**
½ teaspoon **baking soda**
2 tablespoons **butter or margarine**
¾ cup **buttermilk**
2 teaspoons **honey**

●

To make the filling
Preheat the oven to 400°. Lightly coat a 2-quart casserole with no-stick spray.

●

In a self-sealing plastic bag, combine the flour, salt and thyme. Add the turkey and shake to coat.

●

Coat a large no-stick frying pan with no-stick spray. Add the turkey and cook, stirring, over medium heat for 4 minutes, or until lightly browned.

●

Add the broth, celery, carrots, scallions and peppers. Cook for 5 minutes, or until the vegetables soften. Add the parsley, soy sauce and poultry seasoning. Mix well and spoon into the prepared casserole.

To make the crust

Sift the flour, salt (if using), baking powder and baking soda into a large bowl. Using a pastry cutter, cut the butter or margarine into the flour until the mixture resembles coarse meal.

Add the buttermilk and honey, stirring gently to incorporate. Add more buttermilk if the dough is too dry.

Knead lightly in the bowl for 3 to 5 minutes, or until the dough is no longer sticky. Turn out onto a lightly floured surface and roll or pat into a desired shape to cover the casserole. Carefully lift and lay the crust over the filling, gently patting it into place.

Bake for 20 minutes, or until the crust is golden brown and the filling is bubbling.

Hands-on time: 20 minutes
Total time: 40 minutes
Per serving: 443 calories
9.1 g. total fat (19% of calories)

4.6 g. saturated fat
66 mg. cholesterol
865 mg. sodium

Eggplant Stuffed with Cajun Rice

This Cajun dish has been deliciously lightened with reduced-fat turkey sausage and fresh vegetables. Naturally, there's rice and a little bayou heat.

Makes 4 servings

2 **eggplants, about 1½ pounds each**
1 cup **chopped onions**
½ cup **water**
⅓ cup **corn kernels**
1 **yellow pepper, chopped**
1 cup **hot cooked rice**
4 ounces **reduced-fat Cajun-style turkey sausage links, cooked, drained and chopped**
1 **medium tomato, chopped**
¼ cup **chopped fresh parsley**
½ teaspoon **dried basil leaves**
¼ teaspoon **hot-pepper flakes**
¼ teaspoon **ground cumin**
Salt (optional)
Freshly ground black pepper
¼ cup **dried bread crumbs**

Encore!

Cajun Stuffed Pork Chops

Trim 4 lean loin pork chops of all excess fat, then split horizontally. Stuff each chop with ¼ cup leftover Cajun rice. Secure with toothpicks. Dust the chops with flour seasoned with Cajun seasoning. Sear the chops on both sides in a hot pan coated with no-stick spray. Then bake, uncovered, at 375° for 35 minutes, or until the chops are cooked through. Serve with unsweetened apple sauce or steamed red cabbage sprinkled with balsamic vinegar.

Preheat the oven to 450°.

Halve each eggplant, remove the tops and, using a melon baller, scoop out the flesh, leaving ¼"-thick shells. Chop the eggplant flesh.

Place the shells in boiling water for 2 to 3 minutes to soften. Invert and drain on paper towels.

Coat a large no-stick frying pan with no-stick spray. Add the onions and water. Cook over medium-high heat, stirring occasionally, for 5 minutes, or until the onions soften.

Add the corn, yellow peppers and chopped eggplant. Cook for 5 minutes.

Add the rice, sausage, tomatoes, parsley, basil, pepper flakes and cumin. Cook for 10 minutes, or until the eggplant softens. Season with the salt (if using) and black pepper.

Divide the mixture among the eggplant shells, mounding it as necessary to fit. Coat a 9" × 13" baking dish with no-stick spray and arrange the shells in the baking dish. Sprinkle with the bread crumbs.

Bake for 25 to 30 minutes, or until the topping is browned.

Hands-on time: 25 minutes
Total time: 55 minutes

Per serving: 248 calories
4.8 g. total fat (16% of calories)
0.8 g. saturated fat
15 mg. cholesterol
195 mg. sodium

Turkey Tetrazzini

Apopular Sunday supper, this baked pasta dish boasts mushrooms, peas and chunks of turkey in a creamy low-fat sauce.

Makes 4 servings

1 teaspoon **olive oil**
2½ cups **defatted reduced-sodium chicken broth**
½ cup **chopped onions**
10 ounces **mushrooms, thinly sliced**
¼ cup **unbleached flour**
1½ cups **skim milk**
¼ cup **sherry or apple juice**
4 cups **cooked spaghetti**
1 cup **cooked peas**
2 cups **coarsely chopped cooked turkey breast**
¼ cup **grated Parmesan cheese**
⅓ cup **fresh bread crumbs**

•

Preheat the oven to 350°.

•

Coat a large no-stick frying pan with no-stick spray. Add the oil and ½ cup of the broth. Bring to a boil over medium-high heat.

•

Add the onions and cook, stirring frequently, for 3 minutes. Add the mushrooms and cook for 7 minutes, or until the liquid evaporates.

•

Stir in the flour and cook for 2 minutes. Gradually whisk in the milk, sherry or apple juice and the remaining 2 cups broth.

•

Bring to a boil and cook, stirring constantly, for 5 minutes, or until the sauce thickens.

•

Remove from the heat and stir in the spaghetti, peas, turkey and Parmesan.

•

Coat a 3-quart casserole with no-stick spray. Add the turkey mixture. Sprinkle with the bread crumbs.

•

Cover and bake for 20 minutes. Uncover and bake for 10 minutes, or until heated through and lightly browned.

Hands-on time: 20 minutes
Total time: 50 minutes

Per serving: 467 calories
5.5 g. total fat (11% of calories)
1.7 g. saturated fat
53 mg. cholesterol
553 mg. sodium

Encore!

Turkey Noodle Pancakes

These silver-dollar pancakes are unusual and delicious. Begin by finely chopping 2 cups leftover Turkey Tetrazzini. Combine with 4 eggs (or 1 cup egg substitute) and ¼ cup Parmesan. Drop small spoonfuls into a hot, lightly oiled frying pan and cook until lightly browned on both sides. Serve with cranberry sauce or chutney.

Tamale Pie

This shortcut keeps the flavor but takes the fuss out of a tamale dinner for your favorite rancheros. Adding turkey to ground beef helps cut the fat; if possible, use ground turkey breast.

Makes 4 servings

6 ounces **extra-lean ground beef**
4 ounces **ground turkey breast**
1 cup **chopped onions**
1 small **green pepper, diced**
1 can (15 ounces) **reduced-sodium tomato sauce**
1 cup **reduced-sodium salsa**
1 can (16 ounces) **reduced-sodium kidney beans, rinsed and drained**
1 cup **corn kernels**
2 teaspoons **chili powder**
1 teaspoon **ground cumin**
¼ teaspoon **salt (optional)**
¼ teaspoon **freshly ground black pepper**
3–4 drops **hot-pepper sauce (optional)**
6 **corn tortillas (6″ diameter)**

Preheat the oven to 350°.

Crumble the beef and turkey into a 2½-quart flame-proof casserole. Add the onions and green peppers. Cook over medium heat, breaking up the meat with a wooden spoon, for 6 to 7 minutes, or until the meat is browned.

Add the tomato sauce, salsa, beans, corn, chili powder, cumin, salt (if using), black pepper and hot-pepper sauce (if using). Stir to mix well. Remove from the heat.

Measure 3 cups of the mixture and put it into a bowl. Set aside.

Lay 3 tortillas over the remaining meat mixture in the casserole. Top with half the reserved meat mixture and spread evenly with the back of a spoon.

Top with the remaining 3 tortillas and the remaining meat mixture.

Bake for 30 minutes, or until heated through.

Hands-on time: 20 minutes
Total time: 1 hour

Per serving: 407 calories
5.3 g. total fat (11% of calories)
0.9 g. saturated fat
39 mg. cholesterol
267 mg. sodium

To Your Health

Kidney Beans
Kidney beans are best known for their supporting role in chili, but they're suitable for all types of Tex-Mex fare. Half a cup has nearly seven grams of fiber, 57 percent of the Recommended Dietary Allowance (RDA) for blood-building folate and 26 percent of the RDA for iron.

Egg Noodles with Beef and Cabbage

Warming on a winter evening, this is a family-style treat like Grandma used to make. Cooking noodles and cabbage at the same time saves a step and a pot.

Makes 4 servings

8 ounces **extra-lean ground beef**
1 **small onion, chopped**
1 **small green pepper, chopped**
1 **clove garlic, minced**
2 teaspoons **olive oil**
8 ounces **uncooked medium yolk-free egg noodles**
4 cups **coarsely chopped cabbage**
2 cans (14¼ ounces each) **sodium-free stewed tomatoes**
2 teaspoons **chopped fresh basil**
½ teaspoon **freshly ground black pepper**
4 tablespoons **grated Parmesan cheese**

•

Preheat the oven to 400°.

•

Coat a large no-stick frying pan with no-stick spray. Crumble the beef into the pot. Add the onions, green peppers, garlic and oil. Cook over medium-high heat, breaking up the meat with a wooden spoon, for 4 to 5 minutes, or until lightly browned.

•

Cook the noodles in a large pot of boiling water for 5 minutes. Add the cabbage and when the water returns to a boil, cook for 1 minute, or until the cabbage just begins to soften. Drain the cabbage and noodles in a colander.

•

Coat a 2½-quart casserole with no-stick spray. Spoon the meat and the noodle mixtures into the casserole. Add the tomatoes, basil, black pepper and 3 tablespoons of the Parmesan. Toss to mix.

•

Sprinkle with the remaining 1 tablespoon Parmesan.

•

Bake for 15 minutes, or until hot and lightly browned.

Hands-on time: 15 minutes
Total time: 30 minutes

Per serving: 482 calories
16 g. total fat (30% of calories)
6 g. saturated fat
97 mg. cholesterol
261 mg. sodium

Enchilada Casserole

An attractive avocado-and-olive garnish distinguishes this Mexican casserole. If you like, you can assemble the casserole ahead, refrigerate and bake just before serving.

Makes 4 servings

1 **green pepper, chopped**
8 ounces **ground chicken breast**
1 jar (16 ounces) **salsa**
8 **corn tortillas (6″ diameter)**
1 can (16 ounces) **reduced-sodium red beans or kidney beans, rinsed and drained**
⅔ cup **shredded reduced-fat Monterey Jack cheese**
1 cup **nonfat sour cream**
1 **avocado, pitted and sliced**
12 **black olives, pitted and thinly sliced**

•

Preheat the oven to 350°.

•

Coat a large frying pan with no-stick spray. Add the peppers and cook over medium heat for 5 minutes. Add the chicken and cook, breaking up the meat with a wooden spoon, for 3 minutes, or until the chicken is cooked through.

•

Coat an 8″ × 12″ casserole with no-stick spray.

•

Pour the salsa into a shallow bowl and dip 1 tortilla into the salsa to coat the bottom side. Place the tortilla, salsa side up, on a work surface and top with 2 tablespoons of the beans, 2 tablespoons of the chicken mixture, 2 tablespoons of the salsa and 1 tablespoon of the Monterey Jack. Roll up and place in the casserole, seam side down.

•

Repeat to make 7 more filled tortillas.

•

Top the tortillas with any remaining Monterey Jack. Cover and bake for 20 minutes. Uncover and bake for 5 minutes, or until lightly browned and heated through.

•

Serve with the sour cream, avocados and olives.

Hands-on time: 10 minutes
Total time: 35 minutes

Per serving: 695 calories
20 g. total fat (28% of calories)
5.4 g. saturated fat
71 mg. cholesterol
986 mg. sodium

Stuffed Shells

Here's the Italian flavor your family loves—jumbo pasta shells filled with a meat-and-ricotta mixture, then baked in marinara sauce.

Makes 4 servings

20 **jumbo pasta shells**
4 ounces **extra-lean ground beef**
¼ cup **defatted reduced-sodium chicken broth**
¼ cup **finely chopped onions**
½ cup **chopped red peppers**
2 **cloves garlic, minced**
2 ounces **part-skim ricotta cheese**
½ teaspoon **dried oregano leaves**
1½ tablespoons **chopped fresh basil**
1 jar (14 ounces) **reduced-fat spaghetti sauce**
2 tablespoons **grated Parmesan cheese**

Cook the shells in a large pot of boiling water until just tender. Drain and set aside.

Coat a large frying pan with no-stick spray. Crumble the beef into the pan. Cook over medium-high heat, breaking up the meat with a wooden spoon, for 4 to 5 minutes, or until lightly browned.

Line a platter with several thicknesses of paper towels. Transfer the beef to the plate and drain well.

Wipe out the pan with a paper towel. Return the beef to the pan. Add the broth, onions, peppers and garlic and cook for 5 to 6 minutes, or until the onions are soft. Remove from the heat. Stir in the ricotta, oregano and basil. Stuff the mixture into the cooked shells.

If there's any stuffing left over, mix the spaghetti sauce with it. Spoon the sauce into an 8″ × 12″ baking dish. Arrange the filled shells, open side up, over the sauce and sprinkle with the Parmesan.

Bake for 30 minutes, or until heated through.

Hands-on time: 20 minutes
Total time: 50 minutes

Per serving: 305 calories
9.3 g. total fat (27% of calories)
3.3 g. saturated fat
61 mg. cholesterol
629 mg. sodium

Meatball Oven Dinner

Baking the meatballs and vegetables in a dish lined with foil helps cut down on cleanup time later.

Makes 4 servings

Encore!

Hot Meatball Sandwiches
Split and toast 1 whole-wheat submarine roll for each sandwich. Warm 3 leftover meatballs and ¼ cup sauce in a pan until bubbly. Use to stuff the roll. Serve with reduced-sodium dill pickles, baked tortilla chips and low-fat coleslaw.

6 ounces **extra-lean ground beef**
4 ounces **ground turkey breast**
2 tablespoons **quick-cooking rolled oats**
1 tablespoon **instant minced onions**
2 teaspoons **chili powder**
1 **egg white**
½ teaspoon **salt** (**optional**)
⅛ teaspoon **freshly ground black pepper**
Pinch of garlic powder
1 teaspoon **dried thyme leaves**
2 **large onions, chopped**
2 **large potatoes, cubed**
2 **large carrots, thinly sliced**
1 cup **cubed turnips**
1 cup **reduced-sodium tomato sauce**
½ cup **defatted reduced-sodium chicken broth**
¼ cup **ketchup**
1 teaspoon **Worcestershire sauce**
1 **bay leaf**

Preheat the oven to 400°.

Line a 9″ × 13″ baking dish with aluminum foil and allow the foil to extend over the edges of the pan. Coat the foil with no-stick spray.

In a large bowl, combine the beef, turkey, oats, minced onions, chili powder, egg white, salt (if using), black pepper, garlic powder and ½ teaspoon of the thyme. Mix well.

Form the mixture with dampened hands into 20 meatballs. Place in the prepared pan.

Bake for 8 to 10 minutes, or until browned. Use a large spoon to skim any fat from the bottom of the pan and discard.

Add the chopped onions, potatoes, carrots and turnips to the pan. Gently stir to mix.

In a bowl, mix the tomato sauce, broth, ketchup, Worcestershire sauce, bay leaf and the remaining ½ teaspoon thyme.

Pour the sauce over the meatballs and vegetables. Cover with another piece of foil and seal the edges.

Bake for 1 hour, or until the vegetables are tender. Remove and discard the bay leaf.

Hands-on time: 20 minutes
Total time: 1½ hours

Per serving: 288 calories
3.5 g. total fat (11% of calories)
1 g. saturated fat
39 mg. cholesterol
340 mg. sodium

Shepherd's Pie

Using instant mashed potatoes cuts a step from this hearty stew. Although the meat takes an hour to bake, your hands-on time is quite short.

Makes 4 servings

Filling

10 ounces	**beef round steak, trimmed and cut into thin 2″ strips**
2 cups	**chopped onions**
1 can (8 ounces)	**reduced-sodium tomato sauce**
¾ cup	**defatted reduced-sodium beef broth**
1	**carrot, thinly sliced**
1 package (10 ounces)	**frozen succotash, thawed**
2	**large bay leaves**
1¼ teaspoons	**dried thyme leaves**
¼ teaspoon	**dry mustard**
¼ teaspoon	**freshly ground black pepper**
¼ teaspoon	**salt** (**optional**)

Topping

1½ cups	**water**
1 tablespoon	**butter or margarine**
⅔ cup	**1% low-fat milk**
1½ cups	**instant mashed potato flakes**
2 teaspoons	**instant minced onions**
¼ teaspoon	**salt** (**optional**)
⅛ teaspoon	**garlic powder**
¼ cup	**shredded reduced-fat Cheddar cheese**

To make the filling

Preheat the oven to 375°.

Place the beef in a 3-quart casserole. Bake, stirring occasionally, for 10 minutes, or until the meat is browned. Remove from the oven.

Place the onions in a 2-cup glass measuring cup, cover with wax paper and microwave on high power for 2 to 3 minutes, or until the onions soften.

Add the onions to the casserole. Stir in the tomato sauce, broth, carrots, succotash, bay leaves, thyme, mustard, pepper and salt (if using).

Cover and bake for 1 hour, or until the meat is tender.

To make the topping

In a medium saucepan, bring the water and butter or margarine to a boil. Remove from the heat and stir in the milk, potato flakes, onions, salt (if using) and garlic powder.

Remove the casserole from the oven. Remove and discard the bay leaves.

Drop the potato mixture by large spoonfuls onto the casserole and carefully spread over the beef mixture with the back of a large spoon.

Sprinkle with the Cheddar and bake for 5 minutes, or until the cheese begins to melt.

Hands-on time: 20 minutes
Total time: 1½ hours

Per serving: 403 calories
8.4 g. total fat (19% of calories)
3.9 g. saturated fat
19 mg. cholesterol
331 mg. sodium

Beef and Carrot Stew

Because of the low-fat cut of beef, this stew needs extra oven time to tenderize. A surprise ingredient enhances the gravy, which is also wonderful over egg noodles.

Makes 4 servings

2 tablespoons **unbleached flour**
½ teaspoon **paprika**
¼ teaspoon **freshly ground black pepper**
1 pound **beef top round, trimmed and cut into ½″ cubes**
1 **onion, chopped**
1 **clove garlic, minced**
4 cups **defatted reduced-sodium beef broth**
½ teaspoon **dried thyme leaves**
1 **bay leaf**
8 **carrots, chopped**
8 **pitted prunes, coarsely chopped**
2 tablespoons **chopped fresh parsley**

Preheat the oven to 375°.

Combine the flour, paprika and pepper in a self-sealing plastic bag. Add the beef and shake to coat.

Place a Dutch oven over medium-high heat for 2 minutes. Add the beef and cook, stirring, for 5 minutes, or until browned. Add the onions and garlic. Cook, stirring occasionally, for 5 minutes, or until the onions soften.

Add the broth, thyme and bay leaf. Bring to a boil. Add the carrots, prunes and parsley.

Return to a boil, cover and bake for 1 hour, or until the beef and carrots are tender and the gravy has thickened. Remove and discard the bay leaf.

Hands-on time: 25 minutes
Total time: 1½ hours

Per serving: 380 calories
6 g. total fat (15% of calories)
2 g. saturated fat
101 mg. cholesterol
724 mg. sodium

Pork and Roasted Vegetables

This homey oven dinner gets a fast start because you partially cook the vegetables in the microwave. Meat-and-potatoes lovers, this one's for you.

Makes 4 servings

12 ounces **pork loin, trimmed and cut into thin 1"-wide strips**
1¼ teaspoons **dried thyme leaves**
¾ teaspoon **dried rosemary leaves**
¾ teaspoon **salt** (**optional**)
¼ teaspoon **freshly ground black pepper**
1½ cups **cubed rutabagas**
4 **onions, quartered**
2 **potatoes, cut into 1" pieces**
3 **carrots, cut into ½" slices**
2 **cloves garlic, sliced**
3 tablespoons **defatted reduced-sodium beef broth**
1 tablespoon **canola oil**

Preheat the oven to 350°.

In a medium bowl, toss together the pork, thyme, rosemary, salt (if using) and pepper.

Combine the rutabagas and onions in a large microwave-safe bowl. Cover with wax paper and microwave on high power for a total of 4 minutes; stop and stir after 2 minutes.

Add the potatoes, carrots and garlic; stir to mix. Cover and microwave for a total of 8 minutes; stop and stir after 4 minutes.

Mix in the broth and oil. Add the pork and mix well.

Transfer to a 9" × 13" baking dish and spread evenly.

Bake, stirring occasionally, for 45 minutes, or until the meat is tender and the potatoes are light brown. If the vegetables and meat seem dry, add a little more broth during the baking time.

Hands-on time: 15 minutes
Total time: 1¼ hours

Per serving: 307 calories
7.1 g. total fat (21% of calories)
1.4 g. saturated fat
60 mg. cholesterol
104 mg. sodium

Curried Pork-and-Pineapple Dinner

Think of this as a one-pot luau! It calls for a Dutch oven, but if you don't have one, start the dish in a large frying pan and switch to a lidded casserole.

Makes 4 servings

4 **boneless center-cut loin pork chops
(4 ounces each), trimmed**
2½ tablespoons **reduced-sodium soy sauce**
2 teaspoons **curry powder**
½ teaspoon **canola oil**
1 **large onion, chopped**
1 **small sweet red pepper, coarsely chopped**
2 teaspoons **minced fresh ginger**
⅓ cup **pineapple juice**
2 cups **pineapple chunks**
1 **large sweet potato, peeled and cubed**

Preheat the oven to 375°.

In a medium bowl, combine the pork, 1 tablespoon of the soy sauce and ½ teaspoon of the curry powder. Set aside for at least 5 minutes.

In a Dutch oven, combine the oil, onions and peppers. Cook over medium-high heat, stirring, for 4 to 5 minutes, or until the onions are light brown.

Reduce the heat slightly and add the pork and ginger. Cook, turning the chops several times, for 5 minutes, or until nicely browned.

Add the pineapple juice, pineapple chunks, sweet potatoes, the remaining 1½ tablespoons soy sauce and the remaining 1½ teaspoons curry powder. Bring to a boil. Cover and transfer to the oven.

Bake for 25 to 30 minutes, or until the meat and sweet potatoes are tender.

Hands-on time: 15 minutes
Total time: 40 minutes

Per serving: 248 calories
8.5 g. total fat (30% of calories)
2.6 g. saturated fat
51 mg. cholesterol
375 mg. sodium

To Your Health

Pineapple

A one-cup serving of pineapple offers 40 percent of the daily allowance of vitamin C and almost two grams of healthful fiber. Scientists say that bromelain, a powerful enzyme in pineapple, can help prevent cancer cells from growing, aid in burn healing, relieve stomachaches, reduce inflammation, prevent the blood clots that lead to heart attack and stroke and even clean up arteries clogged with plaque.

Seafood, Tomato and Feta Bake

Shrimp and fish bake with tangy feta cheese and chopped tomatoes to make a memorable casserole. If you don't have cod, substitute another lean white-fleshed fish.

Makes 4 servings

> 1 cup **chopped onions**
> ½ cup **water**
> 2 cups **chopped tomatoes**
> 2 **scallions, chopped**
> 1 cup **cooked rice**
> 4 ounces **cod fillets**
> **or other lean white fish fillets, cubed**
> 5 ounces **feta cheese, crumbled**
> 8 ounces **cooked medium shrimp**
> ⅓ cup **fresh bread crumbs**

•

Preheat the oven to 350°. Coat a 2-quart casserole with no-stick spray.

•

Coat a large no-stick frying pan with no-stick spray. Add the onions and water. Cook over medium-high heat, stirring occasionally, for 3 to 4 minutes. Add the tomatoes, scallions and rice. Lower the heat to medium and cook, stirring occasionally, for 5 minutes.

•

Spread half of the rice mixture in the casserole. Top with the fish and sprinkle with half of the feta. Add the rest of the rice mixture.

•

Cover and bake for 25 minutes. Top with the shrimp and the remaining feta. Sprinkle with the bread crumbs.

•

Bake, uncovered, for 15 to 20 minutes, or until the cheese has melted and the bread crumbs are crisp and brown.

Hands-on time: 15 minutes
Total time: 1 hour

Per serving: 297 calories
9.6 g. total fat (29% of calories)
6 g. saturated fat
132 mg. cholesterol
607 mg. sodium

Greek Baked Fish

Generous use of parsley adds a flavor nip and lovely color to this dish. Note that thin fish fillets cook faster than thicker ones.

Makes 4 servings

2 teaspoons **olive oil**
1 **medium onion, chopped**
1 **clove garlic, minced**
½ teaspoon **dried oregano leaves**
2 teaspoons **lemon juice**
1 can (18 ounces) **cannellini beans, rinsed and drained**
1 cup **chopped fresh parsley**
½ teaspoon **salt** (**optional**)
¼ teaspoon **freshly ground black pepper**
4 **flounder, sole or turbot fillets**
(**3 ounces each**)
3 **plum tomatoes, chopped**

Preheat the oven to 400°.

In a large no-stick frying pan, combine the oil, onions, garlic, oregano and 1 teaspoon of the lemon juice. Cook over medium heat, stirring frequently, for 5 to 6 minutes, or until the onions soften. Add a little water, if necessary, to prevent sticking.

Add the beans, parsley, salt (if using) and pepper.

Transfer the mixture to an 8″ × 12″ baking dish and spread it evenly. Top with the fish. Drizzle the remaining 1 teaspoon lemon juice over the fish.

Cover and bake for 18 to 20 minutes, or until the fish flakes when tested with a fork. Sprinkle with the tomatoes.

Hands-on time: 10 minutes
Total time: 35 minutes

Per serving: 218 calories
4.5 g. total fat (16% of calories)
0.6 g. saturated fat
40 mg. cholesterol
253 mg. sodium

Spinach Lasagna

Mushrooms and good-for-you spinach bring great flavor to this filling low-fat dish. Your family will love it.

Makes 4 servings

¼ cup **defatted reduced-sodium chicken broth**
1 cup **thinly sliced onions**
3 cups **sliced mushrooms**
2 **cloves garlic, minced**
1 package (10 ounces) **frozen chopped spinach, thawed and well-drained**
1 cup **reduced-fat ricotta cheese**
1 cup **1% low-fat cottage cheese**
1 **egg, lightly beaten**
3 cups **reduced-fat spaghetti sauce**
8 **lasagna noodles, cooked for 2 minutes and drained**
1¼ cups **finely shredded part-skim mozzarella cheese**
2 tablespoons **grated Parmesan cheese**

Preheat the oven to 350°. Coat an 8″ × 12″ baking dish with no-stick spray.

Coat a large no-stick frying pan with no-stick spray. Add the broth and place over medium-high heat until hot. Add the onions and cook for 3 minutes. Add the mushrooms and garlic. Cook for 3 minutes, or until the vegetables are softened. Remove the pan from the heat.

In a bowl, stir together the spinach, ricotta, cottage cheese and egg.

Spoon 1 cup of the spaghetti sauce into the baking dish. Top with 4 of the noodles, half of the spinach mixture and half of the mushroom mixture. Sprinkle with ½ cup of the mozzarella.

Repeat with 1 cup of sauce, the remaining 4 noodles, the remaining spinach mixture and the remaining mushroom mixture. Sprinkle with ½ cup of the mozzarella.

Favorite Comfort Food
Once cooled, leftover squares of Spinach Lasagna can be packed into small containers and frozen for up to 3 months. To prevent ice crystals from forming, press a layer of plastic film directly on the lasagna before you put on the container lid. Defrost overnight in the refrigerator, then remove the container lid and microwave the lasagna squares on high power for 4 to 6 minutes before serving.

• Top with the remaining 1 cup sauce. Sprinkle with the Parmesan and the remaining ¼ cup mozzarella.

• Cover and bake for 1 hour. Uncover and bake for 15 minutes longer, or until the cheese is golden and the filling is bubbling hot. Let stand for 5 minutes before serving.

Hands-on time: 15 minutes
Total time: 1½ hours

Per serving: 559 calories
11.7 g. total fat (19% of calories)
5 g. saturated fat
86 mg. cholesterol
1,330 mg. sodium

Baked Penne with Cheese and Vegetables

Cheddar is an unusual but inspired addition to this vegetable-and-pasta bake, especially since it goes so well with cauliflower and zucchini.

Makes 4 servings

5½ ounces **uncooked penne**
1 cup **chopped onions**
1 clove **garlic, minced**
2 cups **diced zucchini**
2 cups **chopped cauliflower**
1 can (15 ounces) **reduced-sodium tomato sauce**
2 teaspoons **dried Italian seasoning**
¼ teaspoon **freshly ground black pepper**
⅛ teaspoon **salt** (**optional**)
1 cup **nonfat ricotta cheese**
½ cup **shredded reduced-fat sharp Cheddar cheese**

Preheat the oven to 375°.

Bring a large pot of water to a boil. Add the pasta, onions and garlic. Cook for 5 minutes. Add the zucchini and cauliflower. Cook for 5 to 7 minutes, or until the pasta is just tender.

Drain and transfer to a large bowl. Stir in the tomato sauce, Italian seasoning, pepper and salt (if using).

Coat an 8″ × 12″ baking dish with no-stick spray. Spread half of the pasta mixture in the dish. With a large spoon, arrange dollops of ricotta over the pasta and then spread them out with the back of the spoon to make a fairly even layer.

Top with the remaining pasta mixture. Sprinkle with the Cheddar.

Bake for 12 to 15 minutes, or until the mixture is heated through.

Hands-on time: 10 minutes
Total time: 40 minutes

Per serving: 304 calories
3 g. total fat (8% of calories)
1.3 g. saturated fat
12 mg. cholesterol
277 mg. sodium

Easy Freeze

Creamy Penne Leftovers
This baked pasta dish is a good candidate for freezing. Allow the pasta to cool, then spoon 1- to 2-cup portions into microwave-safe freezer containers, sealing tightly. Defrost by microwaving for 4 minutes on high power, then transfer to a no-stick frying pan. Add several tablespoons of chicken broth to prevent sticking, cover the pan and warm the pasta over medium heat, stirring frequently, until bubbly.

Potato-Vegetable Frittata with Cheddar

A frittata is the Italian answer to an omelet. It's a great way to serve up some of your favorite vegetables and let your oven do half the work.

Makes 4 servings

1½ teaspoons **butter or margarine**
1 cup **finely chopped onions**
⅔ cup **chopped sweet red peppers**
½ cup **chopped broccoli**
1 cup **defatted reduced-sodium chicken broth**
1¾ cups **diced potatoes**
2 **eggs**
3 **egg whites**
¼ cup **skim milk**
1 tablespoon **Dijon mustard**
¼ teaspoon **freshly ground black pepper**
¼ teaspoon **marjoram leaves**
6 tablespoons **shredded reduced-fat sharp Cheddar cheese**

●

Preheat the oven to 350°.

●

In a large no-stick frying pan, combine the butter or margarine, onions, red peppers and broccoli. Cook over medium heat, stirring frequently, for 5 minutes, or until the onions soften.

●

Add the broth and potatoes. Cook, stirring frequently, for 15 to 20 minutes, or until the potatoes are just tender and almost all the liquid has evaporated. If the mixture is too dry, add a bit more broth or water.

●

Coat a 9″ deep-dish pie plate with no-stick spray. Add the potato mixture.

●

In a bowl, beat together the eggs, egg whites, milk, mustard, black pepper, marjoram and 3 tablespoons of the Cheddar. Pour over the vegetables and sprinkle with the remaining 3 tablespoons Cheddar.

●

Bake for 10 minutes. Reduce the heat to 325° and bake for 10 minutes, or until the frittata is barely set in the center when the dish is jiggled.

●

Let stand for 5 minutes before cutting.

Hands-on time: 15 minutes
Total time: 40 minutes

Per serving: 190 calories
6 g. total fat (29% of calories)
2.8 g. saturated fat
116 mg. cholesterol
420 mg. sodium

Three-Pepper Frittata Casserole

Two cheeses and the bright, bold colors of peppers create appeal in this warming supper entrée. It's on the table in 30 minutes.

Makes 4 servings

½ cup **diced onions**
1 **sweet red pepper, chopped**
1 **green pepper, chopped**
1 **yellow pepper, chopped**
3 **cloves garlic, minced**
⅓ cup **white wine or apple juice**
½ cup **crumbled feta cheese**
1 cup **reduced-fat ricotta cheese**
1½ cups **fat-free egg substitute**
¼ cup **chopped fresh parsley**
½ teaspoon **dried basil leaves**
¼ teaspoon **salt**
¼ teaspoon **freshly ground black pepper**

•

Preheat the oven to 400°.

•

Coat a large ovenproof frying pan with no-stick spray. Add the onions and cook over low heat, stirring frequently, for 5 minutes.

•

Add the red, green and yellow peppers, garlic and wine or apple juice. Raise the heat to medium-high and cook, stirring frequently, for 5 minutes, or until the peppers soften. Remove the pan from the heat.

•

In a small bowl, combine the feta, ricotta, egg substitute, parsley, basil, salt and black pepper. Pour over the vegetables.

•

Bake for 15 to 20 minutes, or until the eggs are set and the frittata is puffed and lightly browned. Cut into wedges to serve.

Hands-on time: 10 minutes
Total time: 30 minutes

Per serving: 165 calories
4.8 g. total fat (26% of calories)
2.1 g. saturated fat
20 mg. cholesterol
419 mg. sodium

Fresh Tomato and Black Bean Salsa
(page 296)

The Weekend Pantry

Two-Way Beef-and-Vegetable Soup

This hearty soup begins with homemade stock that you can turn into either a Hungarian soup or a barbecue-flavored soup.

Makes 10 servings

Soup Base

1½ pounds	**beef round, trimmed and cut into bite-size pieces**
4½–5 pounds	**beef marrow bones**
10 cups	**water**
2 cups	**chopped onions**
2 cups	**thinly sliced cabbage**
2	**large cloves garlic, minced**
4	**reduced-sodium beef bouillon cubes**
½ cup	**dried navy or Great Northern beans, rinsed and sorted**
¼ cup	**pearl barley**
2	**large bay leaves**
2 teaspoons	**dried thyme leaves**

Hungarian Beef-and-Vegetable Soup

1 pound	**all-purpose potatoes, cubed**
2 teaspoons	**caraway seeds**
1 teaspoon	**paprika**
1 teaspoon	**salt (optional)**
¼ teaspoon	**freshly ground black pepper**
⅛ teaspoon	**ground celery seed**
2 cups	**frozen mixed vegetables**
1 can (14½ ounces)	**reduced-sodium tomatoes (with juice)**

Barbecue-Style Beef-and-Vegetable Soup

1 pound	**all-purpose potatoes, cubed**
¼ cup	**ketchup**
1½ tablespoons	**sugar**
1 tablespoon	**cider vinegar**
1 teaspoon	**dried basil leaves**
1 teaspoon	**dried thyme leaves**
1 teaspoon	**salt (optional)**
¼ teaspoon	**freshly ground black pepper**
⅛ teaspoon	**ground cloves**
2 cups	**frozen mixed vegetables**
1 can (8 ounces)	**reduced-sodium tomato sauce**

To make the soup base
Preheat the broiler.

In a large roasting pan, combine the beef and bones. Broil 3″ to 4″ from the heat, turning the pieces occasionally, for 10 to 15 minutes, or until lightly browned.

Using a slotted spoon, transfer the pieces to a large soup pot.

Add the water, onions, cabbage, garlic, bouillon cubes, beans, barley, bay leaves and thyme. Bring to a boil over high heat. Reduce the heat and simmer for 2 hours, or until the broth thickens. Remove and discard the bay leaves, bones and any detached bone marrow or gristle.

Cover and refrigerate overnight. Lift the congealed fat from the surface and discard.

Bring to a boil over medium heat. Proceed with one of the variations below.

To make Hungarian beef-and-vegetable soup
Add the potatoes, caraway seeds, paprika, salt (if using), pepper and celery seed to the soup base in the pot.

Simmer, stirring frequently, for 30 minutes, or until the potatoes are tender.

Add the mixed vegetables and tomatoes (with juice), breaking up the tomatoes with a spoon. Simmer for 5 minutes.

To make barbecue-style beef-and-vegetable soup
Add the potatoes, ketchup, sugar, vinegar, basil, thyme, salt (if using), pepper and cloves to the soup base in the pot.

Simmer, stirring frequently, for 30 minutes, or until the potatoes are tender.

Add the mixed vegetables and tomato sauce. Simmer for 5 minutes.

Hands-on time: 15 minutes
Total time: 3 hours plus chilling time

Per serving (Hungarian Beef-and-Vegetable Soup):
252 calories
4.2 g. total fat (14% of calories)
1.2 g. saturated fat
43 mg. cholesterol
124 mg. sodium
Per serving (Barbecue-Style Beef-and-Vegetable Soup):
256 calories
3.9 g. total fat (13% of calories)
1.2 g. saturated fat
43 mg. cholesterol
121 mg. sodium

Chili Con Carne

Chili is so popular and so easy to prepare that it's worth making a big potful at a time. If you have leftovers, mix the chili and rice for easy reheating later.

Makes 9 servings

12 ounces **extra-lean ground beef**
8 ounces **ground turkey breast**
2 cups **chopped onions**
2 **large cloves garlic, minced**
2 cans (16 ounces each) **reduced-sodium tomatoes (with juice)**
1 jar (16 ounces) **reduced-sodium mild or regular salsa**
3 cans (15 ounces each) **reduced-sodium kidney beans, rinsed and drained**
2 tablespoons **chili powder**
¼ teaspoon **salt (optional)**
¼ teaspoon **freshly ground black pepper**
1–3 tablespoons **sugar (optional)**
4 cups **hot cooked rice**

•

Place a Dutch oven or large pot over medium heat. Crumble the beef and turkey into the pot. Add the onions and garlic.

•

Cook, stirring with a wooden spoon to break up the meat, for 5 minutes, or until the meat is lightly browned.

•

Add the tomatoes (with juice), breaking them up with a spoon. Add the salsa, beans, chili powder, salt (if using) and pepper. Mix well.

•

Bring to a boil, reduce the heat, cover and simmer, stirring occasionally, for 1 hour.

•

Using a large spoon, skim and discard any fat from the top of the chili. Taste the chili. If it's too acidic, add the sugar.

•

Serve over the rice.

Hands-on time: 15 minutes
Total time: 1¼ hours

Per serving: 260 calories
3.6 g. total fat (12% of calories)
0.8 g. saturated fat
35 mg. cholesterol
150 mg. sodium

The great thing about chili is that it lends itself to endless variations. You can dress up a bowl of plain chili with any number of toppings to suit your preference of the moment. Or you can modify a basic recipe in myriad ways to accommodate what's on hand and what your family likes. Below are ideas for both types of alterations.

Chili Toppings

Here are six ways to spruce up a bowl of plain chili. The amounts given are for a single serving, so each person in your family could conceivably enjoy a different taste sensation at the same meal.

Cincinnati Four-Way Chili

Top with ⅓ cup cooked spaghetti, 1 tablespoon shredded low-fat Cheddar cheese, grated onion to taste and a dash of ground cinnamon.

San Francisco Chili

Spoon 2 tablespoons shredded low-fat mozzarella or farmer's cheese into each bowl, then add the chili. **Top** with chopped cilantro. **Serve** with toasted sourdough bread.

Crunch and Spice Chili

Crush ½ cup chili pepper–flavored or plain baked tortilla chips on each serving.

Italian Chili

Stir in 2 tablespoons reduced-fat pesto and 2 tablespoons grated Parmesan cheese.

Tex-Mex Chili

Add 1 teaspoon diced jalapeño peppers (wear plastic gloves when handling), 2 tablespoons low-fat sour cream and 2 teaspoons minced cilantro.

Albuquerque Chili

Add 2 to 3 tablespoons cooked and diced tomatillos and 1 teaspoon red or green chili sauce.

Chili Variations

Here are half a dozen ways to customize the basic chili recipe on page 293 to your liking.

Turkey Chili

Use all ground turkey instead of the combination of turkey and beef.

Vegetarian All-Bean Chili

Replace the meat with 2 cups sliced mushrooms. **Add** 15 ounces canned pinto beans plus additional chili powder to taste.

Chili and Polenta

Omit the rice. **Top** each bowl of chili with a square of polenta that you've grilled or pan-sautéed.

Chili and Noodles

Omit the rice and serve the chili over cooked egg noodles.

Black Bean Chili

Substitute canned black beans for the kidney beans and top the chili with nonfat yogurt and plenty of chopped cilantro.

Italian White Bean Chili

Replace the turkey and beef with ground chicken. **Replace** the kidney beans with white beans, such as navy or cannellini beans. **Add** 2 tablespoons reduced-fat pesto. **Serve** over orzo or other small pasta instead of the rice.

Spicy Southwestern Soup

Here's a tasty, no-fuss soup that can be made in a slow-cooker. It's great to have on hand for weekend company or just to serve in the week ahead.

Makes 8 servings

10–12 ounces **extra-lean ground beef**
1 **large green pepper, diced**
6 cups **defatted reduced-sodium chicken broth**
1½ cups **reduced-sodium mild picante sauce**
1 tablespoon **instant minced onions**
1 tablespoon **chili powder**
1 teaspoon **ground cumin**
1 teaspoon **sugar**
½ teaspoon **dried oregano leaves**
Freshly ground black pepper
1 can (16 ounces) **reduced-sodium kidney beans, rinsed and drained**
1 can (15 ounces) **chick-peas, rinsed and drained**
2½ cups **frozen corn kernels**
¼ cup **uncooked white rice**
Salt (optional)

•

Crumble the beef into a Dutch oven or large pot; add the green peppers. Place over medium heat and cook, stirring to break up the meat with a wooden spoon, for 5 minutes, or until the meat is lightly browned.

•

Transfer the mixture to a large plate lined with paper towels. Pat with more towels to remove excess fat. Transfer to a 6-quart Crock-Pot or other slow-cooker.

•

Add the broth, picante sauce, onions, chili powder, cumin, sugar, oregano and black pepper. Mix well. Stir in the beans, chick-peas, corn and rice.

•

Cover and cook on the high setting for 4 to 5 hours (or on the low setting for 6 to 7 hours), until the rice is tender.

•

Taste the soup. If it's too acidic, add a little more sugar. Season to taste with the salt (if using).

Hands-on time: 15 minutes
Total time: 5 hours

Per serving: 241 calories
4.8 g. total fat (18% of calories)
1.8 g. saturated fat
22 mg. cholesterol
428 mg. sodium

Fresh Tomato and Black Bean Salsa

Here's a versatile, substantial salsa to serve with Tex-Mex dishes or to offer as a snack with nonfat corn chips.

Makes 3 cups

1¼ cups **coarsely chopped tomatoes**
1 cup **canned black beans, rinsed and drained**
¼ cup **loosely packed chopped fresh cilantro**
1 small **jalapeño pepper, minced**
  (wear plastic gloves when handling)
¼ cup **chopped scallions**
2 tablespoons **red-wine vinegar**
1 small **clove garlic, minced**
¼ teaspoon **dried oregano leaves**
¼ teaspoon **salt**

•

In a glass bowl, mix the tomatoes, beans, cilantro, peppers, scallions, vinegar, garlic, oregano and salt.

•

Cover and refrigerate for at least 15 minutes to allow the flavors to blend.

Hands-on time: 10 minutes
Total time: 25 minutes

Per ½ cup: 32 calories
0.4 g. total fat (8% of calories)
0 g. saturated fat
0 mg. cholesterol
153 mg. sodium

To Your Health

Black Beans

Black beans add chewiness to soups, casseroles and rice dishes. Originally found in South American and Caribbean dishes, they are now a staple in American kitchens. Half a cup of cooked beans has at least six grams of fiber, 64 percent of the Recommended Dietary Allowance (RDA) for blood-building folate and 18 percent of the RDA for iron.

Marinara Sauce

Double or triple the recipe for this garlic-flavored spaghetti sauce if you like. It freezes well and is perfect on pasta or as a baste for chicken or fish dishes.

Makes 6 cups

¼ cup **defatted reduced-sodium chicken broth**
2 teaspoons **olive oil**
1½ cups **chopped onions**
10 **cloves garlic, minced**
8 cups **canned chopped Italian tomatoes (with juice)**
⅓ cup **chopped fresh parsley**
2 tablespoons **tomato paste**
2 tablespoons **dried basil leaves**
1 teaspoon **dried oregano leaves**
Freshly ground black pepper

•

In a Dutch oven or large pot, bring the broth and oil to a simmer over medium heat. Add the onions and garlic. Cook, stirring, for 5 minutes, or until the vegetables soften.

•

Add the tomatoes (with juice), parsley, tomato paste, basil, oregano and pepper. Bring to a boil. Reduce the heat and simmer, stirring occasionally, for 30 minutes.

•

Remove from the heat and let cool for 10 minutes. Working in batches, puree in a blender.

•

If serving immediately, reheat. Otherwise, cover and refrigerate for up to 3 days or freeze for up to 3 months.

Hands-on time: 10 minutes
Total time: 45 minutes

Per ½ cup: 56 calories
1.3 g. total fat (18% of calories)
0.1 g. saturated fat
0 mg. cholesterol
294 mg. sodium

Barbecue Sauce

Get out the grill and celebrate summer with this easy Southern barbecue sauce. It's nice and lean, so you can slather it on meats, vegetables, poultry or fish.

Makes 4 cups

1 cup **dry sherry or defatted reduced-sodium chicken broth**
2 teaspoons **olive oil**
3 cups **finely chopped onions**
2 cups **finely chopped celery**
½ cup **finely chopped green peppers**
6 **cloves garlic, minced**
6 ounces **tomato paste**
½ cup **reduced-sodium ketchup**
2½ teaspoons **ground red pepper**
Juice of ½ lemon
1 tablespoon **white-wine vinegar**
1 tablespoon **mustard**
1 tablespoon **honey or packed brown sugar**
1 tablespoon **Worcestershire sauce (optional)**

In a Dutch oven or large pot over medium-high heat, warm the sherry or broth and oil. Add the onions, celery, green peppers and garlic. Cook, stirring frequently, for 5 minutes, or until the vegetables soften.

Add the tomato paste, ketchup, red pepper, lemon juice, vinegar, mustard, honey or brown sugar and Worcestershire sauce (if using). Simmer over medium heat, stirring occasionally, for 2 hours.

Remove from the heat and let cool for 10 minutes. Working in batches, puree in a blender.

Use immediately or transfer to glass jars with tight-fitting lids and refrigerate for up to 2 weeks.

Hands-on time: 15 minutes
Total time: 2½ hours

Per ¼ cup: 60 calories
0.8 g. total fat (11% of calories)
0.1 g. saturated fat
0 mg. cholesterol
156 mg. sodium

Creamy Dill Dressing

Indulge yourself with this creamy dressing spiked with fresh dill and garlic. Reduced-fat dairy products help keep the fat content down.

Makes 3 cups

1 cup **1% low-fat cottage cheese**
¾ cup **water**
½ cup **part-skim ricotta cheese**
¼ cup **olive oil**
3 tablespoons **plain nonfat yogurt**
¼ cup **lemon juice**
¼ cup **chopped fresh dill**
3 tablespoons **cider vinegar**
1 tablespoon **Dijon mustard** (**optional**)
1 **clove garlic, minced**
Salt (**optional**)
Freshly ground black pepper

●

In a blender, combine the cottage cheese, water, ricotta, oil and yogurt. Puree until smooth.

●

Add the lemon juice, dill, vinegar, mustard (if using) and garlic. Blend briefly to mix. Taste and season with the salt (if using) and pepper.

●

Use immediately or transfer to a glass jar with a tight-fitting lid and refrigerate for up to 1 week.

Hands-on time: 10 minutes
Total time: 10 minutes

Per 2 tablespoons: 36 calories
2.8 g. total fat (67% of calories)
0.6 g. saturated fat
2 mg. cholesterol
46 mg. sodium

Creamy Dill Dressing (page 299) and Italian Dressing

Italian Dressing

Here's a savory Italian dressing you can afford to love! It's seasoned with tomato juice, garlic and fresh herbs.

Makes 2 cups

½ cup **reduced-sodium tomato juice**
½ cup **balsamic vinegar**
¼ cup **lemon juice**
¼ cup **defatted reduced-sodium chicken broth**
¼ cup **chopped fresh parsley**
3 tablespoons **olive oil**
1 tablespoon **canola oil**
1 teaspoon **minced fresh oregano**
1 teaspoon **paprika**
2 **cloves garlic, minced**
Freshly ground black pepper

●

In a medium bowl, whisk together the tomato juice, vinegar, lemon juice, broth, parsley, olive oil, canola oil, oregano, paprika, garlic and pepper.

●

Use immediately or transfer to a glass jar with a tight-fitting lid and refrigerate for up to 1 week.

Hands-on time: 5 minutes
Total time: 5 minutes

Per 2 tablespoons: 41 calories
3.4 g. total fat (73% of calories)
0.4 g. saturated fat
0 mg. cholesterol
10 mg. sodium

Tangy Marinade

This makes enough marinade for 2 pounds of meat, poultry or fish. Use it when grilling, baking, broiling or braising these foods.

To use the marinade, pour half of the amount in a shallow glass baking dish large enough to hold whatever you plan to cook in a single layer. Arrange the pieces in the dish and pour the remaining marinade over the top. Cover and refrigerate for at least 1½ hours. Marinate meat and poultry pieces for up to 24 hours; marinate fish for up to 2 hours.

Drain off about half the marinade and reserve it for basting. Cook the meat, poultry or fish, basting liberally about halfway through the cooking period. Discard any remaining marinade.

Makes 1½ cups

⅔ cup **defatted reduced-sodium chicken broth**
¼ cup **ketchup**
2 tablespoons **lemon juice**
2 tablespoons **Worcestershire sauce**
1½ tablespoons **canola oil**
1 tablespoon **packed brown sugar**
1½ teaspoons **paprika**
4 **large bay leaves, broken in half**
2¾ teaspoons **dry mustard**
½ teaspoon **dried thyme leaves**
½ teaspoon **ground allspice**
1 **large clove garlic, minced (optional)**
¼ teaspoon **freshly ground black pepper**
¼ teaspoon **onion salt (optional)**

•

In a small bowl, whisk together the broth, ketchup, lemon juice, Worcestershire sauce, oil and brown sugar. Mix in the paprika, bay leaves, mustard, thyme, allspice, garlic (if using), pepper and onion salt (if using).

•

Use immediately or transfer to a glass jar with a tight-fitting lid and refrigerate for up to 1 week. Remove and discard the bay leaves before serving.

Hands-on time: 10 minutes
Total time: 10 minutes

Per ¼ cup: 39 calories
2.3 g. total fat (50% of calories)
0.4 g. saturated fat
0 mg. cholesterol
138 mg. sodium

Ham Stock

A stock like this gives you the smoky flavor of ham without much fat or sodium. Use it for all types of soups. It's especially good as a base for split-pea soup.

Makes 8 cups

1 **large ham bone or 3 large smoked pork hocks, sliced**
8 cups **water**
2 **large onions, sliced**
1 **large carrot, cut into large pieces**
1 **large stalk celery, cut into large pieces**
2 **cloves garlic, minced**
1 **large bay leaf**
1 teaspoon **dried thyme leaves**

•

In a large heavy pot, combine the ham bone or pork hocks, water, onions, carrots, celery, garlic, bay leaf and thyme. Cover and bring to a boil over high heat. Reduce the heat and simmer for 1½ hours.

•

Strain through a colander into a large saucepan and discard all ingredients except the broth.

•

Measure the stock. If necessary, add water to make 8 cups or boil down to get 8 cups.

•

Cover and refrigerate overnight. Remove any congealed fat from the surface.

•

Use immediately, refrigerate for up to 4 days or freeze for up to 2 months.

Hands-on time: 15 minutes
Total time: 1¾ hours

Per cup: 8 calories
0.1 g. total fat (10% of calories)
0 g. saturated fat
0 mg. cholesterol
44 mg. sodium

Credits

We wish to thank the following companies, based in New York City, who donated props for the photography in this book.

Broadway Panhandler

• Fish-and-Pasta Stew (page 78): Le Creuset white pot

Dean & DeLuca

• Gazpacho with Shrimp (page 52): soup bowls
• Spaghetti Carbonara (page 70): plates and bowl
• Spinach, Red Peppers and Egg Noodles (page 184): basket
• Creamy Dill Dressing and Italian Dressing (page 300): glass bowls and tray

Takashimaya New York

• Indonesian Rice with Chicken (page 24): large bowl and chopsticks
• Winter Squash and Potato Chowder (page 108): two bowls, plate and spoon
• Spanish Fish Soup with Orzo (page 100): glass and napkin
• Beef, Kasha and Noodle Varnishkas (page 148): bowl

Index

Note: **Boldface** page references indicate photographs.

F

Fennel
Baked Fish with Fennel, 236
Feta cheese
Seafood, Tomato and Feta Bake, 279
Shrimp and Feta Skillet Dinner, 76
Fish. *See also* Shellfish
Baked Cod in Spanish Sauce, 231
Baked Fish with Fennel, 236
Braised Catfish, Sweet Potatoes and Vegetables, 164
Creole Fish Chowder, 103
Fish, Potato and Vegetable Stew, 156
Fish and Pasta Stew, **78**, 79
Fish and Vegetables in Spicy Orange Sauce, **232**, 233
Greek Baked Fish, **280**, 281
health benefits of, 101
Herbed Fish and Vegetables, **234**, 235
Individual Seafood Salads in Tomato Baskets, 134
Linguine with Fresh Salmon and Tomato Sauce, 77
Oven-Baked Fish and Chips, **196**, 197
Red Potato and Tuna Salad, 131
Rice with Creamy Spinach, Salmon and Dill, 253
Salmon and Potato Salad with Dill Dressing, 135
Seafood, Tomato and Feta Bake, 279
Sole with Vegetables and Sliced Almonds, 252
Spanish Fish Soup with Orzo, **100**, 101
Torta Niçoise, 224
Tuna-Noodle Casserole, 198
Flounder
Greek Baked Fish, **280**, 281
Oven-Baked Fish and Chips, **196**, 197

Sole with Vegetables and Sliced Almonds, 252
Focaccia
Pesto Focaccia, 221
French-style dishes
Garlic French Chicken, **158**, 159
Frittatas
Potato-Vegetable Frittata with Cheddar, 286
Three-Pepper Frittata Casserole, 287
Fruits
Curried Turkey, Vegetables and Fruit, 160
Fusilli
Shrimp and Feta Skillet Dinner, 76

G

Garbanzo beans. *See* Chick-peas
Garlic
Garlic French Chicken, **158**, 159
health benefits of, 159
Roast Chicken Stuffed with Garlic, 190
Shrimp in Garlic Sauce with Tomatoes, **162**, 163
Garnishes, 7
Gazpacho
Gazpacho with Shrimp, **52**, 53
German-style dishes
Braised Pork and Sauerkraut with Apples, 202
German Beef, Barley and Cabbage Soup, 96
German Green Bean, Potato and Ham Dinner, **56**, 57
Ginger
Ginger Chicken, 42
Gouda cheese
Barley Salad with Smoked Cheese, 183
Goulash
Hungarian Goulash, 195
Grains. *See specific grains*
Great Northern beans
Italian Bean Soup, 95

K

Kabobs
Minted Lamb Kabobs with Pita, **48**, 49
Vegetable Kabobs with Herb Butter, 237

Kasha
Beef, Kasha and Noodle Varnishkas, **148**, 149
health benefits of, 149

Kidney beans
Bean and Vegetable Enchilada Bake, **176**, 177
Chili Con Carne, **292**, 293
health benefits of, 267
Mexican Red Rice and Beans, 174

Kugel
Spinach, Red Peppers and Egg Noodles, **184**, 185

L

Lamb
Minted Lamb Kabobs with Pita, **48**, 49

Lasagna
Spinach Lasagna, 282–83
Vegetable Lasagna, **258**, 259

Legumes. *See specific legumes*

Lemons
Greek Lemon-Rice Salad, 138

Lentils
Curried Chicken-and-Lentil Soup, 89
Curried Lentil-and-Onion Stew, 171
health benefits of, 107
Lentil and Potato Soup, 107

Lima beans
Microwave Beef-and-Vegetable Stew, 248

Linguine
Creamy Pasta with Vegetables and Ham, 73
Japanese Chicken and Noodles, 95
Linguine with Fresh Salmon and Tomato Sauce, 77
Linguine with Savory Mushroom Sauce, 80
Vegetables in Creamy Tomato Sauce over Pasta, 84

Lo mein
Pork Lo Mein, 165

M

Macaroni
Macaroni and Cheese with Vegetables, **200**, 201

Marinades
Tangy Marinade, 302

Meal planning, 1–11

Meatballs
Meatball Oven Dinner, 272–73
Mexican Meatball Soup, 92
Spaghetti and Meatballs, **192**, 193

Meats. *See specific meats*

Mediterranean-style dishes
Mediterranean Soup with Peppers, 95
Torta Niçoise, 224

Mexican-style dishes
Bean and Vegetable Enchilada Bake, **176**, 177
Chili Chicken Soup, 94
Chili Con Carne, **292**, 293
Easy Chicken-and-Black-Bean Skillet, **54**
Ede's Chicken Enchiladas, 240
Enchilada Casserole, 269
Fresh Tomato and Black Bean Salsa, 296
Mexican Chicken Salad, 121
Mexican Meatball Soup, 92
Mexican Red Rice and Beans, 174
Microwave Hot-Cha-Cha Beef, **246**, 247
Salsa Cheese Soup, 111
Tamale Pie, **266**, 267
Tortilla Soup, 93
Turkey Quesadillas, **242**, 243
Vegetable Quesadillas, 62